2198

Architecture
A Place for Women

Ellen Perry Berkeley, Editor

Matilda McQuaid,

Associate Editor

Smithsonian Institution Press
Washington and London

Designed by Lisa Buck Vann

Library of Congress
    Cataloging-in-Publication Data

Architecture: a place for women / Ellen
    Perry Berkeley, editor,
Matilda McQuaid, associate editor
p.   cm.
Includes index.
ISBN 0-87474-231-5 (pbk.)
1. Women architects—United States—
    Employment.
2. Women architects—United States—
    Psychology.
I. Berkeley, Ellen Perry.
II. McQuaid, Matilda.
NA1997.A74 1989
720'.88042—dc19
88-29299   CIP

Cover image: Detail of photograph shown
on p. 19, infra.

∞ The paper used in this publication
meets the minimum requirements of
the American National Standard for
Permanence of Paper for Printed Library
Materials Z39.48-1984.

8   7   6   5   4   3   2

96   95   94   93   92   91

Manufactured in the United States of
    America

Contents

v

Contents

Contents

8

The Cambridge School 87
An Extraordinary Professional Education
DOROTHY MAY ANDERSON

9

The Essence of Design 99
Lessons from Two Amateurs
ADELE CHATFIELD-TAYLOR

10

An Elusive Pioneer 107
Tracing the Work of Julia Morgan
SARA HOLMES BOUTELLE

11

Task Force on Women 117
The AIA Responds to a Growing Presence
JUDITH EDELMAN

12

A Feminist Experiment 125
Learning from WSPA, Then and Now
LESLIE KANES WEISMAN

PART III.
SUGGESTING VARIOUS POSSIBILITIES

Introduction 137

13

The Buried Treasure 139
Women's Ancient Architectural Heritage
MIMI LOBELL

14

Restoring a Female Presence 159
New Goals in Historic Preservation
GAIL LEE DUBROW

15

From Muse to Heroine 171
Toward a Visible Creative Identity
ANNE GRISWOLD TYNG

16

Ad-Architects 187
Women Professionals in Magazine Ads
DIANE FAVRO

17

A Feminist Approach to Architecture 201
Acknowledging Women's Ways of Knowing
KAREN A. FRANCK

PART IV

ENVISIONING FUTURE ROLES

Introduction 219

18

Architects without Labels 221
The Case Against All Special Categories
CHLOETHIEL WOODARD SMITH

19

Out of Marginality 229
Toward a New Kind of Professional
ROCHELLE MARTIN

Contents

20

Room at the Top? 237
Sexism and the Star System in Architecture
DENISE SCOTT BROWN

21

Educating for the Future 247
A Growing Archive on Women in Architecture
MATILDA MCQUAID

22

The Studio Experience 261
Differences for Women
ANNE VYTLACIL

Index 271

Preface

Women have had a recognized place in the profession of architecture since 1888, when Louise Blanchard Bethune became the first woman elected to membership in the American Institute of Architects.

This book celebrates more than these one hundred years of women in architecture. The first essay in the book celebrates a remarkable earlier achievement, forty years before Bethune's: the authorship by a woman of the first history of architecture to be published in the United States. And the final essays in the book bring fresh perspectives to a future—to a series of futures—whose indications are visible only sparsely in the present.

The place of women in this field has never been more interesting than it is now, with more women than ever before studying to become architects and moving into positions of prominence in their profession. The concerns that prompted this book—what the profession of architecture may mean to women, and what women may mean to the profession of architecture—are the concerns that will occupy many women (and men) for years to come. Passing a centennial not only gives a chance to look back; it also gives an opportunity to look ahead.

The idea for a book of essays on women in architecture came from Tony P. Wrenn, the archivist of the American Institute of Architects; it was proposed by him in March 1986 as part of the Bethune centennial. His earlier efforts on behalf of women had already seen the AIA's Archive of Women in Architecture established in 1984 and staffed by Matilda McQuaid.

It was Matilda McQuaid, in the spring of 1986, who undertook most of the early work for the book: reaching out to possible essayists, identifying possible volume editors, and carrying the book forward by her belief in it and her hopes for it. I became volume editor in June 1986, contacting additional essayists and proceeding in all ways to make the book a reality. As volume editor, I occasionally overruled the associate editor; but I marveled at our unanimity on decisions large and small, and I valued her good judgment and good spirits throughout our collaboration. The book is, in every sense, the work of two individuals and not an official product of the AIA; the manuscript was not shaped or reshaped, approved or disapproved, by any committees, staff members, or officers of the AIA.

I am a critic and journalist, not a scholar or historian, and the volume under my editorship necessarily bears my stamp. I brought few commitments with me to this undertaking. One was a philosophy of inclusiveness: while I do not agree with every viewpoint of every essay we commissioned, I believe in the tolerance for different views that has historically been the hallmark of the liberal tradition. The reader will thus find some essays that profoundly irritate, some that simply educate, and some that speak deeply and in memorable ways to the reader's cherished values. Different readers, of course, will put the essays into different categories.

I brought, too, a commitment to a readable prose, to a style without jargon or pedantry that would make the volume accessible to the most diverse readership. The book is written for women in general, including those who are not architects; for architects in particular, including those who are not women; and for historians and other scholars, including those who are neither women nor architects.

Finally (but of course initially), I brought to this volume a belief in the ability of women and in the growing presence of women in the profession of architecture. Although problems and difficulties are mentioned throughout this volume, the overall tone of the book is one of celebration and hope, not bitterness or despair.

I have already indicated the importance to this project of Matilda McQuaid, my colleague and friend. Together we extend our profound appreciation to the following: To Tony P. Wrenn, for unfailing support and for significant efforts on behalf of the volume (including initial contact with the Smithsonian Institution Press); to Amy Pastan, acquisitions editor of the Smithsonian Institution Press, for valuable criticism and the painstaking effort necessary to turn a manuscript into a book; to Kathy Kuhtz, former acquisitions editor of the Smithsonian Institution Press, for early and constant enthusiasm about the volume; to Therese Ildefonso, director of membership development and special interests at the AIA, and to Judith Schultz, curator of exhibitions at the Octagon Museum, for important assistance from time to time; to Nora Richter Greer, senior editor of *Architecture* magazine for extensive information gathered through special interviews; to Patricia L. Putis and her Heritage Secretarial Service, for unfailingly high standards in the typing of the manuscript; and finally to the essayists themselves, for efforts all of us recognize as unusual.

For the institutional funding that permitted individuals to undertake this work, we are indebted first to the Graham Foundation for Advanced Studies in the Fine Arts, whose early grant gave us needed credibility with other funding sources. We are indebted also to the American Architectural Foundation, for a much-needed sum from the College of Fellows Fund of the American Institute of Architects. Finally, we acknowledge with gratitude a grant from the Design Arts Program of the National Endowment for the Arts in Washington, D. C., a federal agency.

E.P.B.

Introduction

ELLEN PERRY BERKELEY

Women are too practical to be good architects," says a man I run into occasionally—a man of otherwise thoughtful opinions. He has just learned of the subject of this book. How reminiscent of H. L. Mencken's *In Defense of Women*, which in 1922 outrageously conceded to women a superiority of mind that made them unsuited to the sordid demands of the professions. Women hold positions of substantial responsibility in architecture today, in private offices and public agencies, and they are walking off with highest design honors in school and beyond. Yet my friend is unaware, or (like the rest of Mencken's spiritual heirs) unconvinced.

Women are filling the architecture schools as never before, making up 30 percent of the bachelor's programs and 40 percent of the master's programs in 1985–86.[1] They are moving into the profession in record-breaking numbers, making up 11.3 percent of the nation's architectural personnel in 1985, up from 4.3 percent in 1975.[2] They are suddenly numerous enough to be appearing as *Jeopardy!* contestants.

Yet the savvy Alex Trebek of that TV show could only repeat the familiar stereotype when he introduced one of these women to the nationwide audience. "You want to design *houses*, do you?" he asked this student of architecture. "No," she answered, "*all* kinds of buildings." Trebek gave her the look of polite disbelief he might give an elderly great-aunt who announces her intention to climb the Matterhorn. "It is not altogether *impossible*, my dear," this look says, "but it is, well, *unusual*." Louise Blanchard Bethune must have seen this look often, not only when she announced her wish to become an architect but also, as an architect, when she announced her wish not to do houses.

I mention the recent comments of these two men not to chastise men (both comments could easily have come from women), but to suggest the peculiar ways in which things change. Attitudes do not keep up with events, or events with attitudes. Thus for the vastly increased and increasing number of women in this profession, the times are peculiar and uneven. The gains, however large, have not been fully consolidated. Women's membership in the American Institute of Architects, for instance, which made the giant leap from zero to one in 1888 but was still only 250 in 1974, was suddenly past 3,700 by the end of 1987. The mood of most of these women is to "get on with it" and not dwell on "grievances." Yet as recently as 1987 a session on women at the AIA's national convention became what was later recalled as "one long gripe session." Pervasive sexual harassment may be a thing of the past, but many women could still write an entire résumé in terms of incidents major and minor.

The times, being uneven, are difficult to characterize, and labels are of little help. It is said that we live in "post-feminist" times. But is the women's movement dead (having been killed off by its own excesses and by the efforts of a populace roused against it), or is the feminist cause a solid part of our national agenda in ways that Americans could hardly have imagined a few decades ago? I think the latter, although it does not escape notice that in the profession of architecture (as in the society at large) decent people of almost every political persuasion, believing firmly in the right of women to be whatever they want to be, are eager to avoid identification with "the feminist cause." The complex reasons for this need not concern us here. Still, it is confusing when feminists are not "feminists."

Women today call themselves "architects" rather than "women architects," except when making a special point. But special points are often made, and men can be forgiven for not knowing which label to use. Fortunately, it is now rare to hear men needing to distinguish between themselves as "architects" and the newcomers as "women architects." And we have moved on from the condescending term "architectress," which enjoyed a brief usage in the early 1950s in a savage pair of articles by the dean of Harvard's Graduate School of Design.[3]

Yet today we see a new label. As late as 1987, an architecture school in the Midwest was telling its students that it could find no "outstanding women" to serve as visiting critics. Does this school ask all its men to be outstanding? And, having hired them, does it find them to be so? With the certainty of doubtful answers on these two questions, it would seem that what is operating here is a double standard: men are expected to be competent while women are expected to be outstanding. Many of the early women thought they had to be twice as good to get half as far. The times have changed surely, but the double standard is still strongly entrenched in likely and unlikely places.

Oddly enough, there is dual support for the double standard. It is not only forced on women by the men who feel forced to hire them ("OK, we'll hire a woman, if we can manage to find someone 'outstanding' enough."). The double standard is also readily accepted by some women, for the understandable reason that they find it pleasant, at very least, to consider themselves among the few "outstanding" ones.

We need look no further than the celebration of the Bethune centennial in 1988 for a striking example of the double standard. The AIA traveling exhibition of a century of women's architectural work was titled "That Exceptional One" and special buttons were imprinted with these words from thirty years ago. In the 1950s, Pietro Belluschi had written that he could not recommend his profession to women, but if he saw a really determined woman he would wish her well; "she could be that exceptional one."[4] The phrase was revived for 1988 by the women of the AIA's Women in Architecture Committee—with some misgivings, I am glad to report. At the time, in 1987, only 7.1 percent of AIA members were women and the number of button-wearers on any occasion would therefore be small, seeming to fulfill Belluschi's dismal expectations about the rare "one" who could make it.[5] In its title and its buttons, this exhibition seemed to be saying that the AIA wanted its women to know their place—and know it as a small place.

I suspect that the use of the double standard is an over-compensation on the part of some men (and some women) who, for different reasons, have not been at all sure that women could be taken seriously. I am heartened by the many women who consider the title of the AIA exhibition an error. But women architects and the profession as a whole are not helped when women are the only ones to whom the label "exceptional" is applied. The real step forward will come when women are not only numerous in the profession, as now appears to be happening, but when these women are judged and accepted in the same ways as are men.

To confront the double standard, however, is tricky. According to the new conventional wisdom as stated by women in architecture, women should not have to be outstanding; they will have "arrived" in this profession when ordinary and even mediocre women can attain membership; after all, some men are only mediocre architects. This dovetails nicely with the goals and quotas of affirmative action, which work on the premise that a profession made up equally of women and men is more important than a profession made up of excellent practitioners, whatever their secondary characteristics. It is better to be accepted for your gender than be rejected for it, say the women who favor an officially mandated affirmative action and have been favored by it. But to the women who want merit to remain the only consideration, affirmative action has some troubling consequences, not least of them an undermining in the "affirmed" person of a sense of legitimation, a sense of pride in earned achievement.

The double standard will fall of its own dead weight, when men and women no longer consider it necessary. But women will truly have arrived when the vote on affirmative action is overwhelmingly negative, and that may take a good while longer.

Of course, there are many women in the profession today who are outstanding by anyone's measure. These are the women who, in the past fifty or one hundred years, would have been distinguished from the men primarily by their gender. Today, such women are visible not only as some of the first women to do what they are doing but also as some of the first architects to break new ground in various ways. Here are a few of the hundreds of interesting women in architecture today:

Chicago architect Diane Legge Lohan is the first woman partner of Skidmore Owings & Merrill, with responsibility for large projects such as the *Boston Globe*'s new printing plant. "The more I practice, the harder it seems to design a good building, let alone an outstanding building. I hope I have enough patience to do a few great buildings." Although she sees as much difference between individuals as she does between the genders, she thinks that women deal with other people differently from men. "We accommodate. We try to resolve a conflict before there's a confrontation. But women are learning from men when it's necessary to be tough, confrontational, stubborn."

Roberta Washington, in New York City, left a firm specializing in health care facilities to open her own office in Harlem. She renovates brown-stones there as her bread-and-butter work; she finds different satisfactions in designing housing for recovered alcoholics, former drug addicts, and the homeless. "I want to be known as a good architect, not a good female architect, not a good black architect."

Elected to the Raleigh, N.C., city council, Norma DeCamp Burns has helped to make the city's planning document (originally only a guide) into an effective tool for regulating growth and insuring quality development. "Women need to be more active in all kinds of groups that make policy, in the business world and in government." At the same time, Burns has shown what quality architecture can add to a community: the Chatham County Social Services Building, designed by her in Burnstudio Associates, was chosen one of the best buildings of 1985 by the architecture critic of *Time* magazine.

Judith D. Chafee worked for some of the top offices in the East before returning to her native Arizona in 1970; some architects now consider her "the best designer in Tucson," as reported by the architecture critic of the *Tucson Citizen*. Elected a Fellow of the AIA in 1983, she has won numerous awards for her fine desert residences. "The only thing that is important is excellence in architecture. That's what women should be concerned with. That's what men should be concerned with. The whole situation has to do with the liberation of both sexes."[6]

Margaret D. Woodring has been teaching since 1980 at the University of California, Berkeley, where she runs the International Program that she developed. "Some of the most interesting work in my practice deals with development of low-income housing using the tax system as a basis of subsidies. . . . I'm a product of the sixties, more liberal and socially concerned than the norm today. And yet, because I spent the seventies in the realm of public finance (mostly in transportation), I feel that understanding finance and economics is critical before we make our next set of advances in social housing, transportation, urban recreation—you name it. This position sometimes separates me from my sixties pals."

Rosaria Piomelli was the first woman to serve as dean of an architecture school in the United States (City College of the City University of New York). "My being a woman was always a mixed blessing for the job. On the one hand, attention was bestowed on me. On the other hand, this may have fostered resentment among my colleagues. I believe, though, that attention was generated not only from my gender but also from the agenda I was implementing at the school." Her last term as dean was the fall of 1982. "It is important that we do not get so enamored of the title or the power as to accept costly compromises to maintain them. There must be no regret in letting go."

Polly Welch, a partner in the Boston firm of Welch & Epp Associates (basically, as Welch describes it, "two independent practices combined for the sake of professional, intellectual, and emotional support"), is an officer in the multidisciplinary Environmental Design Research Association. She had worked in a traditional firm, but found that "the rewards for which we worked—being in the magazines—were not those I found satisfying. I wanted to find out how people really used the buildings I was designing." She has chosen not to offer traditional architectural services but instead to provide research, programming, and evaluation. "These services are currently viewed as tangential to the design process, but I think they will all eventually be incorporated into design as architects are held more accountable for the performance of their buildings over time." Welch sees a building not as an artifact, an object created at a moment in time, but as the physical representation of an ongoing process. She wonders whether this is related to a gender difference; she finds that the latter approach fulfills her need "to nurture, to facilitate growth."

Lynda Simmons, one of the pioneers in creating humane and affordable housing in New York City, has been president of the nonprofit Phipps Houses since 1982 (before that, as director of development, she created 1,610 apartments in the Bellevue South renewal area of Manhattan). Caring about her tenants and her buildings in a comprehensive way, she founded the Phipps Community Development Corporation to provide social services and engender a sense of community among Phipps tenants. One byproduct of that effort, as Simmons tells it, is that they have not had to paint the halls in ten years; she knows of no other subsidized apartments where that can be said.

Beverly A. Willis, who came to the profession from the field of art and without a degree in architecture, has been licensed for twenty years and has served as president of the California Council of the AIA. She became a Fellow of the AIA in 1980; only twenty-five women before her had received this honor. Although she was once controversial for saying she would not hire women, her office has recently been as high as 75 percent women. Her San Francisco office is small, bringing in outside people when needed; in nine months she and a crew of twenty-eight designed and did all construction documents for a $100-million community in Hawaii. Her work includes one of the earliest preservation projects in San Francisco (the award-winning 1980 Union Street) and major new projects such as the San Francisco Ballet building, the country's first new building designed specifically for a ballet company.

Jane Leoncavallo Hough, in 1986, became the first woman to be chief architect of the public schools of Washington, D.C. She has a staff of up to twenty, an annual budget of $40 million, and an overall plant of 18 million square feet. Her office primarily does upgrading and converting (adding computer labs, for instance), but one pilot program in six schools provides infant care to allow young mothers to continue their schooling. "They never thought they'd have a woman in this job, but I'm even hiring women now. The men requested it."

Joan Forrester Sprague has shifted her work in the past decade toward nonprofit real estate development for a constituency that has never before been a "client" in a traditional architectural setting: low-income women and their families. A cofounder in 1972 of the nonhierarchical Open Design Office, she was a cofounder in 1981 (and subsequently executive director and president) of the innovative Women's Institute for Housing and Economic Development, Inc., in Boston. She describes WIHED as "a development-assistance organization for groups already assisting low-income women, an entity that takes a comprehensive view of housing, including economic and childcare concerns." The focus of her work with WIHED has been on a new housing type—transitional housing—so called because it bridges the gap between emergency shelter and permanent housing. Sprague became an architect in the 1950s because she wanted to work toward aesthetic and social good. "I have maintained those early goals at a time when architecture has become increasingly defined in terms of form alone and the profession has become centered largely on promoting and perpetuating itself, losing ideals of social good along the way." Early in her career, she saw her place as a "helper" of men. Today, she says, "I have found my strengths and identity as a woman. Founding organizations that grew from my roots of womanhood, I have used my design skills to redefine my personal and professional roles as well as create physical space."

These are all noteworthy women, and they are only a random selection. But the times are uneven. When the AIA held its national convention in New York City in 1988, Saks Fifth Avenue joined in the celebration. Along three sides of the department store were windows with female manikins—wearing nightgowns, bridal gowns, bathing suits, and street dresses. At or near the important corner next to St. Patrick's Cathedral were the five windows celebrating architecture: the architect-manikins looked creative and concerned and fashionable as they beheld their drawings and models. But all of the manikins attired to look like architects were male; that is still what an architect looks like, to many.

To many, too, "an architect" is equated still with the central figure of Ayn Rand's novel *The Fountainhead*. For countless women in architecture, however, Howard Roark is immediately and forever damned because he is "macho," which, like all code-words, is used without explanation or substantiation. Women architects seem to be caught in a paradox: Roark regarded as macho stereotype is in other respects the nonconformist these same women might often emulate. More importantly, Roark's story addresses the larger issues of power and integrity that may soon become central for women as they rise in this profession. To the extent that women too easily despise Roark and too quickly identify with his enemy Toohey, the real villain of the piece (a man who cares only for power and fears anyone with integrity), women may be misunderstanding these issues in their own lives. Those who care about honest discourse will want to dispense with the word "macho." Sexist stereotyping has never been productive.

The 1990s will witness increasingly richer dialogue as the old watchwords fade into disuse. We have already come a long way from the rhetoric of the 1970s, when participants came to an otherwise admirable Women's School of Planning and Architecture, for instance, as to a religious tent meeting, breathless to hear and speak the One True Word. When doubt seemed to bedevil a believer in such gatherings, she was in effect banished to the rear of the tent, virtually excluded from the group. (I have seen this in too many women's groups to call it a product of the outcast's personality.) To challenge the word of a feminist in those days was to question the validity of the entire gender. Any conventional folly spoken by a woman was considered valid in the 1970s as long as it stemmed from a proper disdain for "the system."

Today, all but the most willful are able to see their world with more subtlety, and we are already hearing lively things. Joan Goody (of Goody, Clancy & Associates, Architects, of Boston) raises fresh questions about the role and attributes of women architects in ways that would not have been possible even as late as the 1970s.[7] Although most architects are men, she says, most have played the female role in relation to their powerful patrons. Architects, she continues, have a fair number of the traditional female attributes (they are sensitive, artistically creative, and malleable) and the traditional female flaws (they are temperamental, spendthrift, and late). Although the client may sound exasperated at his architect's excesses, the client's tone also suggests that "it takes a strong man to keep this interesting but undisciplined talent under control, and it takes a rich man to afford this decorative luxury—tones and phrases which, alas, the successful male client might use to describe his attractive, expensively clad, and spendthrift wife."

Goody asks: What happens when a woman assumes the role of architect, a role "traditionally male (although in many ways essentially female)"? The client always wants more than a well-crafted building, more than a space well-tailored to daily needs; the client wants "a bit of magic," says Goody, and "much of the magic is in the architect's presentation of himself as the magician. . . . The ability to express confidence, to carry others along on a magical trip, is critical." *Authority* is critical. Yet she suggests that the woman's approach, which involves "a willingness to discuss the options, evaluate the choices, demystify the process, and share the decisions," serves to undercut the authority of the woman architect—making architecture seem to be something "anyone can do." Goody does not ask, but we may, whether men have not known exactly what they have been doing, resisting women's entry into the profession. (Goody does point out that with today's "multi-headed clients," the female traits of patience, compromise, and tenacity have become undeniable assets, essential to the realization of major projects.)

What women bring to the practice of architecture (and whether, in fact, they are coming home to an essentially "female" occupation) will be the subject of an ongoing debate. Louise Blanchard Bethune would have had a few salty comments to make, we can be sure. She would have been amazed at the large numbers of excellent women now taking their place, making their special place, in the profession. She would have been happy to find these women no longer "exceptional."

Notes

1. Figures are from the National Architectural Accrediting Board. With 59 B.Arch. programs reporting, and a total of 13,701 students, 4,368 were women (31.9 percent). With 53 M.Arch. programs reporting, and a total of 3,710 students, 1,499 were women (40.4 percent). These percentages probably reflect the situation for the United States as a whole, but the total numbers are considerably higher; the Association of Collegiate Schools of Architecture identifies 92 schools of architecture in the United States.

2. *The American Woman 1987–88: A Report in Depth*, Sara E. Rix, ed., for the Women's Research and Education Institute of the Congressional Caucus for Women's Issues (New York: W. W. Norton & Co., 1987), 310. According to this document, the Bureau of Labor Statistics listed 130,000 architectural personnel in 1985, but did not specify how many were registered architects.

3. Joseph Hudnut, "The Architectress," *American Institute of Architects Journal* 15 (March 1951):111–16; (April 1951): 181–84, 187–88.

4. Belluschi's full statement: "I cannot, in whole conscience, recommend architecture as a profession for girls. I know some women who have done well at it, but the obstacles are so great that it takes an exceptional girl to make a go of it. If she insisted on becoming an architect, I would try to dissuade her. If then she was still determined, I would give her my blessing—she could be that exceptional one." Thus concluded his article "Should You Be an Architect?" in the series of career articles written for the New York Life Insurance Company in the mid-fifties. The series originally appeared as public service advertisements in *Life, Look, Saturday Evening Post,* and *Scholastic Magazine*. A paperback compilation of the series, copyrighted 1958, had a distribution of two million copies before being discontinued in 1971. The foreword says that older articles were "reviewed and revised" to keep them up to date, but my 1969 edition of the book (its ninth revision) has Belluschi's words as quoted above.

5. As of June 1987, total membership of the AIA was 49,717, of whom 3,531 were women (1,855 regular members and 1,676 associate members). Leading the states was California (698 women, regular and associate members), followed by New York (334), Texas (266), Massachusetts (195), Virginia (134), Florida (133),

and Illinois (123). Nineteen of the states had no more than 20 women members of the AIA.

6. These paragraphs on Diane Legge Lohan, Roberta Washington, Norma DeCamp Burns, and Judith Chafee are drawn from extensive interviews conducted by Nora Richter Greer, senior editor of *Architecture* magazine (official journal of the AIA), and I am indebted to her for permitting the use of this material here.

7. Joan Goody, "Consenting Adults: Client and Architect" (Paper delivered at the 37th International Design Conference in Aspen; Aspen, Colo.: 17 June 1987).

Contributors

Dorothy May Anderson studied at the Cambridge School from 1929 to 1933, alternating her semesters with work for landscape architects Ellen Shipman (New York, N.Y. and Cornish, N.H.), Louise Payson (New York, N.Y.), and Mary P. Cunningham (Boston, Mass.). Between 1935 and 1943 she was resident landscape architect at Smith College, hired to teach and to redesign the campus and other college properties; in 1942 she was granted a master's degree in landscape architecture by Smith on the basis of her Cambridge School certificate. After World War II she served in the U.S. Foreign Service as a regional geographic attaché in Cairo, for eastern Africa, and in Paris, for southwestern Europe. In Washington, D.C., she has worked on freelance projects as landscape architect, geographer, editor, and writer. Her acclaimed book, Women, Design, and the Cambridge School *(Mesa, Ariz.: PDA Publishers, 1980), is the first published history of the Cambridge School.*

Adriana Barbasch, AIA, is a registered architect with her own practice. Until recently she was vice president for development at Milstein, Wittek & Associates, Architects, P. C., of Buffalo, N.Y., having joined the firm in 1966 soon after emigrating to the United States. Ms. Barbasch earned her master's degree in architecture in 1951 from the Institute of Architecture in Bucharest, Romania. Prior to coming to the United States, she worked in Romania and Italy on major planning and architecture projects. Since 1976 she has also been an instructor in design at the School of Architecture and Environmental Design at the State University of New York at Buffalo.

Ellen Perry Berkeley is a writer, formerly a senior editor of Architecture Plus *(1972–75) and the* Architectural Forum *(1967–72) and on the editorial staff of* Progressive Architecture *(1959–67). She is a graduate of Smith College and attended Harvard's Graduate School of Design and the Architectural Association's school in London. She has worked in architecture offices on both coasts. In 1972–73, Ms. Berkeley was awarded a Loeb Fellowship in Advanced Environmental Studies at Harvard. She was a founding member of the Alliance of Women in Architecture in 1972 and of the Women's School of Planning and Architecture in 1974. In the past decade she has continued writing, for various publications, and has taught architecture criticism in workshops at Columbia University, the University of California at Berkeley, the University of Washington, Massachusetts Institute of Technology, and Harvard's Continuing Education Program. She lives in Shaftsbury, Vermont.*

Sidney R. Bland is professor of history at James Madison University, where he has been teaching since 1965. He received his Ph.D. in 1972 from George Washington University, with a dissertation on the National Woman's Party and women's suffrage. Among his areas of specialization are women's history, the New South, and American history from the late nineteenth century to the early twentieth century. "Miss Sue" has been a subject of special interest to Mr. Bland since 1981; his research has resulted in a number of articles and lectures on this pioneer in preservation, and a book is projected.

Sara Holmes Boutelle, founder of the Julia Morgan Association, is an architectural historian who has been researching Julia Morgan for over fifteen years. Ms. Boutelle's work was the basis for the first exhibitions on Morgan (at the Berkeley City Club, the Oakland Museum, and the University of California, Berkeley); her articles on Morgan appear in many publications. Ms. Boutelle received her bachelor of arts degree from Mount Holyoke College and received the certificate from the Sorbonne in Paris. Her book Julia Morgan, Architect *(Abbeville Press, 1988) is the first full-length treatment of the pioneering architect.*

Adele Chatfield-Taylor has been director of the Design Arts Program of the National Endowment for the Arts since 1984. Her work as a professional historic preservationist began in New York City, where she was a founder of Urban Deadline Architects in 1968 and later served on the staff of the New York City Landmarks Preservation Commission. She became the executive director of the New York Landmarks Preservation Foundation in 1980. Ms. Chatfield-Taylor received a B.A. from Manhattanville College and an M.S. from the Graduate School of Architecture and Planning at Columbia University. She had a Prix de Rome from the American Academy in Rome (1983–84) and was a Loeb Fellow at the Harvard Graduate School of Design in 1978–79. She is an adjunct professor of architecture in the Graduate School of Architecture and Planning at Columbia University and frequently lectures on historic preservation, cities, and design.

Lamia Doumato is head of reference at the National Gallery of Art Library, Washington, D.C. She was a contributor to several books—The Comfortable House (Cambridge: MIT Press, 1986), *Dictionary of Women Artists (Boston: G. K. Hall, 1985), and most recently an introduction to a facsimile of the 1848 volume,* History of Architecture, *by Mrs. L. C. Tuthill (New York: Garland Publishing Co., 1988). She has a master's degree in art history from Pennsylvania State University and a master's in library science from Simmons College. She served as chair of the Association of Architectural Librarians in 1987.*

Gail Lee Dubrow is a Ph.D. candidate in urban planning at University of California, Los Angeles, with a concentration in the history of the built environment. She has taught in women's studies programs at the University of Oregon, George Washington University, the University of Maryland at College Park, and California State University at Long Beach and Northridge. Ms. Dubrow has been involved in preservation projects concerning women's history, most notably the Los Angeles Women's History Project. Her dissertation, "Preserving Her Heritage: American Landmarks of Women's History," combines findings from that project with research on women's history landmarks in Boston. Her work has been supported by fellowships from the American Association of University Women Educational Foundation, the Woodrow Wilson Foundation, and the Graduate Division of UCLA. She is coauthor with Dolores Hayden and Carolyn Flynn of The Power of Place: Los Angeles *(Los Angeles: The Power of Place, 1985), a multi-ethnic historical itinerary for Los Angeles.*

Judith Edelman, FAIA, is a partner (along with her husband Harold Edelman, FAIA, and Gerald Buck, AIA) in the Edelman Partnership/Architects in New York City. Their practice includes urban planning, housing, community centers, and historic preservation projects; the firm has won many design awards from the AIA and from organizations such as the National Trust for Historic Preservation and New York's Municipal Art Society. Ms. Edelman served as chairwoman of the AIA's Task Force on Women in Architecture (1974–75) and was vice president of the AIA's New York chapter (1975–77). She was a founding member of the Alliance of Women in Architecture. She has taught at the City College School of Architecture and has been a visiting lecturer at architecture schools in the United States and China. In 1982 she was the first Claire Watson Forrest Memorial Lecturer at the University of Oregon, University of California at Berkeley, and University of Southern California. She has a B.Arch. from Columbia University School of Architecture.

Diane Favro has been, since 1984, an assistant professor at the Graduate School of Architecture and Urban Planning, University of California, Los Angeles. In 1986, she was guest curator and wrote the accompanying catalog for the exhibition "Moving through New Towns," sponsored by Saddleback College and the International New Towns Association. She has several books in progress, two of which are Julia Morgan *(Garland Press), an extensive collection of Morgan's drawings, and* The Urban Image of Augustan Rome *(subject of the dissertation for her 1984 Ph.D. in architecture from the University of California, Berkeley).*

Karen A. Franck has been an associate professor at the School of Architecture, New Jersey Institute of Technology, since 1983. She has a Ph.D. from the Environmental Psychology Program of the City University of New York (1979) and a B.A. from Bennington College (1970). In 1984 she received a grant from the National Science Foundation to study recent social and spatial innovations in American housing. In 1986 she received a grant from the State of New Jersey Department of Higher Education to develop two new courses, on alternative futures and alternative buildings. She is co-editor with Sherry Ahrentzen of the forthcoming book, New Households, New Housing, *to be published by Van Nostrand Reinhold.*

Elizabeth G. Grossman is an assistant professor of art and architectural history at the Rhode Island School of Design, where she has taught since 1973. She is also a visiting professor at the Pembroke Center for Teaching and Research on Women at Brown University. Ms. Grossman received both a master's and a Ph.D. from Brown University and wrote her dissertation on "Paul Cret: Rationalism and Imagery in American Architecture." She is writing a book on the civic architecture of Paul Cret and has published several papers on his work. Her work in general concerns the relationship between the ideology of institutions and the production of architecture.

Louise Hall, AIA, Wellesley '27, graduated from MIT with an S.B. in architecture in 1930. In 1931 she went to Duke University to organize the department of fine arts, and in her own words, "taught for forty-four years on every day of the year except Christmas." She was a professor of architecture from 1963 until her retirement in 1975. In 1954 she earned a Ph.D. in architecture from Harvard Graduate School of Design (Radcliffe College degree); her dissertation was entitled "Artificer to Architect in Anglo-America." She has written articles for professional journals about American architecture and has contributed to guide books on the architecture of North Carolina.

Lisa Koenigsberg has a Ph.D. in American studies from Yale University (1987), an M.Phil. in American studies from Yale University (1984), an M.A. in American studies from Yale (1981), and an M.A. in history from Johns Hopkins (1979). She is an architectural historian working at the Landmarks Preservation Commission, City of New York. She was a guest curator at the Worcester Art Museum for the exhibition "Renderings from Worcester's Past" in 1987 and organized an exhibition for the Yale University Art Gallery on "Selected Images of American Victorian Womanhood" in 1982. Ms. Koenigsberg was a Smithsonian Institution Predoctoral Fellow between 1984 and 1987. Her Ph.D. dissertation is on "Professionalizing Domesticity: A Tradition of American Women Writers on Architecture, 1848–1913."

Mimi Lobell is a tenured associate professor at Pratt Institute, School of Architecture, where she has taught architectural design, history, and various electives since 1972. She has also taught courses on myth and symbol in architecture at the C. G. Jung Foundation in New York. She received her M. Arch. from the University of Pennsylvania in 1966, is registered in New York State, and has worked as a designer in the offices of Marcel Breuer, John M.

Johansen, and others. Ms. Lobell was a cofounder of the Alliance of Women in Architecture in 1972, and her long-standing interest in women and the feminine principle in architecture can be seen in much of her work, including her 1975 design for a Goddess Temple, which has been widely published. She has lectured and published internationally, and her book, tentatively titled Spatial Archetypes: The Hidden Patterns of Psyche and Civilization, *is nearing completion.*

Matilda McQuaid is a curatorial assistant in the department of architecture and design at the Museum of Modern Art, where she works on exhibitions and supervises the Mies van der Rohe Archive. From 1984 to 1986, she worked at the national AIA headquarters as a research consultant for the AIA's 1988 exhibition on women in architecture, and helped to establish the AIA Archive on Women in Architecture. She is working on a master's degree in architectural history from the University of Virginia; her thesis is on Catherine Bauer's book, Modern Housing (1934), *and its effect on architecture during this century.*

Rochelle Martin earned the doctor of architecture degree from the University of Michigan, College of Architecture and Urban Planning, in 1986. Her previous degrees are a B.Arch. from Lawrence Institute of Technology (1977) and an M.A. in history from Wayne State University (1968). She has taught architectural design and history at Kansas State University, the University of Michigan, the University of Nebraska, and Lawrence Institute of Technology.

Lisa B. Reitzes has been an instructor of American art and architecture at Smith College since 1984. She recently completed a Ph.D. in art history at the University of Delaware with a dissertation on the architecture of the Public Works Administration. She has written and coauthored two books on architecture in Idaho and was a contributor to the Macmillan Encyclopedia of Architects *(New York: The Free Press, 1982) and the* Dictionary of Art *(London: Macmillan, forthcoming). She has been conducting research on Minerva Parker Nichols for several years and has lectured on Nichols and other early women architects.*

Denise Scott Brown is an architect, planner, educator, and theorist. A principal in Venturi, Rauch and Scott Brown since 1967, she has been partner in charge of a series of urban design and planning projects throughout the country. She has written and lectured extensively, and her work appears in translation in five languages. Academic research projects designed by Ms. Scott Brown formed the basis for the seminal book Learning from Las Vegas, *which she coauthored with Robert Venturi and Steven Izenour, as well as for the exhibition "Signs of Life, Symbols in the American City," designed by VRSB for the Smithsonian Institution's celebration of the Bicentennial. She is a graduate of the Architectural Association's school in London (1955); she has an M.C.P. (1960) and an M.Arch. (1965) from the University of Pennsylvania.*

Chloethiel Woodard Smith, FAIA, has been a principal in several firms in Washington, D.C. since 1946. Organized as Chloethiel Woodard Smith and Associated Architects in 1963, her practice includes architecture, urban design, and planning. She has been a member of the Commission of Fine Arts and the President's Council on Pennsylvania Avenue and is currently a board member of the National Building Museum. She is a graduate of the University of Oregon with a B.Arch. (1932), and of Washington University with an M.Arch. in city planning (1933).

Anne Griswold Tyng, FAIA, is an associate professor (adjunct) at the University of Pennsylvania where she has taught since 1978. While at Radcliffe (A.B., 1942) she attended the Cambridge School for one year before studying at Harvard (M.Arch., 1944). She began working at the office of Stonorov & Kahn in 1945 and continued to work with Louis I. Kahn for three decades. Ms. Tyng holds a Ph.D. in architecture from the University of Pennsylvania (1975) with a dissertation on "Simultaneous Randomness and Order: The Fibonacci-Divine Proportion as a Universal Forming Principle." She is a member and past officer of the C. G. Jung Center of Philadelphia, and was elected an associate of the National Academy of Design. Her work has been widely published as well as featured in an exhibit at the Octagon Museum (Washington, D.C.).

David Van Zanten is a professor in the department of art history at Northwestern University, where he has been teaching since 1979; from 1971 to 1979 he taught in the history of art department at the University of Pennsylvania. Among his major publications are Designing Paris: The Architecture of Duban, Labrouste, Duc and Vaudoyer *(MIT Press, 1987);* Walter Burley Griffin: Selected Designs *(Prairie School Press, 1970); and a contribution to* The Architecture of the Ecole des Beaux-Arts *Arthur Drexler, ed. (New York: Museum of Modern Art, 1977). He has held visiting lectureships at the University of California, Berkeley (1979) and Cornell (1976), and in 1980 he delivered the Mathews Lectures at Columbia University. Receiving his undergraduate degree from Princeton in 1965, Mr. Van Zanten earned his M.A. and Ph.D. from Harvard, in 1966 and 1970.*

Anne Vytlačil, AIA, is an architect in Washington, D.C., with a practice in residential and commercial projects. From 1978 to 1985 she taught architectural design and professional practice for part of each year at California Polytechnic State University, San Luis Obispo. She was a founding member of Washington Women in Architecture in 1975 and became a member of the Intern Development Program Coordinating Committee (a joint committee of the National Council of Architectural Registration Boards and the AIA) in 1986. Graduating from Radcliffe College magna cum laude, Ms. Vytlačil received her M.Arch. from Harvard in 1962.

Leslie Kanes Weisman is an associate professor and past associate dean of the School of Architecture at New Jersey Institute of Technology. As an educator in both architecture and women's studies, she has taught at the University of Detroit in the School of Architecture, at Brooklyn College in the Women's Studies Program, and at MIT as a visiting associate professor of architecture, planning, and women's studies (joint appointment). She is a cofounder of the Women's School of Planning and Architecture (1974) and of Networks: Women in Architecture (1977), a New York professional organization. She has written a book about women, architecture, and society—a feminist analysis of the man-made environment—to be published by Unwin-Hyman/Pandora.

PART I.

RESEARCHING

THE PAST

Introduction

Lamia Doumato opens this volume by writing about the work of Louisa Tuthill, author of the first history of architecture (1848) in the United States. Mrs. Tuthill hoped for an American architecture that would be appreciated by a cultivated public. Although much of her book was directed to practicing architects, it was dedicated "to the Ladies of the United States of America, the acknowledged arbiters of taste."

Tuthill saw architecture as a subject for women to appreciate but for men to do, yet it is not unlikely that the book found its way into the hands of the determined Jennie Louise Blanchard, for whom architecture would be a vocation. Our second essayist, Adriana Barbasch, has researched the details of Louise Blanchard Bethune's life and work. As we celebrate the one hundredth anniversary of Bethune's election to the AIA in 1888, and her subsequent honor as its first woman Fellow in 1889, it is disappointing to note that no one is trying to save the handful of her remaining buildings.

Bethune came to architecture through apprenticeship, which was usually considered a poor second to academic training. Elizabeth G. Grossman and Lisa B. Reitzes challenge this assumption. They argue persuasively that academic training between 1880 and 1910 (with its model of the "gentleman" architect) was part of the AIA struggle to establish stronger professional authority for itself and its members. In the battle for turf between architects and builders, women were the losers.

We turn next to Lisa Koenigsberg's essay on Mariana Van Rensselaer, one of the most important figures in the emerging tradition of women writing about buildings of their time. The essay suggests that the profession's antipathy to women must be considered when viewing Van Rensselaer's career. Van Rensselaer found a useful niche in mediating between the architectural establishment and the potential client. When she wrote what the professionals wanted to hear, they loved her, but they never let her forget that she was not one of them.

Next, through David Van Zanten's provocative look at Frank Lloyd Wright in his Oak Park studio, we see Wright's use of the kindergarten idea as it was interpreted by the women close to him. Wright made a distinctive commitment to the woman-dominated and "servicing" suburb, Van Zanten hypothesizes, but it was a role for which Wright was ultimately not suited.

Finally, in this group of essays, we meet Susan Pringle Frost, to whom in no small way the city of Charleston, S.C., owes its architectural and economic survival. "Miss Sue" Frost, Sidney R. Bland tells us, was an example of the New Woman who arose at the turn of the century. A crusader for many social causes, she crusaded on her own behalf when she became a realtor. Only partly from her real estate adventures came her passion for saving the decrepit dwellings of Charleston's early history. She did not achieve much in the way of material success, Bland continues, but her idea of saving an entire neighborhood as a vital ongoing community would be widely copied. To this pioneer in preservation, and her courage and energy, the nation owes the survival of more than just the buildings in which the prominent citizens lived.

1

Louisa Tuthill's

Unique

Achievement

First History of

Architecture in the U.S.

LAMIA DOUMATO

In a letter of 15 February 1841, Louisa Tuthill offered the publishing firm of Cary and Hart her recently completed manuscript, a general work on American architecture. This volume, the first history of architecture published in the United States, would not actually appear until 1848 and then under an expanded scope and format.

It is a book on architecture designed for general circulation and not alone for artists. The title will be somewhat as follows; Architecture, Ancient and Modern: The past and present condition of the Art in the United States, with plans for its improvement. The Mss. is ready for the press and has been examined by several literary and scientific gentlemen and (I trust I shall be pardoned for adding) highly approved. The object of it is to improve the public taste by bringing the topic before readers of all classes, and furnishing correct models for imitation. No work of the kind has hitherto appeared in the United States, and you will find, gentlemen, that it is much needed.[1]

A publication of this genre was a deviation from Mrs. Tuthill's existing work—sentimental and moralistic books for "young ladies" to prepare them for marriage and their domestic duties.[2] These publications played a crucial role in the development of family life and were as common in the nineteenth century as cookbooks are today. Louisa Tuthill also edited and wrote a series of children's books with the same blatant moral overtones; these volumes were quite successful, some going into as many as forty editions.

Tuthill did not begin her life with hopes of a career in writing. She was born in New Haven in 1799 into an affluent family, descendants of one of the city's founders. Educated in seminaries at Litchfield and New Haven where the curricula compared with that of Yale College, Louisa Caroline Huggins also received what a contemporary described as "the more general, but not less important element of education, the constant intercourse with people of refined taste and cultivated minds."[3]

In 1817 Louisa married Cornelius Tuthill, a recent Yale graduate whose career as a minister was cut short by an attack of typhus. He turned briefly to literary pursuits, but his health continued to deteriorate, and in 1825 Mrs. Tuthill found herself a widow with four children. Louisa Tuthill's literary talents, which she had earlier disdained, were now a source of both revenue and solace for her.

At this time in America, there were a good number of women writers who produced etiquette books similar to Mrs. Tuthill's. Catherine Beecher, for instance, in 1841 had authored the *Treatise on Domestic Economy For the Use of Young Ladies at Home and In School* which, although it concerned itself more with the economics and day-to-day upkeep of a home than did the writings of the "genteel" Mrs. Tuthill, was nonetheless addressed to the same audience. The issues brought home were just that—issues about the home brought to the home. Another important voice raised to the homemaker was that of Lydia Sigourney, whose *Letters to Young Ladies* had won wide recognition in 1833. Another was Sarah Hale, who (like Tuthill) was widowed early in life; her husband's friends had supported her initial literary venture as editor of the popular journal, *Woman's Companion*.[4]

All these women were well-educated, all were descended from important families, all were pious. But these similarities were not nearly as significant as the existence of an audience ready and waiting to consider their message. The period 1815–1865 was a time of complex change in American life: the mechanization of manufacturing and of agriculture, the availability of swifter means of transportation, and the use of progressive and more efficient business techniques all combined to move America from a traditional to a more modern way of life.[5]

The middle class wanted to preserve its traditional values while embracing selected new ones, and since the home was recognized as the most effective place for inculcating values, it was therefore the place for reconciling old and new. This was a major preoccupation of the era. Music and literature emphasized the vital role of house and home, as in John Howard Payne's exceptionally popular "Home Sweet Home."[6] Music, art, and cultural events were embraced by American womanhood. " 'High art' was enlisted in an effort to improve or reform the American character."[7] Art and taste were blended with religion and morals to create an ideal conception of truth and beauty, and these twin ideals appeared in the writings of many popular authors. Morality became inextricably tied to domestic architecture.

Besides being enterprising and diligent, Louisa Tuthill was perceptive. She understood her society and seized this opportunity to provide the public with its wants. In publishing this first history of architecture she paved the way for two vital American phenomena. First, she established a precedent for female authors writing architecture criticism and history; this was the first attempt by a woman writer to influence style (taste) in architecture. Second, she defended the validity of a truly American architecture (a belief propagated by earlier architecture writers, e.g., Thomas Jefferson and A. J. Davis); she championed an architecture with indigenous regional building materials, with a relationship between art and the American landscape, with trained architects here in the United States—ultimately an architecture for America not dependent on Europe.

Tuthill's influence becomes immediately apparent through the efforts of her long-time acquaintance, Sarah Hale, editor of the popular *Godey's Lady's Book*. In 1849 the magazine boasted an unprecedented forty thousand subscribers.[8] Also in 1849 *Godey's* established a regular feature in each issue—the "Model Cottage" column—which would for the next thirty years influence house styles as strongly as the magazine's fashions would dominate American women's standard of dress.[9] Tuthill's pleas for an American style did not go unheeded by *Godey's* (which published 450 model-house designs between the years 1846 and 1898); in 1854 the magazine announced that all future "Lady's Book Houses" would be by American designers.[10] Another female author following the pioneering tracks of Tuthill was Frederika Bremer, who discussed American architecture in her prefaces to a number of Andrew Jackson

Downing's books. Harriet Monroe and later Mariana Griswold Van Rensselaer and a host of other writers would continue to keep the American public aware of the aesthetics of architecture. Included in this group was Helen Gaut, writer and illustrator for several magazines and newspapers in the United States, who wrote articles on domestic architecture for the *Ladies Home Journal* for more than two decades.[11]

Writing a history of architecture was a formidable task in the 1840s, probably more so than it would be today; the existing sources were fewer and were not easily available. As a well-connected woman of New Haven society, however, Mrs. Tuthill had access to the library of the prominent architect Ithiel Town; his private library, amassed over a thirty-year period, consisted of some ten thousand volumes (many of them rare and valuable), and some twenty thousand engravings by ancient and modern masters.[12] Important publications such as *Views of Ancient Monuments in Central America, Chiapas, and Yucatan* by Frederick Catherwood (published in London in 1844) and Lord Kingsborough's contemporaneous seven-volume folio series on the *Antiquities of Mexico* attest to the seriousness of Tuthill's commitment and to the quality of Town's book collection.

The complete citation as it appears on the title page of the Tuthill volume is: *History of Architecture from the Earliest Times; its Present Condition in Europe and the United States; With a Biography of Eminent Architects and a Glossary of Architectural Terms by Mrs. L. C. Tuthill. With Numerous Illustrations.* The history is composed of 28 chapters in 426 pages; supplementing the text are 46 engravings and 102 woodcuts. The preface is followed by lists of the plates; completing the book are two appendixes, a chronological table of the principal architects before and since the Christian era, and a glossary of architectural terms.

A glance at the table of contents immediately identifies idiosyncrasies of this volume: no chapters on early Christian architecture or Byzantine architecture; chronological arrangement interrupted by chapters on architectural principles, on building materials, and on qualifications for an architect; an entire chapter devoted to arrangements of a city, i.e., city planning. Future histories of architecture would consist of several volumes and would provide more balanced and comprehensive coverage of periods, cultures, and styles. Tuthill's history could not compare in scope or in thoroughness; however, her intention was not to provide the definitive history of architecture. Her book was initially conceived as a history of American architecture; moreover, her intent was to use the book as a vehicle for promoting her ideals and for developing the architectural profession in the United States.[13] She confirms her motivation not only in the dedicatory statement but also at several points within the text: her desire is to appeal to American womanhood to establish and maintain high standards for their native architecture. In her writing she combines verse, flowery sentiment, sociological insight, social history, explanation of terms, and personal ideology. Always, Louisa Tuthill is subjective, and this need to include her own highly colored observations renders her account interesting and thought-provoking.

Her history has no formal bibliography or list of sources, but she provides references to useful works in footnotes throughout the book. Here, Tuthill is concise to a fault, often listing only the author's last name and the first few words of the title, e.g., Britton's *Architectural Antiquities,* Pugin's *Specimens of Gothic Architecture,* and Loudon's *Architectural Encyclopedia.* Perhaps she assumes that her audience would be well acquainted with these popular books.

Unfortunately Mrs. Tuthill is not discriminating enough to adjust her style for books that could not have been "household terms" for her readers, e.g., Jahu's *Biblical Archaeology,* Callaud in his *Journey to Meroe,* Gau in his *Nubia.* Perhaps she assumes that few, if any, readers would consult references even if given the opportunity to do so.

Her essays on current topics in art and her awareness of American architecture are her strong points; this is where Louisa Tuthill shines. As a roundabout way of introducing the concept of an art school in the United States (a cause espoused by Ithiel Town, Lydia Sigourney, and a number of the New Haven intellectuals), she presents the factors that have hindered the progress of art in America: she relates most problems to a lack of developed "taste" in the United States. Why should artist or artisan develop his art to a superlative point when no one is there to recognize his achievement? Tuthill sees this phase of American life ending as more people travel to Europe and come home with an appreciation of (and desire for) the finer things experienced on their sojourn; it is unnecessary for art objects, architectural elements, or drawings to be carted back from Europe when Americans are an industrious and talented lot and perfectly capable of providing products as good as— or better than—their European counterparts.

"In order that the fine arts may be successfully cultivated, taste must be diffused among the higher classes of the community," she writes.[14] And, she continues, "Among the arts of design, architecture must precede painting and sculpture: they are but the hand maidens who deco-rate her palaces, her capitols, her churches."¹⁵ There is nothing of the democratic ideal in Louisa Tuthill's writings. She lives in a world of hier-archies, both in thought and in actuality.

Tuthill encourages the development of the architectural profession. "To the young men of our country, Architecture offers a lucrative and honorable profession. Instead of devoting so large a proportion of tal-ent and active energy to the three learned professions, and to commer-cial pursuits, it is high time to direct them into other channels. This Art opens a fair field for laudable ambition."¹⁶ (She would have been star-tled to know that only a generation later "young *women* of the country" were beginning to follow this advice.) In her respect for professional-ism, Louisa Tuthill distinguishes herself from contemporary women authors who advocated self-help in the home; the Beechers, for instance, antagonized architects by including sketches for cupboards and closets that the housewife could make on her own.

An equally important issue for the author is her unequivocal belief that Americans should employ American architects to build American houses. Even the English architectural prototype, acknowledged by her as part of the American heritage, is rejected because she believes that a truly American architecture must be indigenous: " . . . an American archi-tect must possess the power to adopt what is suitable to our soil, cli-mate, manners, civil institutions and religion without servile imitation."¹⁷

Perhaps her statement did not pass unheeded. Beginning with Richardson in the 1870s, we find prestigious American architects reas-sessing seventeenth-century American house types, materials, and ele-ments and reinterpreting them into a new eclectic style. This trend con-tinued in the works of Emerson, Price, and finally through the 1890s with McKim, Mead, and White. The practice of borrowing and integrat-ing elements of early American architecture into new buildings of the 1870s–1890s was so marked as to reverse the usual patterns of influence and to make American achievements in architecture highly desirable and emulated in Europe.¹⁸

Although Louisa Tuthill refuses to identify the important profes-sionals of her day, she accepts the task of "merely mentioning" some of the principal public buildings in the United States. In some instances she goes further to provide location and give a sentence or two on style, measurements, and unique architectural elements; and in the course of this survey, she names a few architects, among them Thomas U. Walter,

John Notman, Richard Upjohn, James Renwick, and (understandably) the firm of Town and Davis.

Tuthill's entreaties to working architects do not end with a discussion of their studies, an enumeration of their intellectual qualities, and a publication of their work. She has a more serious matter to discuss— building materials—and she devotes an entire chapter to it. After defining the indigenous marbles, stones, metals, and trees, she offers these words of caution: "Instead of cutting down and wasting trees ... farm houses might be constructed of the stones that now encumber the soil ... There has hitherto been a great want of economy in this respect, and it is therefore the more earnestly urged upon the attention of the community."[19] Since none of the author's other writings shows a regard for frugality, we can conclude that she was genuinely concerned with preservation and conservation of the country's natural resources.

Although much of the volume is seemingly directed at practicing architects, Mrs. Tuthill makes clear her prime motivation for writing this book in her dedicatory statement: "To the Ladies of the United States of America, the acknowledged arbiters of taste, this work is respectfully inscribed."[20] Very little in this statement is unusual for nineteenth-century publications. Educating the female of the Northeast and Midwest was a common goal, attested to by the number of publications directed at women. The uniqueness of Louisa Tuthill's concept is concern for visual rather than verbal education; her intention is to provide American women with sufficient knowledge of the art of architecture to enable them to make aesthetic decisions. She presents convincing arguments. "Every person has an individual interest in Architecture as a useful art and all who cultivate a taste for the Fine Arts must give it a high place among them. The best way of effecting improvement in any art or science ... is to multiply as far as possible those who can observe and judge."[21]

She believes in the basic and enriching value of a knowledge of architecture. For women, she writes, a taste for architecture is as vital as a taste for flowers. To Louisa Tuthill, and to her readers, architecture provides a sense of history and a link to understanding elements of the past: religion, government, social institutions, science, and art.

Despite the fact that Mrs. Tuthill's history of architecture did not enjoy the numerous editions or great popularity attained by some of her less significant books, it emerges as a noteworthy contribution to nineteenth-century architectural history.[22] She realized that she had made a unique contribution in publishing the first history of architecture in the United States. Undoubtedly she also realized that she had raised many vital issues: the importance of an informed consumer; the need for a school for the proper training of American architects; the significance of function as the most important element of a building; and finally, the existence of architecture as an integral part of daily life.

Could she know that she was launching a line of women architecture writers and critics, stronger at some periods than others, but nonetheless continuing into our own time? Could she realize that she was preparing women readers for the next few generations of architectural thought? Prophetically, the ideals proposed in her history—the insistence on professionally trained architects (which would, of course, come with the founding of the AIA in 1857), the use of indigenous regional building materials, and the development of a uniquely American architecture—were the wave of the future. Mrs. Tuthill's study for "the Ladies of the United States of America" fully documents the philosophy of American and European architecture in her time and ably provides a transition from that time into the epochs to come.

Notes

1. The original letter from Mrs. Tuthill to publishers Cary and Hart is in the collection of the Historical Society of Philadelphia. The manuscript discussed in her letter of 1841 has not survived, but we know from the context of the letter that it was a history limited to American architecture. In the seven intervening years before the book was published, Mrs. Tuthill expanded her work to make it a history of world architecture.

2. In these etiquette books, Mrs. Tuthill intended to present to the public what was socially and tastefully acceptable in America. In this sense, her history of architecture is not so different from her earlier writings. Her work included books for children as well as collections of essays by other authors.

3. John S. Hart, *Female Prose Writers of America* (Philadelphia: E. H. Butler and Co., 1852), 100.

4. After publishing nine volumes, Mrs. Hale's magazine was bought by Godey in 1837 (with Mrs. Hale retained as editor) and merged with his *Lady's Book*. Ultimately, the title would be changed to *Godey's Lady's Book*.

5. David Handlin, *The American Home* (Boston: Little, Brown and Co., 1979), 4.

6. Ibid.

7. Dominic Ricciotti, "Popular Age in *Godey's Lady's Book*," *Historical New Hampshire* 27 (Spring 1972): 3.

8. Frank L. Mott, *A History of American Magazines* (Cambridge: Harvard University Press, 1966), 351.

9. Ruth E. Finley, *The Lady of Godey's: Sarah Josepha Hale* (Philadelphia: J. B. Lippincott, 1931), 138.

10. Gwendolyn Wright, *Moralism and the American Home* (Chicago: University of Chicago Press, 1980), 11.

11. John William Leonard, ed. *Woman's Who's Who of America, 1914–1915* (Detroit: Gale Publishers, 1976) 63.

12. Lydia Sigourney, "The Residence of Ithiel Town, Esquire," *Ladies' Home Companion and Literary Expositor* 10 (1839–1840): 123.

13. Although the book purports to be about the "present condition [of architecture] in Europe and the United States," Tuthill has only one chapter devoted exclusively to European architecture, and precious little to say in its favor. She disposes of Italy, Spain, and Portugal with the judgment that no recently built structures can compare with those of former ages. She dismisses London as having only Wren's legacy to boast of, and St. Petersburg and Moscow as owing a debt of thanks to their emigrant Italian architects. Only Paris emerges in her book as a place of taste and magnificence in its public buildings. Small wonder that Tuthill sought to emulate the Ecole des Beaux Arts when she proposed an American school to train architects.

14. Louisa C. H. Tuthill, *History of Architecture* (Philadelphia: Lindsay and Blakiston, 1848), 248.

15. Ibid., 249.

16. Ibid., ix.

17. Ibid., 222.

18. James D. Kornwolf, "American Architecture and the Aesthetic Movement" in Metropolitan Museum of Art catalog, *In Pursuit of Beauty: Americans and the Aesthetic Movement* (New York: Rizzoli, 1986).

19. Tuthill, 256.

20. Ibid., ix.

21. Ibid.

22. Curiously, the history received no critical mention at the time. Despite a search through numerous periodicals on microfilm, I am unable to find any review or references to the work. Even her friend Sigourney seems to have deserted her on this one. But writers viewing it with the advantage of historical hindsight have proved more capable of appreciating its value. Alan Gowans, in his award-winning *Images of American Living* (Boston: J. B. Lippincott, 1964), criticizes Tuthill's search for the picturesque but quotes her book as a source of established taste for the period. Henry-Russell Hitchcock includes her book in his *American Architectural Books* (New York: Da Capo Press, 1976), and Talbot Hamlin praises her book in *Greek Revival Architecture in America* (New York: Oxford University Press, 1944), calling it "remarkable for its sane, common-sense and forward-looking criticism."

2

Louise

Blanchard

Bethune

The AIA Accepts Its

First Woman Member

ADRIANA BARBASCH

In 1881, young Jennie Louise Blanchard announced the opening of her architectural office at the Ninth Congress of the Association for the Advancement of Women held in Buffalo. That congress also heard an address by Belva Ann Lockwood, soon to be the first woman candidate for president of the United States.

Running on the National Equal Rights Party ticket, Lockwood lost her second of two bids for the presidency in 1888; she never ran for president again but remained a successful lawyer and activist for fifty years. She appears on the seventeen-cent stamp issued in 1986. Another election of 1888 was more favorable to women. Jennie Louise, now Louise Blanchard Bethune, became the first woman to be voted a member of the American Institute of Architects.

Born in 1856 in Waterloo, New York, Jennie Louise Blanchard was the daughter of Dalson Wallace Blanchard, a mathematician and school principal of French Huguenot descent, and Emma Melona Blanchard, (née Williams), a school teacher whose Welsh ancestors had come to Massachusetts in 1640.¹ Her only brother died at an early age.

Jennie Louise Bethune (née Blanchard), 1856–1913. She was the first woman to be accepted into the American Institute of Architects, 1888, and first woman to be made a Fellow of the AIA, 1889. Photograph courtesy of Buffalo and Erie County Historical Society

As was common for girls in those times, Jennie Louise was educated at home. With her parents' undivided attention, she probably received a more complete education than was possible at any girls' school. During these formative years, too, she acquired a self-reliance that led her to disregard many conventional limitations throughout her life.[2]

The Blanchards moved to Buffalo in 1866, to better jobs, and Jennie Louise spent her next eight years at the Buffalo High School, graduating in 1874. It was here that she expressed interest in architecture and showed ability in drawing houses and other buildings.

For two years she studied in preparation to enter the newly opened architecture course at Cornell University, but in 1876 she decided to enter the profession in the more traditional way, by apprenticing as a draftsman in a professional office. She was hired by Richard A. Waite, a well-established office in Buffalo and learned her trade through hard work: six days a week at the drafting board, on construction sites, and studying the vast amount of material in the office library.

She soon advanced to become R. A. Waite's assistant. She had mastered technical drafting, construction detailing, and the art of architectural design. She had received a man's education and had proven her ability in a man's profession. At the young age of twenty-five, she decided to open her own office.[3]

The city of Buffalo in 1881 was enjoying its most prosperous era. For the fifteen years after the construction of the Erie Canal in 1825, Buffalo had been the largest port of emigration to the West.[4] As the tide of pioneers began to slow, the ships turned around to bring in their harvests and make Buffalo the largest grain-handling port in the world. With the invention of the steam-powered grain elevator in 1842, Joseph Dart revolutionized the grain trade and Buffalo became—after Chicago—the nation's second busiest railway center.[5]

By 1881, the population of Buffalo was 155,000; it would reach 352,000 at the turn of the century. Banks, real-estate businesses, and manufacturing enterprises were flourishing. An early public transportation system of horse-drawn carriages became, in 1896, a trolley system totalling 169 miles within the city limits. Buffalo claimed to be the best paved city in the world in 1897, with more than 200 miles of streets surfaced with asphalt and stone. The city boasted one of the most comprehensive park systems (nearly 1,000 acres designed by Frederick Law Olmsted), a New York State University and several colleges, over thirty newspapers and periodicals in six languages, and a well-developed cultural life.[6] To house this phenomenal development, architects from other cities flocked to Buffalo. New and existing offices needed every person qualified to do the work.

Jennie Louise Blanchard's apprenticeship had evolved under the most auspicious conditions. This was a time, furthermore, women were actively pursuing emancipation. In October 1881, the Ninth Congress of the Association for the Advancement of Women convened in Buffalo, with 975 women and 25 men voicing their beliefs and examining the scientific, artistic, and professional fields for their acceptance of women. The opening of Bethune's office, announced during this Congress, marked what is considered the entry into the field of the first professional woman architect in the United States.[7]

Robert Armour Bethune, a Canadian-born draftsman and former colleague from R. A. Waite, became Louise's partner and husband in December 1881. The hiring of draftsman William L. Fuchs, in 1882, seems to have coincided with the birth of Louise's only child, Charles William, in 1883. (Fuchs apprenticed in the office until 1883 when he became the third partner.)

Although it is difficult to know precise authorship of work in any partnership, we are told in an article of 1893 that Louise Bethune "had been in business for sixteen years" and that "for some years she had taken entire charge of the office work and complete superintendence

Lockport Union High School, 1890, Lockport, New York, Louise Bethune, architect. No longer standing, this is one of only ten buildings done by Bethune's partnership for which she alone can be definitively credited. Photograph courtesy of Lockport Public Library.

of one-third of the outside work".[8] Yet one hundred years later, despite her numerous and significant contributions to Buffalo's architecture, Louise Bethune is remembered just vaguely and then only in connection with the Hotel Lafayette, keystone of her career.

Her office produced a continuous stream of industrial, commercial, and educational buildings of all sizes and types.[9] Many notable industrial buildings are in good condition today and are still in use for their initial purposes (e.g., the Iroquois Door Plant Company warehouse and the large Chandler Street complex for the Buffalo Weaving Company).

Between 1881 and 1904, when the City of Buffalo commissioned fifty-four new school buildings and twelve major additions to existing schools, Louise Bethune's office can be credited with the design of eighteen of these—plus the Lockport Union High School and a large addition to the old Griffith Institute in Springville.[10]

Her firm also built a number of structures for other uses: the woman's prison for the Erie County Penitentiary; grandstands for the Queen City Baseball and Amusement Company (later the Offerman

Baseball Stadium); the first building for the Seventy-fourth Regiment Armory (later converted into the Elmwood Music Hall); the transformer building for the first power line in the nation, bringing electricity from Niagara Falls to Buffalo's trolley system,[11] the Kensington Church in Buffalo; the Denton & Cottier music store, one of the first structures in the United States with a steel frame and poured concrete slabs; the police precinct station on Louisiana Street; a four-story multiple dwelling with stores; and a railroad station in Blackrock, now part of Buffalo.

Most of the firm's designs are utilitarian and indicate tight budget controls, at the same time showing good sense of proportion, discreet handling of decorative elements, and thorough knowledge of construction technology. It is only in a few projects that Louise Bethune shows her talent for classical detailing in elegant materials.

Above all, Louise Bethune has been praised for the design of the Lafayette Hotel, her authorship clearly acknowledged in writings of her

Detail, Lafayette Hotel. Observers may read the initials carved in stone as a decorative treatment of the Lafayette "L" or as the signature of Jennie Louise Bethune. Photograph by Joseph Stallone, courtesy of Adriana Barbasch

Hotel Lafayette, 1902–1904, Buffalo, New York, Louise Bethune, architect. Seriously deteriorated in the eighties, this building is considered the keystone of Bethune's career. Photograph by Joseph Stallone, courtesy of Adriana Barbasch

time. Originally planned for the Pan-American Exposition, the 225-room hotel was delayed by financial woes and change of ownership, and opened finally in 1904. With hot and cold water in all bathrooms, and telephones in all rooms, the seven-story hotel offered "the best that science, art and experience can offer for the comfort of the travelling public."[12] Four years later, an addition doubled the size of the hotel, and fifty years later it was still operating as a luxury 400-room hotel, run by three successive generations of the same family. Today it is a rooming house, in dire need of restoration.[13]

In contrast to the amazing range and variety of these projects, the office produced very few single-family residences, mostly for clients whose names are connected with other commissions. Louise Bethune had a strong dislike for single-residence architecture; she rejected the pigeon-holing of women to house design and, from her own experience, knew it to be the worst-paying and most frustrating job for any architect.[14]

Her professional reputation brought her enthusiastic admission to the Western Association of Architects in 1885. The board of directors, which included some of her eminent colleagues from Buffalo—Louis H. Sullivan, Daniel Burnham and John M. Root who all had offices then in Buffalo and knew her work well—first decided on the general principle of accepting women as members. "If the lady is practicing architecture and is in good standing, there is no reason why she should not be one of us." Louise Bethune's application was then voted on. "She has done work by herself and been very successful. She is unanimously elected a member."[15]

She was a major organizer in 1886 of the Architects Association in Buffalo, called the Buffalo Society of Architects until 1891 when it became the Buffalo Chapter of the American Institute of Architects. In 1888, she was elected to membership in the American Institute of Architects; in 1889, she became its first woman Fellow when the Western Association of Architects was merged with the Institute.[16] She was an active AIA member throughout her career and held chapter office as Vice-President and Treasurer.[17]

A woman of strong professional principles, she consistently supported the Architects' Licensing Bill, which, after twenty-five years of debate, became the law to enforce rigid preliminary examinations for the practice of architecture. And in 1891 she refused to compete for the design of the Woman's Building for the World's Columbian Exposition in Chicago, because it was against her principle of "Equal Remuneration for Equal Service." (Male architects were "appointed" to design major buildings and were paid $10,000 for artistic services only, with all construction drawings made at the expense of the Fair. Women architects were asked to compete for the artistic design and to provide all construction documents for a "prize" of $1,000.)[18]

Although there are conflicting dates for Louise Bethune's retirement, some as early as the 1890s, the Buffalo City Directories carried her name in the business section until 1910. She had moved close to her son's home in 1907; her husband's residence was shown as the place of business until 1911, when he moved out to join her. (It is possible that her early change of address was due to a kidney disease that required special care by her son, a urologist.) Louise Bethune died in 1913 at the age of fifty-seven.

Her will, containing a codicil dated 4 January 1908 and settling her share of the firm with the two remaining partners, confirms 1908 as the date of retirement. According to this codicil, written in her own handwriting, Jennie Louise Bethune had been sole owner of the office until the other two partners became financially involved, "since 1886 in the case of Robert A. Bethune and since 1893 in the case of Wm. L. Fuchs."[19]

She had been a pioneer and a highly principled professional. Her beliefs are stated in her speech of 6 March 1891 before the Women's Educational and Industrial Union: "[Women] meet no serious opposition from the profession nor the public. Neither are they warmly welcomed. They minister to no special needs of women, and receive no special favors from them."[20]

She continued with these thoughts, as reported in one of the local newspapers. While there had always been a need for women in the medical fraternity and while she believed there was a strong necessity for women in the legal profession, she said

there is no need whatever of a woman architect. No one wants her, no one yearns for her and there is no special line in architecture to which she is better adapted than a man . . . [The woman architect] has exactly the same work to do as a man. When a woman enters the profession she will be met kindly and will be welcome but not as a woman, only as an architect.[21]

The professional journal would quote her at some length about the few women in the profession, and about her hopes for their future.

There are among [the women graduates] a few brilliant and energetic women for whom the future holds great possibilities.

There are also a few women drafting in various offices through the country . . . They shirk the brick-and-mortar-rubber-boot-and-ladder-climbing period of investigative education, and as a consequence remain at the tracing stage of draftsmanship. There are hardly more successful women draftsmen than women graduates, but the next decade will doubtless give us a few thoroughly efficient architects from their number.[22]

She was far from being a rabble-rouser. To the women who heard her luncheon comments, she made clear the principles of her own career.

The objects of the business woman are quite distinct from those of the professional agitator. Her aims are conservative rather than aggressive, her strength lies in adaptability, not in reform, and her desire is to conciliate rather than to antagonize.[23]

She left those ladies, and she leaves us, with words that showed her belief in herself and her belief in women as architects. "The future of woman in the architectural profession is what she herself sees fit to make it."[24]

Notes

1. Frances E. Willard and Mary A. Livermore, eds., *A Woman of the Century: Fourteen Hundred-Seventy Biographical Sketches accompanied by Portraits of Leading American Women in All Walks of Life* (Buffalo: Charles Wells Moulton, 1893), 80–81.

2. *The National Cyclopaedia of American Biography*, vol. 12 (New York: James T. White & Company, 1904), 9.

3. Madeleine Stern, *We The Women: Career Firsts of Nineteenth-Century America* (New York: Schulte Publishing Company, 1963), 62.

4. Richard C. Brown and Bob Watson, *Buffalo: Lake City in Niagara Land, An Illustrated History* (Buffalo: Windsor Publications, Inc., 1981), 28–33.

5. *Our Police and Our City: The Official History of the Buffalo Police Department from the Earliest Days to the Present Time, Compiled by William H. Dolan, Clerk to the Board of Police, and a History of the City of Buffalo, with Biographies of Typical and Representative Citizens*, ed., Mark S. Hubel (Buffalo: Bensler & Wesley, 1893).

6. Brown and Watson, 44.

7. The statement that she was "the first professional woman architect in the United States" can be found in the following: Stern, 61; Willard and Livermore, 81; *Who's Who in New York, 1904*, 117; *The National Cyclopaedia of American Biography, 1904*, 9; *Notable American Women 1607–1950, Bibliographical Dictionary 1971*, vol. 1, 140.

8. "Some Distinguished Women of Buffalo," *American Woman's Illustrated World*, 7 October 1893. Biographical notes printed during her lifetime credit her as sole architect of the Hotel Lafayette and the Lockport Union High School, and we have a list of buildings submitted with her application for AIA membership: Public School No. 4; Police Station No. 2; Peter Hoffman's Millinery House; and residences for William Mitchell, Spencer Kellogg, H. G. Brooks, A. J. Meyer, and George Waterman.

9. The City of Buffalo recording of building permits started in 1892, and until 1896 did not state complete data on address, owner, construction description, or name of architect. Louise Bethune's projects executed between 1881 and 1896 therefore cannot be definitely determined from building permits. However, by comparing biographical information with Buffalo City Directories, with old city maps, and with the extensive photographic collections at the Buffalo & Erie County Historical Society, I could identify and verify a surprisingly large number of buildings executed by BB&F.

10. G. Morton Weed, *From the Boiler Room: The Buffalo Public Schools, 1807–1984*, (Buffalo: Printed by author, 1984). Public school buildings were recorded with the Board of Education; however, all drawings prior to 1930 have been discarded for lack of storage space. Fortunately, the Historical Society has all yearly reports of the Superintendent of Schools, which contain reproductions of plans and facades of major new projects, with building descriptions and sometimes with architects' names. Mr. G. Morton Weed, a chief engineer custodian of the school system, has done extensive research on the city's public schools and helped me with information and photographs of many schools now demolished. Mrs. Christa Caldwell assisted me in researching the Lockport Union High School; Mr. Alan V. Manchester, the Griffith Institute in Springville.

11. J. N. Larned, *A History of Buffalo: Delineating the Evolution of the City* (New York: Progress of the Empire State Company, 1911). The building permit recorded in 1896 for the construction of the Transformer Building corresponds with the date of the first electric power line from the Niagara Falls hydroelectric plant in Buffalo. This was the first transformer building in the city, and perhaps in the nation, to receive electricity from the Niagara Falls hydro-electric power plant; the building still stands.

12. "The Lafayette, A Fireproof Hotel," *The Illustrated Buffalo Express*, (29 May 1904): 11.

13. A search for information about the Hotel Lafayette led me to John Herlan, great-grandson of W. L. Fuchs. He owns original renderings of the Hotel Lafayette (a splendid Beaux-Arts-style watercolor) and the Denton & Cottier Music Store building, along with several rolled-up linen and tracing paper drawings, many of them water-damaged. Mr. Herlan turned down my offer to have the renderings photographed and the drawings restored.

14. "It is often proposed that [the woman architect] become exclusively a dwelling house architect. Pity her, and withdraw the suggestion. A specialist should become so from intrinsic fitness, not from extrinsic influence. Furthermore, the dwelling is the most pottering and worst-paid work an architect ever does. He always dreads it, not, as someone may have told you, because he must usually deal with a woman, but because he must strive to gratify the conflicting desires of an entire household, who dig up every hatchet for his benefit and hold daily powwows in his anteroom, and because he knows he loses money nearly every time. Dwelling house architecture, as a special branch for women, should be, at the present rate of remuneration, quite out of the question." Louise Bethune, "Women and Architecture" *Inland Architect and News Record* 17 (March 1891): 20–21.

15. George E. Pettengill, "How AIA Acquired its First Woman Member, Mrs. Louise Bethune," *AIA Journal* 63 (March 1975): 35.

16. The Western Association had only one class of membership—Fellow— so between 1889 and 1898, all existing members of the AIA became Fellows and all new members entered at that level. Thus, while Louise Bethune's election to

the AIA was on the merit of her work, her elevation to FAIA was a matter of good timing.

17. Buffalo City Directories 1887, 1888, and 1896.

18. Bethune: 21.

19. Last Will and Testament of Jennie Louise Bethune filed 16 January 1914, Surrogate Court, County of Erie, State of New York.

20. Bethune: 21.

21. "Women in Architecture: One Who Has Been Successful in it Talks to Other Women," *Buffalo Morning Express* (7 March 1881): 6. Other portions of this speech appeared in the *Buffalo Courier*, titled "Woman Architects: No Demand For Them Unless They Are Willing to Do Men's Work" (7 March 1881): 6. To my knowledge, there is no printed record of the entire speech.

22. Bethune: 21.

23. Ibid.

24. Ibid.

3

Caught in

the Crossfire

Women and

Architectural Education,

1880–1910

ELIZABETH G. GROSSMAN

AND LISA B. REITZES

Historians of the phenomenon of professionalization have consistently pointed out the connection between the desire of an occupation to gain professional status and the efforts by that occupation to require educational degrees as credentials.[1] Studies on women in the architecture have shared the assumption that there was a connection between the progress of women in the profession and their access to architecture schools.[2] In this essay, we shall show that between 1880 and 1910 the struggles to distinguish the architectural profession from the building trades made the question of the appropriate architectural training an ideological issue with particular ramifications for women.

The establishment of architecture schools in the United States after the Civil War would seem to have come at an optimum time for women. Collegiate education had already become an expectation of middle-class women,[3] and the architecture schools now seemed to promise women easier access to professional training than the apprenticeship system had offered. Apprenticeship confronted women with the personal prejudices of individual men; the seemingly objective standards of admission of the architecture schools suggested that people would be accepted on their merits, regardless of gender or class.[4] The endorsement of academic education by the American Institute of Architects further suggested that the profession was changing in ways helpful to women's entry.

Louise Blanchard Bethune, the first woman to be admitted to the AIA, seemed to appreciate the possibilities of this nexus of conditions. In a speech for the Women's Education and Industrial Union of Buffalo she linked the fluid state of architectural professionalization to opportunities for women: "Women have entered the architectural profession at a much earlier stage of its existence [than medicine or law] even before it has received legislative recognition. . . . The future of woman in the architectural profession is what she herself sees fit to make it."[5]

Bethune related these opportunities to what she saw as the general availability of academic education, pointing out that "with few exceptions the educational facilities are the same for men and women." Yet she also expressed disappointment at women's failure to capitalize on the apparent benefits of academic training in a profession waiting to receive them. "The total number of [women] graduates from the various schools in the country can hardly exceed a dozen and most of these seem to have renounced ambition with the attainment of the degree."[6]

Bethune may have sensed that conditions for women in architecture were not completely rosy. But instead of considering the underlying reasons for the malaise of her apparently ambitious sisters, she exhorted women to recognize their golden opportunities. Like many women who succeed in "male" fields, Bethune wanted to believe that her profession was at last free of gender bias. Her fulsome gratitude toward the AIA confirms her idealism:

The great architectural societies of the country, the American Institute and its state and city Chapters, are all open to [women] upon proof of qualification. Thank, with me, the noble-hearted men whose far-seeing polity and kindly nature has laid this stepping-stone.[7]

Ironically, at the same time that Bethune was encouraging women to rely on the beneficence of the Institute, the AIA was beginning to narrow its requirements for membership. The process took a few years but, effective in 1901, acting upon an 1897 recommendation of its Committee on Education, the AIA restricted membership to those who passed an examination set by the Institute or to those who presented a "degree from an accredited School of Architecture."[8] Because this decision ended the individualized review of applicants, it must have seemed to offer women a broader invitation to enter the profession, particularly as they were already admitted to four of the nine architecture schools.[9] The AIA's explicit statement that its new admission policy was intended to increase membership should also have seemed an encouraging sign for women.

Yet, as might be expected, the Institute was hardly interested in simply growing in numbers, but was claiming for itself stronger professional authority. The admissions criteria set down in 1901 added fresh currency to the long-standing campaign of architects to distinguish their profession from the building trades. By privileging the academic degree as a certification of "a definite and valuable standard of skill," the AIA was tacitly devaluing the apprenticeship system, which had its roots in the building trades.[10] Apprenticeship had thus far produced most of the nation's practitioners but it was not guided by examinations, much less academic degrees.

In this campaign to strengthen its authority, the AIA also intended to create a new image of "the architect." As articulated in its Report of the President, the AIA took the position that an architectural degree certified not only that an applicant possessed a particular level of skill, but also that the holder of the degree was a person of "established character."[11] Burton Bledstein explains in his study of professionalization in America that the concept of character occupied a central place in the culture of professionalism, but it had rather a different meaning than in society at large:

Character was the deepest self of the man that bound together the whole of the individual. It made possible the self-reliant intellect that could both think irrespective of public approval and exert a supreme effort of human attention to overcome any personal obstacle. The impressiveness of a man's worldly credentials reflected the strength of his inner character, the permanence of his inner continuity, which corresponded to the outer continuity of his career.[12]

What we have here is a circular definition that links career achievement with masculine attributes. Women, because of the social forces hindering their ability to gain "worldly credentials," were not likely to fulfill this professional definition of "character," nor was their "innate" good

Architecture students and faculty at Massachusetts Institute of Technology, 1909. Women tentatively identified are (left to right) Rebecca Hull Thompson, Lahvesia Paxton Packwood, Helen McGraw Longyear, and Florence Luscomb. Increasingly, an academic education became the route by which women entered the profession in these decades. Photograph courtesy of MIT Museum

nature likely to be accepted as a worthy equivalent of the *acquired* professional character sought by the AIA.[13] An academic degree might produce the same level of skill for men and women, but it could not carry the same signification of proper character.

   The equivocal relation of women to the profession was clarified in 1906, when the Committee on Education set forth a definition of the architect making it absolutely clear that architecture was a profession best served by *gentlemen*—and only those with the loftiest cultural and social ambitions at that.

An architect we defined as one ranking in the class of men of culture, learning and refinement, differentiated from the others of his class solely by his function as a creator of pure beauty, as an exponent through material forms of the best secular, intellectual, and religious civilization of his time, and as an organizer and director of manifold and varied industries and activities.

   From these assumptions, it follows necessarily that the objective of architectural education must be the breeding of gentlemen of cultivation, learning, and broad sympathies, who understand the dignity and significance of art both as beauty and as language . . . and who can inspire, organize and direct widely different classes of men.[14]

Clearly, for all that the new AIA policy appeared to be offering women access to the practice of architecture on objective—that is, equal—terms, in actuality what was being constructed was a model of the architect that, at the very least, presented serious barriers to women's inclusion and guaranteed that women's presence would be considered aberrant. Although the Committee on Education did not speak for the entire AIA membership, much less for the profession at large, the Committee was in these years dominated by architecture school educators and graduates. Indeed, the Harvard School of Architecture publicly endorsed the 1906 policy statement.[15] Thus, the Committee represented the values of the schools and the elite of the profession.[16] This was the AIA of "noble-hearted men" that Louise Bethune had earlier recommended to her "sisters" as open to all qualified women.

But Bethune's understanding of what a woman architect must do to succeed in this profession was more pragmatic than suggested by her avid enthusiasm for the AIA. At the same time that she urged women entering the field to take fuller advantage of academic programs, she also warned them not to "shirk" other aspects of their education.[17] More specifically, she insisted that "women who are pioneers in any profession should be proficient in every department" and that "women architects must be practical superintendents as well as designers and scientific constructors."[18]

We might attribute Bethune's model of the woman architect to her own preferences and experience. Though she had prepared herself to enter the architecture program at Cornell, she chose instead to seek an apprenticeship. In her active partnership in Buffalo, she prided herself on having "a practical knowledge of all details of a building."[19] In effect, Bethune was proposing that women must do more than men—be more comprehensively competent—to succeed in architecture.

Bethune's statements about the necessity of practical expertise for women architects were also made, no doubt, in response to the continuing litany of questions about whether women had the physical stamina and practical knowledge to be architects. For example, an 1876 editorial in *American Architect and Building News* alleged that, for women, "the work of superintending would probably be found too laborious and inconvenient, and would certainly involve a change in fashion of raiment; and the preparation of large working-drawings would be almost equally awkward." This editorial concluded its sartorial concerns with the opinion that women, though they might possess "good powers of design," could only aspire to be "valuable co-adjutors to architects."[20]

Because Bethune wanted women to be architects in their own right, she encouraged them to counter these gender-based prejudices by acquiring comprehensive practical skills. But where could women acquire these particular qualifications? During the same time that Bethune was exhorting women to be "complete" practitioners, many architecture schools were widening the distinction in their curricula between the aesthetic and technical training of the student/architect. Indeed, in this period, the AIA Committee on Education specifically recommended more emphasis on the "aesthetic" in architecture school curricula.[21]

Bethune's remarks in 1891 must have taken on particular import for academically trained women in light of the professional stir prompted by Sophia Hayden's nervous collapse during the construction of her design for the Woman's Building at the World's Columbian Exposition. In an all too predictable editorial, *AABN* worried that

the planning and construction of any building, with the accompanying dealing with clients is always liable to be "especially trying." . . . If the building of which the women seem to be so proud . . . is to mark the physical ruin of its architect, it will be a much more telling argument against the wisdom of women entering this especial profession than anything else could be.[22]

A strong rebuttal was made by a successful woman architect, Minerva Parker Nichols of Philadelphia, who had actually lost the Woman's Building competition to Hayden.[23] "It is not fair, because one woman makes a doubtful success, to draw conclusions from her example. . . . Because one woman suffers from exhaustion in the daily wear and tear of her household duty, you would not say that women were unfitted for domestic life."[24] Nichols objected to a gender explanation for Hayden's predicament; she assumed that, given a real chance, women architects would prove as capable as men.

It is time to put aside prejudice and sentimentalism, and judge women's work by their ability. Let the conditions and restrictions be exactly the same as those under which men work , . . . so that the restriction shall be one of ability, and not sex. We do not need women as architects, we do not need men, but we do need brains enough to lift the architecture of this country beyond the grasp of unskilled and unqualified practitioners.[25]

To explain Hayden's failure to prove the capabilities of women, Nichols blamed the training her colleague had received. Hayden had received a

four-year degree from MIT in 1890 but, in Nichols's view, was "unpre-
pared through lack of practical experience" to take on the commission
for the Woman's Building in 1891.[26]

Yet it would be a mistake to assume that Nichols thought academic
training a waste of time for women. In fact, she seemed to see this route
as particularly suited to them and seemed still to perceive apprenticeship as the more common route for men. Yet if a woman could not attend
a school, Nichols saw "no reason why she may not study after the same
fashion *as a man does* [emphasis added], and enter the office of a first-
class architect and thus begin the study of her work in a practical
way."[27]

In describing this "alternative route" for women, Nichols was
describing her own experience since, like Bethune, she had come to
architecture through an apprenticeship. After graduating from the Philadelphia Normal Art School, she entered the office of Philadelphia architect Frederick Thorn, Jr., and while training with him took courses in
architectural drawing and design at the Franklin Institute. When Thorn
retired four years later, Nichols took over the business, continuing her
education at the Philadelphia Museum and School of Industrial Arts.[28]
Thus she did not go from the academy to the office, but rather, as was
usual for men, supplemented her practical training with course work.
The favorable aspects of her own academic experiences undoubtedly
made Nichols idealistic about the options presented to women by the
architecture schools. But the concern that she and Bethune expressed,
about the lack of practical expertise of school-trained women, realisti-
cally echoed the views of male architects who would be the colleagues
and employers of women entering the field.

To obtain the kind of practical experience that Nichols and Bethune
endorsed, however, women coming out of the schools (like men) had to
enter what amounted to an "internship" in an architect's office—a period
the AIA would later formally define as the "candidacy."[29] The difficulty
was that, in seeking to fulfill this requirement, women aspirants were
back in the position of having to be accepted by an individual mentor,
the very impediment that admission to an architecture school was supposed to eliminate.

Nichols was peculiarly optimistic about the chances for school-
trained women to continue their training in an office—"there are very
few architects who would not be willing to offer a helping hand to any
woman whom they saw earnestly attempting to join their ranks"[30]—but
her own circumstances had been fortuitous. After inheriting her

mentor's active Philadelphia practice, Nichols went on to have a prosperous, if relatively short, career as an architect best known for her suburban houses and for her work with women's organizations.[31] For our purposes, what is most significant about Nichols is the extravagant support she received from the builders' community in Philadelphia. *The Philadelphia Real Estate Record and Builders' Guide*, which identified itself as "devoted to real estate, building, architectural and insurance interests," gave an entire front page to Nichols's career in 1890. Earlier this journal had proudly announced her entry into the profession as "the only [woman] in this city who has chosen this useful occupation,"[32] and it followed her work until she left the city in 1896.

The *PRERBG* used Nichols's established success to substantiate its claim that "a position [in architecture] is waiting for every woman [who] makes herself capable of filling it." This article emphatically stated that gender had not been a factor in the fortunes of "the only woman architect in Philadelphia":

Strange to say the fact of being a woman has never, at any time, been a serious drawback, nor in any way handicapped her while pursuing her line of work. On the contrary, words of encouragement and good fellowship have at all times been freely extended, both by the public in general and her fellow architects. . . . As to builders, mechanics, and all with whom she has come in contact, the only advantage any of them has taken in dealing with a woman has been added care on their part in executing the work called for by her plans and specifications.[33]

The enthusiasm of the *PRERBG* shows the local builders' community to be far more receptive to women at this time than the part of the profession that espoused the AIA model of architecture. Indeed, the builders actively recruited women into architectural practice.

However, as with the AIA model of the "qualified" architect, the definition of "capable" that the *PRERBG* offered in support of Nichols was specific and value-laden. Nichols was praised because she "[did] not come before the public with the plea that she is a woman, and therefore to be helped and supported, but as fully prepared as the generality of her co-laborers."[34] In other words, this journal's remarkable endorsement of Nichols lay not only in the fact that she was adequately trained, but also in the fact that she was trained in such a way as not to set her apart from the community in which she worked. For the *PRERBG*, this meant training through apprenticeship, not through an elite academic program.

The *PRERBG* clearly believed that apprenticeship trained a person to be an architect and not merely a builder. In its commentary on the results of the 1891 competition for the Woman's Building, the journal predictably endorsed Minerva Parker Nichols's design, but it also asserted that the other top competitors (Sophia Hayden, Lois Howe, Laura Hayes) were not "professional architects and therefore the competition cannot be classed as one based on true architectural merit."[35] Hayden and Howe had both recently graduated from MIT, and therefore, by *PRERBG* standards, lacked practical experience, and Laura Hayes had received no formal training in architecture at all.[36] Among these women, only Nichols had come to the competition with full credentials.

In sum, Bethune's and Nichols's advocacy of academic education and practical experience for women derived from their belief that a woman's success in the profession depended on her becoming a "complete architect." But the professional struggles between architects and builders were in effect rendering that model of the architect meaningless. Instead of seeking a larger conception of the profession, each of these factions actually sought authority for its own more limited definition of the field. Women, not surprisingly, got caught in this male battle for professional turf.

The efforts of certain architects, in this period, to define a profession of architecture apart from building focused on the credibility of academic education. This locus of the conflict became, it seems, a quagmire of options for women. The willingness of at least some schools to admit women offered the hope, perhaps for the first time, that women would be judged equally with men. Yet, because one of the stated functions of this education was to construct a model of the "gentleman" architect, this route hardly offered women entrance into a gender-free realm.

Furthermore, once these women graduated, they faced the difficulty of finding an office in which to intern, to acquire that "practical experience" they were assumed as a sex to be lacking, regardless of their previous education. It seems likely that if a woman applied for internship to an architect who valued school training, the "gentlemanly" model would work against her. On the other hand, if she sought employment from the ranks of architects who were not themselves academically trained, these practitioners would be suspicious, not only of her training but also of her inappropriate architectural ambitions.[37] It was commonplace in this period, for instance, to assume that women who did enter the profession should "specialize" in domestic architecture.[38] Yet the schools, in their curricula and underlying philosophy, encouraged students to aspire to design buildings for the great cultural institutions of the country.[39]

If a woman who wished to become an architect in this period understood from the start that the professional status promised by the academic degree was not intended for her, she could choose to try to enter an apprenticeship with an established, sympathetic architect. If she joined a small firm of local reputation and became a house designer, she could hope for professional acceptance and an active, profitable career. However, for some ambitious, middle-class women—for whom professional identity was increasingly linked to higher education—this "traditional" route must have seemed an unattractive option. For, insofar as they embraced the AIA definition of the architect, these women might have seen apprenticeship as a process jeopardizing both their professional and class status.[40]

Given the prospects that professionalization and academic education actually opened for women in this period, is it any wonder that, as Louise Bethune observed, most of the women who graduated from the schools "renounced ambition with the attainment of the degree" or that, according to the *PRERBG*, "In Philadelphia, while most of the trades and professions are ably represented by a number of bright and intelligent women, that of architecture has but one follower."[41]

Notes

We wish to acknowledge the contributions, at various stages of this project, of Baruch Kirschenbaum, Sharon Hartman Strom, Sandra Tatman, Patricia Wright, and the librarians of the Art and Music Department of the Providence Public Library.

1. See, for example: Burton T. Bledstein, *The Culture of Professionalism: The Middle Class and the Development of Higher Education in America* (New York, W. W. Norton & Co., 1976). Most definitions of a profession include requisite specialized or advanced training. By 1921, a federal government effort to distinguish professional and nonprofessional work even went so far as to state that "College education is at least presumptive evidence that an applicant is a professional worker," as Elizabeth Kemper Adams quoted in her *Women Professional Workers: A Study Made for the Women's Educational and Industrial Union* (New York: Macmillan Company, 1921), 8.

2. See, for example: Susana Torre, ed., *Women in American Architecture: A Historic and Contemporary Perspective* (New York: Whitney Library of Design, 1977);

Doris Cole, *From Tipi to Skyscraper* (Boston: i press, 1973); and Gwendolyn Wright, "On the Fringe of the Profession: Women in American Architecture," in *The Architect: Chapters in the History of the Profession* ed. Spiro Kostof (New York: Oxford University Press, 1977).

3. See Barbara Miller Solomon, *In the Company of Educated Women: A History of Women and Higher Education in America* (New Haven: Yale University Press, 1985), Chap. 4.

4. For a discussion of women's assumptions about the meritocratic nature of the professions, see Penina Migdal Glazer and Miriam Slater, *Unequal Colleagues: The Entrance of Women into the Professions, 1890–1940* (New Brunswick: Rutgers University Press, 1986), 10–14.

5. Louise Blanchard Bethune, "Women and Architecture," *The Inland Architect and News Record* 17 (March 1891): 20–21.

6. Ibid., 21.

7. Ibid., 21.

8. *Proceedings of the Thirty-Fifth Annual Convention of the American Institute of Architects* 35 (1901–2), 11.

9. As of 1901, the following schools admitted women: Cornell University (1871); Syracuse University (1871); University of Illinois (1873); and MIT (1883). For additional discussion of these programs, see Torre, 55–56. For general information on architecture schools at this time, see Turpin Bannister, ed., *The Architect at Mid-Century: Evolution and Achievement* (New York: Reinhold Publishing Corporation, 1954), 96–98, and Arthur Clason Weatherhead, *History of Collegiate Education in Architecture in the United States* (Los Angeles: By the author, 1941).

10. *Proceedings* 35, 11.

11. Ibid. This phrase was used by AIA President Robert Peabody in his address to the Annual AIA Convention in 1901. He stated that "we seek to make membership a sign of established character."

12. Bledstein, 158.

13. For the various dimensions of the connection between women's education and women's character, see Solomon, Chap. 2.

14. *Proceedings* 40 (1906–7), 27.

15. For the Harvard endorsement, see *Architectural Record* 22 (March 1907): 135. This article asserts that the AIA statement represented "the ideals" of Harvard's Department of Architecture "from the first." It is interesting to speculate about the connection between this fervent embrace of AIA ideology and Harvard's lengthy refusal to admit women.

16. For the roster of members of the Committee on Education, see the list of Standing Committees in *Proceedings* (1890–1910). Henry F. and Elsie Rathburn Withey, *Biographical Dictionary of American Architects, Deceased* (1956; reprint, Los Angeles: Hennessey & Ingalls, Inc., 1970) provides biographical information on the individual architects mentioned.

17. These practical aspects are Bethune's often-quoted "brick-and-mortar-rubber-boot-and-ladder-climbing period of investigative education." Bethune: 21.

18. Quoted in Madeleine Stern, *We the Women: Career Firsts of Nineteenth-Century America* (New York: Schulte Publishing Company, 1963), 65.

19. Stern, 65.

20. Editorial, *American Architect and Building News* 1 (30 September 1876): 313.

21. For an overview of curricular shifts in architecture programs in this period, see Bannister, 96–100. See also: Caroline Shillaber, *Massachusetts Institute of Technology School of Architecture and Planning, 1861–1961* (Cambridge: MIT, 1963) and Richard Oliver, ed., *The Making of an Architect, 1881–1981* (New York: Rizzoli, 1981). For the views of the Committee on Education, see *Proceedings* 40, 30.

22. Editorial *AABN* 38 (26 November 1892): 134.

23. For a detailed description of the circumstances and outcomes of the competition for the Woman's Building, see Jeanne Weimann, *The Fair Women* (Chicago: Academy Chicago, 1891).

24. Minerva Parker Nichols, "A Woman on the Woman's Building," *AABN* 38 (10 December 1892): 169.

25. Ibid.

26. Ibid.

27. "Representative Women: Minerva Parker Nichols," *Woman's Progress* 1 (May 1893): 59. In this article, Nichols specifically encouraged women to "take the four year course at the Boston School of Technology [MIT]."

28. Biographical information on Minerva Parker Nichols may be obtained from articles in *The Philadelphia Real Estate Record and Builders' Guide* (14 August 1889; 26 March 1890) and in *Woman's Progress* 1 (May 1893): 57–60, as well as in Frances E. Willard and Mary A. Livermore, eds., *A Woman of the Century: Fourteen Hundred-Seventy Biographical Sketches accompanied by Portraits of Leading American Women in All Walks of Life* (Buffalo: Charles Wells Moulton, 1893). Concerning Nichols's academic training, the University of Pennsylvania began architectural instruction in 1874 and established its School of Architecture in 1890, but it did not admit women to its architectural degree programs until 1949.

29. Bannister, 332–33, in the 1954 report of the Committee on Education, *The Architect at Mid-Century*, the "candidacy" is defined as the period in which the aspirant "seeks to acquire the practical knowledge, skills, and judgment which are the prerequisites to full professional status." The Report states that "school and office training must complement each other in the attainment of professionally competent personnel."

30. "Representative Women": 60.

31. See *PRERBG*, various notices 1889–1896. Nichols's house in Cynwyd, Pa. was published in *American Architect and Building News* 39 (11 February 1893): 95. For information on Nichols's work for the New Century Club in Philadel-

phia, see Trades League of Philadelphia, *The City of Philadelphia* (Philadelphia: G. S. Harris & Sons, 1894). Twenty-three drawings of various works by Minerva Parker Nichols are at the Arthur and Elizabeth Schlesinger Library on the History of Women in America, Radcliffe College.

32. *PRERBG* (14 August 1889): 378.

33. *PRERBG* (26 March 1890): 1. Over the years, the *PRERBG* conscientiously noted in many of the announcements of her projects that Nichols superintended the construction of buildings she designed.

34. *PRERBG* (14 August 1889): 378.

35. *PRERBG* (1 April 1893): 193.

36. Torre, 71–73. Illustrated here are the Howe and Hayes competition drawings, and the Nichols design for the Isabella Pavilion (later submitted to the competition).

37. Bannister, 98. In accounting for the small proportion of architects who were academically trained by 1900, the AIA Report identifies "the suspicion of many practitioners" as a significant factor.

38. For discussion of the "rigid categorization" of women in architecture offices and practice, see Wright, "On the Fringe of the Profession," 280–81.

39. While the incompatibility of academic training and actual practice might have been more striking for women, a similar situation existed for most students coming out of the schools, which in this period were mostly intensifying their attachment to instructional methods and philosophies of the Ecole des Beaux-Arts. Gwendolyn Wright, in *Moralism and the Model Home: Domestic Architecture and Cultural Conflict in Chicago, 1873–1913* (Chicago: University of Chicago Press, 1980), 212–20, discusses the general schism between academic curricula and the "standard practice" of architecture at this time.

40. For a discussion of the relationship of formal education, apprenticeship, and class, see: Milka Bliznakov, "Women Architects" in *The Structurist* 25/26 (1985/86): 121–27.

41. *PRERBG* (26 March 1890): 1.

4

Mariana Van

Rensselaer

An Architecture Critic

in Context

LISA KOENIGSBERG

Mariana Van Rensselaer (1851–
1934) was part of a tradition of American women who wrote about extant
architecture, a tradition that flourished for several literary generations
between 1848 and 1913.[1]

These women writers constitute a tradition, heretofore unrecognized, in that they fulfilled the same role and occupied the same position with respect to their readers and to the professional establishment.[2] As such, they comprise what might be called the "related
regulated occupation" of writing about existing architecture.[3] They
wrote for a general public, in an occupation made possible because architects needed allies and popularizers to separate themselves from builders and to define themselves as professionals. These writers (including
Van Rensselaer) often served as intermediaries between the general public of potential clients and the professional establishment, translating
many of the profession's views for a lay audience.[4] This related occupation was also regulated in that its practitioners were often unofficially

Augustus Saint-Gaudens, Mrs. Schuyler Van Rensselaer, *bronze bas-relief, 1888; gift of Mrs. Schuyler Van Rensselaer, 1919. Photograph courtesy of Metropolitan Museum of Art*

(but carefully) examined by members of the professional establishment for adherence to appropriate standards.

Van Rensselaer was one of this tradition's most important figures (although she was also known as a historian and a writer on pictorial arts), and this essay will place her within the context of the architectural world. Gender played a critical role in this world during her era, and I contend that the general professional antipathy to women should be considered when viewing her role as a writer on architecture.

Van Rensselaer's privileged background, like that of other women writers about architecture, provided her with an alternative education

that enabled her to write on this subject for a general public of potential clients. As the child of an Alley and a Griswold, both members of
established New York families, wealth and social prominence were
Mariana's birthright. With this social station came education by private
tutors, an early knowledge of art and culture, and summer visits to such
fashionable places as Newport, Rhode Island. When, in 1868, her parents went abroad to live in Dresden, Mariana accompanied them. There
she met and, in 1873, married Schuyler Van Rensselaer (b.1845), a
Harvard- and Freiburg-educated mining engineer from an equally distinguished family. Returning to America, the couple made their home
in New Brunswick, New Jersey—birthplace of their only child George
Griswold (1875–94)—until Schuyler's death in 1884. From 1885 until her
own death, Van Rensselaer lived once again in Manhattan. During her
adult life, she continued to travel to Europe and spent many summers
in Marion, Massachusetts, and other summer colonies.

Van Rensselaer—like the other women—referred often to the places
where she had travelled and lived. Her journeys provided her with experiences on which to base several articles on German architecture for
American Architect and Building News (hereafter *AABN*), as well as a series
on English cathedrals and another series on French churches for *Century*.[5] In addition, many of Van Rensselaer's writings discuss her native
New York.[6] She also considered the architecture of the summer colonies near Boston, and of Newport, places with which she was quite
familiar.[7]

As an expression of her feminine identity and as a gesture to her
general audience (which included women), some of Van Rensselaer's
writings on contemporary architecture emphasized the home, as did
architectural writings of the other women writers in this tradition. In
so doing, she ensured the continued importance of the concept of
domesticity, a nineteenth-century notion that the home was a woman's
realm and haven.[8] For example, she stressed dwellings in five articles in
the "Recent Architecture in America" series (1884–86), devoting more
attention to domestic structures than to any other type. In her biography of Henry Hobson Richardson, she separated the domestic commissions, tending to treat all other buildings chronologically. In "The Development of American Homes," she again emphasized the home, thus
acknowledging that her readers were more likely to commission or purchase a home than any other type of building.[9]

Van Rensselaer's alternative education (itself due to her gender,
although made possible by her privileged background) uniquely suited

her for her role as an intermediary between the general public and the professional—and generally male—architectural world. Few women from her milieu received higher educations during these years.[10] She was also essentially excluded from professional school by virtue of her sex. In contrast, architects and male professional writers on architecture, who often came from equally prominent social backgrounds, began to pursue apprenticeships, attend universities and professional architecture schools, and assume editorial positions.[11] In 1881, rejecting a suggestion by Sylvester Rosa Koehler, editor of the *American Art Review*, that she begin a new magazine (after financial problems halted publication of his own journal) Van Rensselaer said "as . . . with almost all of my sex, I have family duties which must take precedence of all others." She added, "People say that the fact of being a woman need not limit one's activity, but I do not find it so!"[12] Her opposition to women's suffrage, documented by her pamphlet *Should We Ask for the Suffrage?* (1894), is further evidence of her belief in women's different role and responsibilities.[13]

The full-scale professionalization of architecture provided opportunities for Van Rensselaer by creating an increased need for mediators between the professional architectural establishment and the potential client; that is, a need for advocates of the profession's concerns. For example, it was of supreme importance to the profession that architects (rather than builders) be employed; accordingly, in Van Rensselaer's eyes, the professional architect (always male) was indispensable: "Instead of blaming our architecture for being 'too professional', we should blame it for being not by a thousand degrees professional *enough*."[14] She also contrasted the "thoughtless, untrained, 'popular' " pursuit of architecture with the architect's "educated, deliberating, theorizing" mind, employing the evocative term "scientific" to suggest command of a body of theoretical and systematized knowledge, one of the main characteristics of a professional and one that separates an architect from a builder.[15]

Endorsement of particular architects and styles was an additional aspect of Van Rensselaer's role as a writer on architecture. Although her writings were certainly didactic, many can also be seen as "prescriptive" tools that told "the wide general public of future clients, . . . the patrons," which architects and styles to select.[16] Thus, she served as a publicist within an increasingly competitive consumer economy in which home-ownership had become part of the very definition of middle-class status.[17]

Although Van Rensselaer praised other styles and the work of other architects, through the publication of the Richardson biography in 1888 she enthusiastically promoted Richardson and his work in the Romanesque style, first epitomized for her by his Trinity Church (1872–77) in Boston. However, in 1892 she announced that although Richardson's architecture would never be forgotten, its style was no longer the most "original" and "pleasing to the public eye."[18] She then solely endorsed the Renaissance style exemplified by McKim, Mead, and White's Boston Public Library (1887–95), proclaiming that the art which "was reborn with the birth of modern civilization" was the proper style for the twentieth century.[19] Along with the architects whose work she championed, Van Rensselaer urged a schematized treatment of interiors in which "the same style, the same spirit . . . the same fundamental ideas prevail throughout."[20] She advocated the gradual creation of a national style forged out of the vocabulary of the past, but noted that uniquely American circumstances would dictate certain specifically American solutions, such as the American "country dwelling."[21]

However, professionalization also created unforeseen difficulties for Van Rensselaer, whose writings were often evaluated by members of the professional establishment to ensure that they upheld standards deemed appropriate by them. Her works were lauded when they served the profession's needs; for example, for her endorsement of the profession in "Client and Architect," an essay first published in *North American Review* (1890) and, at the AIA convention of that year, recommended for reprinting and distribution to its members, Van Rensselaer was made an honorary member of the AIA in 1890.[22] However, even writings by Van Rensselaer, who was clearly perceived as an advocate of the profession's interests, were negatively reviewed when they did not stress what the profession deemed important. For example, *Architectural Record* dismissed the book version of *English Cathedrals* (1892) as "ephemeral [and] . . . popular," while *AABN* sniffed that the book "smacks of the magazine and so, almost, . . . of the literary hack."[23]

Van Rensselaer was certainly aware that members of the professional establishment evaluated her writings. Throughout her career, she was concerned about her ability to discuss technical matters and feared that her writings would not satisfy a professional audience.[24] Even in the introduction to *English Cathedrals*, a work aimed at the layman, she assumed a deferential tone toward the professional establishment; referring to herself as "an amateur" Van Rensselaer "confess[ed] that this is a book for amateurs, not architects" who, she hoped would put her "sketch" into "the hands of... the untravelled, unprofessional American."[25]

Perhaps because of her anxieties about writing in a more technical vein and for a professional audience, Van Rensselaer did not publish most of her work on architecture in *AABN*.[26] Instead, many of her writings on architectural topics appeared in *Century* magazine, one of the most important post-Civil War general monthlies aimed at what she termed "that easily bored creature, the Average Reader."[27] As a contributor to *Century*, Van Rensselaer was pressured to keep her essays light in tone because Richard Watson Gilder, her editor, feared that her contributions on architecture were too dry and technical for his readership.[28]

To understand fully Van Rensselaer's role as a writer on architecture, she must be placed in the professional context within which she attempted—but felt unable—to operate. The professional establishment's hostility to women between the mid-1800s and the early 1900s should be seen as an additional and daunting obstacle, one of which she must have been cognizant. Since the professional press is an extension of the architectural establishment, Van Rensselaer's reticence about publishing on architecture in *AABN* should be viewed as an aspect of women's difficulties in gaining acceptance within the profession. Van Rensselaer's female contemporaries generally did not enroll in America's recently established architecture departments and schools, which "pointedly discouraged" or refused to consider women's applications.[29] Women often faced difficulties when competing for fellowships and in joining professional associations.[30] Women architects frequently had difficulty securing varied types of commissions. In addition, their work often went unrecognized; perhaps as a response, some women eventually began to form their own firms.[31]

Furthermore, at least through 1900, the editors of *AABN*, which was "designed as a vehicle of expression for the architectural profession," and which Van Rensselaer (as a contributor) would have read, felt that American women should not become architects, suggesting that they instead pursue "various forms of decorative art" and decoration.[32] This journal recommended that instead of pursuing careers as architects, "all lady clients and wives of clients ... take pains to instill [in architects] the requisite knowledge" of "the requirements of houses which women acquire by living in them," although they noted, reluctantly, that anonymous work in support of architects could conceivably be done by women.[33] The editors subsequently opined that few women could "endure the strain" of being *"practising* architects as the word is under-stood by male practitioners."[34] Sophia Hayden, architect of the Woman's Building at the World's Columbian Exposition, who had "broken down mentally" and had possibly acquired "brain fever" from overwork, was used to exemplify purported feminine weakness.[35]

Undeterred by Minerva Parker Nichols's spirited defense of women's right to pursue careers as architects, *AABN's* editors later main-tained that "in an American school, it might be predicted that the girls, although industrious and faithful, would not, as a rule, succeed in the intense labor necessary to perform architectural work of real value," although they admitted that French women might succeed in the hot-house atmosphere of Paris.[36] By reprinting an extract from a paper that appeared in the Royal Institute of British Architects' *Journal*, the edi-tors at least put before their audience, if they did not directly endorse, the notion that if architecture "can maintain its original place among the sciences" it "may yet successfully resist the blandishments of the better half of human kind," that is, of women.[37] In effect, the journal proposed a division with men controlling the "science" and "art" of structure and architecture, while women might influence taste through suggestion and by practicing the arts of decoration.

In fact, it was easier for women to specialize in domestic commis-sions—or to become interior decorators and landscape architects—than it was for them to pursue careers as professionally trained architects with well-rounded practices.[38] In 1900, there were only 100 women archi-tects, as opposed to 10,500 male architects; such a statistic demonstrates women's problems in gaining acceptance within the profession.[39] Even women who were professionally trained often worked almost exclusively on the domestic commissions deemed appropriate for women archi-tects.[40] The women's clubs and women's pavilions that became popular in the late nineteenth century created a new type of commission fre-quently awarded to women architects, who were employed to design a home away from home for their own sex.[41] In effect, women architects had thrust upon them (and often accepted) the domestic slant evident in some of Van Rensselaer's writings and in books and articles by other women writers in the tradition.

A brief survey of some major architectural journals reveals that, during the years when Van Rensselaer wrote about architecture (and even as late as 1910), few American women appear to have written about the subject in these pages. American women's writings on architecture were not often published in *AABN*, although two women, the Countess von Krackow and Sophia Beale (neither American), were published frequently. The journal considered Beale's book on Paris churches (much of which had appeared in their pages) "historical and archaeological," rather than architectural; von Krackow wrote about the culture and architecture of the German-speaking lands.[42] A sampling of the western journals, *Inland Architect* and *Western Architect*, also reveals few articles by American women writers, and they appear not to have contributed to *Brickbuilder*, a journal published in Boston.

Similarly, few American women seem to have published articles on architecture in *Architectural Record*. Katharine C. Budd, the one who published the greatest number of articles on architectural concerns in that periodical during the first decade of the twentieth century (some related to domestic topics and some accompanied by drawings she herself had executed), studied privately with William R. Ware of Columbia University and in Paris and appears to have become the first woman member of the New York chapter of the AIA.[43] Thus, professional training, which was not readily available to women during this period, seems to have been an important factor for those American women who were seeking to publish about architecture in these journals.

The paucity of published work on architecture by American women in these professional journals during this period suggests that the hostility expressed toward American women as practitioners might well apply by extension to American women as writers for such journals. At the very least, the profession's prejudice against American women as architects seems to have served as a barrier that American women were reluctant to cross in order to write on architecture, particularly contemporary American architecture. Not surprisingly, it appears to have been easier for them to publish on the arts of decoration and the pictorial arts in these same professional magazines.[44] Although Van Rensselaer was reluctant to write about architecture in *AABN*, she did contribute a significant number of articles on pictorial and decorative arts, the latter clearly deemed suitably feminine by the profession and by that periodical.[45] Her last contributions to *AABN* discussed landscape gardening, which was considered more "suitable employment" for women.[46]

Van Rensselaer must have perceived a professional antipathy to women as architects and as writers on architecture for the professional press. This awareness probably contributed to her lack of confidence in addressing the profession about its own "art."

In the late 1880s, Van Rensselaer became a major participant in the rebirth of American interest in landscape gardening, about which she published numerous articles, including an important study of Frederick Law Olmsted, and *Art-Out-of-Doors*.⁴⁷ Writing on landscape architecture allowed Van Rensselaer to resolve her confusion and anxieties over structure and signalled her involvement with what was considered a more appropriate feminine concern: "women and gardening, as opposed to women and building, were naturally connected.⁴⁸ Insisting that no house was too small for an architect and no yard or garden was too small for a landscape architect's arts, Van Rensselaer once again discussed the domestic realm.⁴⁹ In keeping with her notions on interiors, she prescribed harmony between the "grounds and the house" and between the "homegrounds and the outer landscape."⁵⁰

Van Rensselaer also served as an advocate for what she termed the emerging "profession" of landscape architecture (as she had promoted the profession of architecture). Olmsted figured as her prototype for the new professional, and she urged readers interested in pursuing careers as landscape architects to travel and seize the "chance to enter an office like Mr. Olmsted's." She also stressed the need for "a school of gardening art."⁵¹

Directly translating many of Olmsted's concerns into her writings and thus serving as an intermediary between a new professional establishment and its potential client, Van Rensselaer expressed the hope, in *Art-Out-of-Doors*, that as "we have learned not to confound an architect with a builder, or with the carpenter . . . soon, perhaps, we shall be wise enough not to confound a landscape-gardener with a mere grower of plants."⁵² Praising her efforts, Olmsted noted, "we have had five young men coming to us for 'advice' about entering our profession, all referring to your articles.⁵³

Most important in this context, her new interest in landscape was related to her concern for pictorial arts and enabled her to view architecture as an element within the larger composition, the landscape. She maintained that if the trees and shrubs "form a picture, it will give us the same sort of satisfaction that we get from a good landscape on canvas."⁵⁴ The landscape gardener/architect should "accept Nature's frame, outlines, and materials, and paint his pictures according to her local specifications."⁵⁵ By discussing architecture as an element in a composition, she freed herself of the burden of understanding architecture's technical and structural aspects; and at the same time she moved farther away from the area deemed unsuitable for women by the architectural establishment.

During the middle years of her life, Van Rensselaer was active in New York's social causes; she also began writing fiction. After the turn of the century, she returned to writing poetry.[56] In addition, her two-volume *History of the City of New York in the Seventeenth Century* appeared (1909). Despite such a shift in emphasis, her important earlier writings establish her as a major tastemaker of the last quarter of the nineteenth century and place her squarely within the tradition of American women writers on architecture.

Notes

1. All information on Van Rensselaer's life is derived from Lois Dinnerstein, "Opulence and Ocular Delight, Splendor and Squalor: Critical Writings in Art and Architecture by Mariana Van Rensselaer" (Ph.D. diss., City University of New York, 1979) and Cynthia Kinnard, "The Life and Works of Mariana Griswold Van Rensselaer, American Art Critic" (Ph.D. diss., Johns Hopkins University, 1977); see also, Cynthia Kinnard; "Mariana Griswold Van Rensselaer (1851–1934): America's First Professional Female Art Critic," in *Women as Interpreters of the Visual Arts, 1820–1979*, ed. Claire Richter Sherman, with Adele Holcomb (Westport and London: Greenwood Press, 1981), 181–205.

2. For further discussion of this tradition, see: Lisa Koenigsberg, "Professionalizing Domesticity: A Tradition of American Women Writers on Architecture, 1848–1913" (Ph.D. diss., Yale University, 1987). The dates of 1848 and 1913 marked the publication, respectively of Louisa C. Tuthill's *History of Architecture* and Elsie de Wolfe's *The House in Good Taste*.

3. This term was suggested by William Goode, "The Theoretical Limits of Professionalization," in *The Semi-Professions and their Organization*, ed. Amitai Etzioni (New York: The Free Press, 1969), 272, 284.

4. On Van Rensselaer's role as a popularizer, see Kinnard, "Life and Works," 260, 296, and Dinnerstein, 81.

5. See, for example: "From Bayreuth to Ratisbon—Notes of a Hasty Trip," a thirteen-part series published in *AABN* during 1882 and 1883. The thirteen articles on English cathedrals were published in *Century* from 1887 to 1892 and the five articles on French churches appeared in *Century* from 1894 through 1899.

6. See, for example: The following pages in the "Recent Architecture in America" series in *Century*: "City Dwellings, I," 9 (February 1886): 548–58; "City Dwellings, II," 9 (March 1886): 677–78, 682–87; "Commercial Buildings," 6 (August 1884): 511–23.

7. On summer colonies and their architecture, see Van Rensselaer, *Henry Hobson Richardson and His Works* (1888; reprint, New York: Dover Publications,

1969), 105; "American Country Dwellings, II," *Century* 10 (June 1886): 208–10. On Newport architecture, see, for example: Ibid. 211–20.

8. Nancy Cott, *The Bonds of Womanhood: Woman's Sphere in New England 1780–1835* (1977; reprint, New Haven: Yale University Press, 1979), 63–100; Kathryn Kish Sklar, *Catherine Beecher: A Study in American Domesticity* (1973; reprint, New York: W. W. Norton and Co., 1976).

9. Van Rensselaer, "The Development of American Homes," *The Forum* 12 (January 1892): 667–76.

10. Helen Lefkowitz Horowitz, *Alma Mater: Design and Experience in the Women's Colleges from their Nineteenth-century Beginnings to the 1930s* (New York: Knopf, 1985), 147.

11. William B. Rhoads, "The Colonial Revival" (Ph.D. diss., Princeton University, 1974) vol. I, 453. On William R. Ware, founder of Columbia and MIT schools of architecture and a prolific author, see: John Barrington Bayley and Henry Hope Reed, "Introductory Notes for the Classical America Edition," *The American Vignola* (reprint, New York: Norton and Co., 1977), xi. On William Rotch Ware, editor of *AABN*, see: Henry F. Withey and Elsie Rathburn Withey, *Biographical Dictionary of American Architects, Deceased* (1956; reprint, Los Angeles: Hennessey & Ingalls, Inc., 1970), 633. On the education of Herbert Croly, editor of *Architectural Record*, see: David Levy, *Herbert Croly of the New Republic* (Princeton: Princeton University Press, 1985), 72–85. On Montgomery Schuyler, see William H. Jordy and Ralph Coe, eds. and "Introduction," *American Architecture and Other Writings by Montgomery Schuyler* (Cambridge: The Belknap Press of Harvard University Press, 1961), I, 3–11.

12. Van Rensselaer to Sylvester Rosa Koehler, 26 September 1881, Koehler Collection, Archives of American Art, Smithsonian Institution, quoted in Dinnerstein, 35–37.

13. Van Rensselaer, *Should We Ask for the Suffrage?* (New York: J. J. O'Brien & Son, 1894); Kinnard, "Life and Works," 283, 295.

14. Van Rensselaer, "American Country Dwellings, I" *Century* 10 (May 1886): 12.

15. Van Rensselaer, "American Country Dwellings, I": 10, 11; Magali Sarfatti Larson, *The Rise of Professionalism: A Sociological Analysis* (Berkeley: University of California Press, 1977), 40; Dell Upton, "Pattern Books and Professionalism: Aspects of the Transformation of Domestic Architecture in America, 1800–1860," *Winterthur Portfolio* 19 (Summer and Autumn 1984): 111.

16. Van Rensselaer, "American Country Dwellings, I": 14. On Van Rensselaer as an educator, see: Kinnard, "Life and Works," iv, 296, and Dinnerstein, 75, 77.

17. Gwendolyn Wright, *Moralism and the Model Home: Domestic Architecture and Cultural Conflict in Chicago, 1873–1913* (Chicago: University of Chicago Press, 1980), 80.

18. Van Rensselaer, "The Development of American Homes," 675 and *Henry Hobson Richardson*, 20–21, 56.

19. Van Rensselaer, "The New Public Library in Boston: Its Artistic Aspects," *Century* 28 (June 1895): 262; "St. Paul's," *Century* 21 (March 1892): 665.

20. Van Rensselaer, "American Country Dwellings, II": 219.

21. Van Rensselaer, "American Country Dwellings, I": 3; "American Country Dwellings, II": 207; "American Country Dwellings, III" *Century* 10 (July 1886): 426, 428.

22. Van Rensselaer, "Client and Architect," *North American Review* 151 (September 1890): 319–28. *Proceedings of the Twenty-fourth Annual Convention of the American Institute of Architects*, 22–24 October 1890, (Chicago: Inland Architect Press, 1891), 126.

23. *Architectural Record* 2 (January–March 1893): 390; *AABN* 40 (1 April 1893): 11–12.

24. Van Rensselaer to Olmsted, 7 April 1888, and Olmsted to Van Rensselaer, 12 June 1886, Olmsted Papers, Manuscript Division, Library of Congress; "Berlin and New York" *AABN* 18 (18 July 1885): 27; Kinnard, "Life and Works," 111–12.

25. Van Rensselaer, *English Cathedrals*, ix, x.

26. Kinnard, "Life and Works," 52, 67, 69, 111, 246.

27. Van Rensselaer to Mr. Carey, 30 May [1896/9?], Century Collection, New York Public Library; Kinnard, "Life and Works," 111–12.

28. Van Rensselaer to Gilder, 20 March [1894], Century Collection, New York Public Library; Kinnard, "Life and Works," iv, 232, 238, 296 and Dinnerstein, 74.

29. Gwendolyn Wright, "On the Fringe of the Profession: Women in American Architecture," in Spiro Kostof, ed., *The Architect: Chapters in the History of the Profession* (New York: Oxford University Press, 1977), 280, 291.

30. For example, it was not until after World War II that the American Academy in Rome allowed women to hold fellowships in the Fine Arts and abandoned the rule prohibiting married male Fellows; see Lucia Valentine and Alan Valentine, *The American Academy in Rome* (Charlottesville: University Press of Virginia, 1969), 57, 108. On Lois Lilley Howe's election to the AIA, see C. H. Blackall to Glenn Brown, 7 September 1907, AIA, Archives, RG 803 Box 10 Folder 2.

31. Judith Paine, "Pioneer Women Architects," and "Sophia Hayden and the Woman's Building Competition"; Susan Fondiler Berkon, "Marion Mahony Griffin"; and Sara Boutelle, "Julia Morgan," in Susana Torre, ed., *Women in American Architecture: A Historic and Contemporary Perspective* (New York: Whitney Library of Design, 1977), 54–69, 70–87. On women's partnerships, see Paine, "Pioneer Women Architects," 66; on women as anonymous designers, see Wright, "On the Fringe," 290–91.

32. Vincent J. Scully, Jr., *The Shingle and the Stick Style: Architectural Theory and Design from Downing to the Origins of Wright* (1955; rev.ed. New Haven: Yale

---

University Press, 1971), 34; *AABN* 1 (30 September 1876): 313; *AABN* 23 (9 June 1888): 265.

33. *AABN* 1 (30 September 1876): 313.

34. *AABN* 19 (5 June 1886): 61–62.

35. "Chicago," *AABN* 38 (26 November 1892): 134.

36. Minerva Parker Nichols, "A Woman on the Woman's Building," *AABN* 38 (10 December 1892): 170; *AABN* 69 (21 July 1900): 18.

37. "Female Competition," *AABN* 30 (27 December 1890): 197.

38. Wright, "On the Fringe," 280–83 and Paine, "Pioneer Women Architects," 69.

39. Burton Bledstein, *The Culture of Professionalism* (1976; reprint, New York: W. W. Norton, 1978), 120.

40. Wright, "On the Fringe," 280–83; Paine, "Pioneer Women Architects," 69.

41. Paine, "Sophia Hayden,"; Darlene R. Roth and Louise E. Shaw, *Atlanta Women: From Myth to Modern Times* (Atlanta: Atlanta Historical Society, 1980), 25; Paine, "Pioneer Women Architects," 69.

42. After checking the major biographical dictionaries, I have been unable to establish Countess von Krackow's nationality; the name may be a European pseudonym. For the review of Beale's book, *AABN* 42 (18 November 1893): 91.

43. Unidentified newspaper clipping from Budd's papers, in Vicky Opperman to Matilda McQuaid, 1 March 1986; Judith Paine to George Pettengill, 24 June 1974; both in the Women in Architecture Archive, AIA; I am grateful to Matilda McQuaid for sharing this biographical information with me; see also Paine, "Pioneer Women Architects," 69. Budd's articles for *Architectural Record* include "Japanese Houses" 19 (January 1906): 1–26; "The Kitchen and Its Dependent Services. I. With Sketches by the Author" 23 (June 1908): 463–76.

44. See, for example: Candace Wheeler, "Decorative Art," *Architectural Record* 4 (April-June 1895): 409–13; Helen Campbell, "Household Furnishings," *Architectural Record* 6 (October–December 1896): 97–104; Mildred Stapley, "The Art and Practice of Consistent Forms of Decorative Treatment, The Jacobean Period," *AABN* 97 (2 March 1910): 97–102.

45. Van Rensselaer's articles on decorative arts, in *AABN*, include "Artistic Embroidery–Work by the 'Associated Artists,' " 14 (15 and 22 September 1883): 127–28, 140–41. For the many reviews and articles on the pictorial arts that Van Rensselaer published in *AABN*, see bibliographies in Kinnard "Life and Works" and in Dinnerstein.

46. *Garden and Forest* (12 October 1892): 482, cited by Deborah Nevins, "The Triumph of Flora: Women and American Landscape, 1890–1935," *Antiques* 127 (April 1985): 913. See also: Catherine R. Brown and Celia Newton Maddox, "Women and the Land: 'A Suitable Profession,' " *Landscape Architecture* 72 (May 1982): 64–69; Van Rensselaer, "Landscape Gardening," *AABN* 22 (1 October and 3 December 1887): 157–59 and 263–64; *AABN* 23 (7 January 1888): 3–5.

47. In 1888, Van Rensselaer was a founding contributor to *Garden and Forest*; Olmsted was the subject of a major essay in *Century* 24 (October 1893): 860–67 and much of the final chapter of *Art-Out-of-Doors: Hints on Good Taste in Gardening* (New York: Charles Scribner's Sons, 1893).

48. Nevins, 905.

49. Van Rensselaer, "Landscape Gardening, VI," *Garden and Forest* I (4 April 1888): 63–64. See also *Art-Out-of-Doors*, 51–135.

50. Van Rensselaer, *Art-Out-of-Doors*, 67.

51. Ibid., 371–2.

52. Ibid., 354; see, for example: Olmsted to Van Rensselaer, June 1893, Olmsted Papers, Manuscript Division, Library of Congress; Kinnard, "Life and Works," 260, 296.

53. Olmsted to Van Rensselaer, 9 April 1888, Olmsted Papers, Manuscript Division, Library of Congress.

54. Van Rensselaer, *Art-Out-of-Doors*, 28.

55. Ibid., 41.

56. Kinnard, "Life and Works," 273.

5

Frank Lloyd

Wright's

Kindergarten

Professional Practice

and Sexual Roles

DAVID VAN ZANTEN

Women were important in Frank Lloyd Wright's career in Oak Park, Illinois (1889–1909). He emerged as an architect building homes in an increasingly woman-dominated suburb; his chief draftsman, Marion Mahony, was one of the first university-educated American women architects; Wright's aunts, Jane and Ellen Lloyd Jones, had been his first clients in 1887 and were important clients again in 1902; their work as experimental teachers paralleled that of his mother, Anna, and his wife, Catherine, and was basic to his own architectural education.

It would seem fruitful to examine Wright's early work in this context, that of the turn-of-the-century American suburb and its female ethos. Nancy Cott and Gwendolyn Wright have outlined this on a broad plane and Leonard Eaton, Norris Kelly Smith, and Anthony Alofsin have started more focused work.[1] In this short sketch, I would like to focus on Wright's Oak Park practice, working from the research of Eaton and Smith to suggest a chain of hypotheses: 1) that Wright's conscious commitment to the suburb is distinctive and fundamental to his whole enterprise in Oak Park; 2) that within this commitment is the assumption that his objective was to teach as well as provide a professional service, and to teach through design exercises that were lucid, elastic, and nurturing; and 3) that this conception of design as nurture is essentially feminine and led him into a conflict between the (organizing) urban and the (nurturing) suburban, eventually frustrated him so much that in 1909 he dramatically threw it all over.

For Wright to propose nurture as his basic manner of professional practice was to reverse the method established in Chicago, the city of corporate organization, especially by Daniel Burnham, who insisted upon a quasi-military specialization and delegation and the insertion of authorized details.[2] Nurture was the function of the suburb: after the men left each morning for the quantified, competitive, gridded, industrially fabricated Loop, the women set to homemaking and childrearing in the nature-filled suburb. And this distinction between organizing and nurturing was the difference between business and art, as Wright himself would state in his 1898 business card.

In 1898 Wright added a separate and very strikingly designed office, with a drafting room accommodating about twelve draftsmen, to his home in Oak Park.[3] The new structure had a separate, monumental entrance on Chicago Avenue, as well as a library intended to be open to the public as "a free circulating art library." Wright's office had previously been in the Loop (first in the Schiller Building, then in Steinway Hall, and finally in the Rookery), and it was unheard of in Chicago for an ambitious architect to establish himself in the suburbs. His friends and competitors—Dwight Perkins, Myron Hunt, Robert C. Spencer— all worked out of Loop offices, although they were all principally domestic architects living in and designing for the elite suburbs. One leading Prairie School firm came out of the Loop—Thomas Tallmadge a leading citizen of Evanston and Vernon Watson a respectable resident of Oak Park working extensively after 1905 in both localities from offices at 188 Madison Street. A few lesser-known architects who did maintain suburban offices, such as Eben Ezra Roberts in Oak Park, worked only in the immediate vicinity and maintained offices in the local bank building near the railroad station.[4]

Wright explained his initiative in a business card and it was reproduced in the 9 February 1898 issue of *Construction News*:

The practice of architecture as a profession has fine art as well as commercial elements ; . . .

56

To develop in a better sense this fine art side in combination with its commercial condition the architect should place himself in an environment that conspires to develop the best there is in him. The first requisite is a place fitted and adapted to be protected and set aside from the distractions of the busy city. The worker is enabled on this basis to secure the quiet concentration of effort essential to the full success of a building project—the intrinsic value of which is measured by that effort.

To practice the profession of architecture along these lines, in the hope of reaching these better results, a complete architectural workshop has been constructed in Oak Park. . . .

Wright's structure was domestic in scale and intimate, with its principal space—the drafting room—dominated by a large brick fireplace. It was less a "workshop" than a "living room" as Alfred Granger labelled it in *House Beautiful* in 1899 or a "studio" as Robert C. Spencer called it in *Architectural Review* in 1900.[5] The latter designation has stuck to this day. Living room and Studio expressed the collegial atmosphere that Wright tried to cultivate among his draftsmen and delineated in his 1908 article "In the Cause of Architecture."

These young people have found their way to me through natural sympathy with the work, and have become loyal assistants. . . . The few draftsmen so far associated with this work have been taken into the draughting room in every case almost wholly unformed, many of them with no particular previous training, and patiently nursed for years in the atmosphere of the work itself, until, saturated by intimate association, at an impressionable age, with its motifs and phrases, they have become helpful.[6]

For about a year and a half Wright established profit-sharing.[7] Most importantly, the method of design he developed in the Studio around 1900—his "Prairie Style"—functioned as a geometric system of composition that the draftsmen could use individually to elaborate Wright's general indications.[8] There was no production line or division of labor, Wright wrote in 1908; instead he tried having each draftsman carry a selected design through from beginning to end:

This year I assign to each a project that has been carefully conceived in my own mind, which he accepts as a specific work. He follows its subsequent development through all its phases in drawing room and field, meeting with the client himself on occasions, gaining an all-round development impossible otherwise, and insuring an enthusiasm and a grasp of detail.

57

Significantly, Wright's system of Prairie design was already in 1900 linked by Robert C. Spencer to the abstract block compositions taught in the kindergarten method of elementary education established in the United States during the 1860s[9] and adopted by Wright's mother in raising him. Spencer's observations have usually been understood narrowly by historians, as explaining the specific aesthetic characteristics represented in Wright's style. It would seem logical, however, to propose in the context of the educational concept of his Studio that Wright saw it as pedagogical, as a way of achieving compositional lucidity and comprehensibility so as to structure the draftsman's individual elaboration of a scheme. That is to say that Wright saw the Studio on Chicago Avenue as the professional mirror of the kindergarten maintained by his wife Catherine in the great vaulted playroom on the opposite side of the Oak Park house or of the kindergarten education he himself had received from his teacher-mother Anna (living in Oak Park next door on Chicago Avenue), or of the experimental kindergarten-oriented Hillside Home School his aunts established in Spring Green, Wisconsin (housed in the large building that Wright erected for them in 1902–1903). The principle of the kindergarten was to educate children not by discipline and memorization but by play—by recognizing play as the reflection of the natural curiosity and enthusiasm that might be harnessed by a sensitive teacher to become learning. A basic component was the "gift," the carefully designed toy of abstract form that might guide the child's creativity without restricting it: cubic blocks, for example, to be set in patterns on a grid. (It is play with these blocks that is often cited as influencing Wright's own sense of design.) At the Hillside Home School this method was expanded to constitute an entire pre-college program.[10]

Wright was not the only architect considering the establishment of the kindergarten paradigm in architecture at that moment: in 1902–1903 Louis Sullivan was publishing his "Kindergarten Chats," in the *Interstate Architect and Builder* in Cleveland, addressed to young draftsmen, citing the kindergarten as the model for design education as well as demonstrating what he meant, more broadly, in his essays.

I have described Wright's attitude in the Studio as nurturing and noted how he shared design responsibility—even profits—with his draftsmen. He tried to be very giving, as his mother, wife, and aunts were with their numerous children, and as was the whole ethos of the suburb. But as is well known, Wright's commitment collapsed in 1909 and he abandoned his wife and children, his Studio and his men, his whole suburban world, to flee to Europe with an Oak Park client's wife. Afterwards he was sad, if unrepentant, in describing how he had left, as Anthony Alofsin has documented. But he was angry at his former draftsmen, who went out on their own after 1909 and who (he felt) merely copied his style. In 1914 he published an article entitled "In the Cause of Architecture," reflecting bitterly on the optimism of six years before:

Half-baked, imitative designs—fictitious semblances—pretentiously put forward in the name of a movement or a cause, particularly while novelty is the chief popular standard, endanger the cause, weaken the efficiency of genuine work, for the time being at least; lower standards of artistic integrity permanently; demoralize all values artistically; until utter prostitution results.[11]

What went wrong? Were not the Studio draftsmen *supposed* to learn and apply Wright's system? Even in the optimistic delineation of his 1908 article there was a note of condescension when he called his draftsmen "assistants" and "helpful." Wright was a powerful, willful artist and—in the end—wanted willing executants more than grateful pupils. There was always too much of the Burnham in him. The basic problem seems to have been that the nurturing of six children, twelve draftsmen, and dozens of Oak Park clients was not, in the end, what he wished to do, regardless of his mother, wife, and aunts.

A look at the position Wright was now in leads us back to his great predecessor: Henry Hobson Richardson, with his office in his house in Brookline, Massachusetts. Here had been a man who did big work in a quiet, collegial setting, creating a new seemingly "American" architecture in friendly collaboration with powerful businessmen and grateful draftsmen. He had died young in 1886, and Root, Sullivan, and Wright were in awe of his accomplishment. But Wright discovered that this could not be reproduced in Chicago in 1900. Patrician Brookline was not middle class, domestic Oak Park. Richardson's apprentices were fundamentally different from Wright's callow kindergartners. Architecture had ceased to be crafted and nurtured; with Burnham it had come to be produced.[12]

Writers have never ceased to be struck by the distinction between the suburbs and the city in the industrial age but are usually quick to attribute this to a simple dichotomy between wealth and order versus poverty and chaos. It would be more interesting to explore such distinctions as marks of social (and sexual) structure. The emerging downtowns and suburbs of the industrial city around 1900 were social zones of unstated and only symbolically indicated meaning. Wright's problem is that in abandoning the Loop (the conventional professional zone) he stumbled into another zone (that of the suburb-home-nursery) just as structured as the first, and just as hostile to him, although for different reasons. By 1909 all he could do was to flee to the unappropriated territory of Europe, then Wisconsin.[13]

Notes

1. Nancy F. Cott, *The Bonds of Womanhood: 'Woman's Sphere' in New England, 1780–1835* (New Haven: Yale University Press, 1977); Gwendolyn Wright, *Moralism and the Model Home: Domestic Architecture and Cultural Conflict in Chicago, 1873–1913* (Chicago: University of Chicago Press, 1980); Norris Kelly Smith, *Frank Lloyd Wright: A Study in Architectural Content* (Englewood Cliffs: Prentice Hall, 1966); Leonard Eaton, *Two Chicago Architects and their Clients: Frank Lloyd Wright and Howard Van Doren Shaw* (Cambridge: MIT Press, 1969); Anthony Alofsin, *Frank Lloyd Wright: The Impact of Europe* (Ph.D. diss., Columbia University, 1987). Also, Robert C. Twombley, *Frank Lloyd Wright, his Life and Architecture* (New York: John Wiley & Sons, 1979), especially chapter 2 and Brendan Gill, *Many Masks: A Life of Frank Lloyd Wright* (New York: G. P. Putnam's Sons, 1987). This essay is a sketch of a lengthier study I have underway.

2. Harriet Monroe, *John Wellborn Root: A Study of his Life and Work* (New York: Houghton Mifflin, 1896), especially 121–24; Charles Moore, *Daniel Burnham: Architect; Planner of Cities* (New York: Houghton Mifflin, 1921), II, chapter 26. Also, my essay, "The Projecting of Chicago as a Commercial City and the Rationalization of Design and Construction," in *Chicago and New York: Architectural Interactions* (Chicago: Art Institute of Chicago, 1984).

3. Frank Lloyd Wright Home and Studio Foundation, *The Plan for Restoration and Adaptive Use of the Frank Lloyd Wright Home and Studio* (Chicago: University of Chicago Press, 1977).

4. Perkins, Hunt, and Tallmadge were prominent residents of Evanston and built extensively there, yet none ever maintained an office in Evanston or listed himself in the professional section of the city business directories. On the situation in Oak Park, see Paul E. Sprague, *Guide to Frank Lloyd Wright and Prairie School Architecture in Oak Park* (Oak Park: Oak Park Landmarks Commission, 1976). The celebrated precedent for Wright's move was Henry Hobson Richardson who, during the 1870s and 1880s, maintained his office attached to his house in Brookline, Mass. The structure itself, however, had no architectural pretense.

5. Alfred Granger, "An Architect's Studio," *House Beautiful* (December 1899); Robert C. Spencer, "The Work of Frank Lloyd Wright," *Architectural Review*, (April

1900): 61–72. Contemporaneously it was published in the 1900 *Chicago Architectural Club Catalogue* with a similar short explanation.

6. *Architectural Record* 23 (March 1908): 155–65, especially 164.

7. Wright mentions this in a letter to the Australian government in response to their inquiry about his former draftsman, Walter Burley Griffin (specifically, about Griffin's contribution to the Wright office), after Griffin won the competition in 1912 to design the Australian capital of Canberra. See Donald Leslie Johnson, *The Architecture of Walter Burley Griffin* (Melbourne: Macmillan, 1977), 22.

8. I treat this at length in the essay "Schooling the Prairie School: Frank Lloyd Wright's Prairie Style as a Communicable System," in *The Nature of Frank Lloyd Wright*, ed. Carol Bolen, Robert Nelson, Linda Seidel (Chicago: University of Chicago Press, 1988), 70–84.

9. Spencer, "The Work of Frank Lloyd Wright." Also, Grant Carpenter Manson, *Frank Lloyd Wright to 1910: The First Golden Age* (New York: Reinhold, 1958), 6–10; Stuart Wilson, "The Gifts of Friedrich Froebel," *Journal of the Society of Architectural Historians* 26 (December 1967): 238–41; Edgar Kaufmann, Jr., "Form Become Feeling, A New View of Froebel and Wright," *Journal of the Society of Architectural Historians* 40 (May 1981): 130–37.

10. On the Hillside Home School, see Mary Ellen Chase, *A Goodly Fellowship* (New York: Macmillan, 1940), chapter 4.

11. "In the Cause of Architecture (Second Paper)," *Architectural Record* 35 (May 1914): 405–14, especially 407.

12. The transformation of the architectural profession in the 1890s is a large topic. See, on Richardson's office, James O'Gorman, *H. H. Richardson and His Office* (Cambridge: Harvard University Library, 1974). Also: Andrew Saint, *The Image of the Architect* (New Haven: Yale University Press, 1983).

13. The distinction between the downtown and the suburb, viewed censorially, appears as early as Friedrich Engels's *Condition of the Working-Class in England* (first English edition, London: 1892). On social marks and zones, see also: Mary Douglas, *The World of Goods* (New York: Basic Books, 1979) and Paul Fussell, *Abroad: British Literary Travelling Between the Wars* (New York: Oxford University Press, 1980).

6

"Miss Sue" of

Charleston

Saving a Neighborhood,

Influencing a Nation

SIDNEY R. BLAND

Arguably the most important asset of Charleston, South Carolina, is its architecture, a celebrated montage of more than three thousand historic structures. Generation after generation has perpetuated the popular "single houses," the one-room-wide structures that are set endwise to the street and sequester their inhabitants within a network of iron gates, colonnaded piazzas, and walled courtyards. The closely clustered houses account for much of the charm of this port city; the integrity of streetscapes has served as a potent argument for historic preservation.

In recent times, Charleston's historical character has generated a dramatic economic revival, enriching the coffers of the treasury by more than $1.6 billion annually. Historic districts keep absorbing more of the architectural richness of the peninsula. Charleston owes the survival of its architectural riches (and the expansion of its economic riches) in no small way to the foresight, energy, perseverance, and achievement, of one woman: Susan Pringle Frost. Because her ideas later affected the entire preservation movement, the nation is also in debt to "Miss Sue."

Portrait of Susan Pringle Frost, 1873–1960,
pioneer in preservation. Photograph courtesy of
Preservation Society of Charleston

Preservation has always been an important concern of Charlestonians. (The city seal states: "She guards her buildings, customs and laws.") But a concerted preservation spirit did not begin to emerge in Charleston until after Alice Ravenel Huger Smith and her father published *The Dwelling Houses of Charleston* in 1917; and that spirit did not coalesce into truly effective community planning until over a decade later, with passage of the zoning ordinance in 1931 establishing the first historic district in the United States. Throughout much of the first quarter of the twentieth century there were few who fought to preserve the Charleston architecture from what the Smiths labeled "incongruous" new construction. Susan Pringle Frost was, for all intents and purposes, alone in her crusade to restore the fine old homes of Charleston's slums.

Susan Frost (1873–1960) emerged in the public sphere as the result of the same factors that brought other "new women" in the New South out of the shadows. The poverty that followed the Civil War was a key factor. When her once-prosperous family went bankrupt with failures in the rice industry, Frost was forced to work outside the home, learning shorthand and typing prior to becoming a legal secretary. Her sixteen years as a stenographer for a federal district court judge heightened her social awareness. Her impeccable lineage, highlighted by direct ties to noted Revolutionary War merchant Miles Brewton, and to many other of the city's finest (Pinckneys, Mottes, Pringles, Bulls, and Alstons), brought with it the customary benefits of formal schooling and travel and, upon adulthood, entry into financial, political, and cultural circles.

Southern women's lives were also changing after the Civil War because of women's clubs. Such associations were proliferating rapidly, and they served as "the nurseries for leadership, the incubators for the 'new woman', and a major tool for social change throughout the region."[1] For Susan Frost, this sisterhood engineered both civic and feminist commitment.

She was an active participant in the vigorous Progressive-era Charleston Federation of Women's Clubs. She joined efforts pressuring the city to hire matrons for the police station and jail and to appoint women to such bodies as the Playground Commission and the Board of Education. She was on the committee that gained women admittance to the College of Charleston in 1918. She also belonged to the equally active, 250-women-strong Civic Club and supported its crusades for a public library, a Negro kindergarten, child welfare, public health, and urban beautification. As head of the club's City Betterment Committee she especially raised the area's consciousness of its endangered architecture.

Civic concerns and club work, an emerging independence as a professional, and a penchant for challenging the cultural role ordained for women—all these propelled Susan Frost into feminist activity. She founded and headed the Equal Suffrage League of Charleston for three years, then fell under the sway of the militant National Woman's Party and its controversial leader Alice Paul.[2] Capitalizing on Frost's social standing (and admittedly admiring her self-proclaimed motto, "With the help of God I will leap over the wall"), the Woman's Party made the South Carolinian a member of its advisory council and convinced her to picket in Washington.

For all her travels with a federal judge, and all her club and feminist activism, however, Susan Frost had only begun to set Charleston atwitter. Tempted by the lure of profits from an early-twentieth-century real-estate boom, and with neither job security nor financial stability fully assured, "Miss Sue" borrowed a handful of capital and in 1909 quietly ventured into real estate. Soon licensed by the state of South Carolina (among the earliest women to be licensed) and buoyed by a few early sales, Frost went public with her new career in 1918. She became the first woman on the Charleston Real Estate Exchange, and her initial commissions brought another "first"—a woman driving her own automobile, chauffeuring prospective customers through the city's narrow alleyways.[3] She achieved still more visibility when she broke the sex barrier and opened a small office in the professional district on Broad Street. Women's toilet facilities did not yet exist in that male bastion.

Assuredly, Susan Frost's interest in saving old dwellings emerged as a sequel to her real-estate business. It also had other roots: her involvement in the health and beautification programs of the women's clubs to which she belonged; her family and social ties, in Charleston and elsewhere, to those with preservation inclinations;[4] and, perhaps most important of all, her identity with the larger community of Charleston and the mood of its people. A co-worker pinpointed the connection:

Her appreciation of Charleston architecture . . . was founded on a sentimental love for the old city. She saw it partly through a golden haze of memory and association, not only for its buildings, and streets, and vistas, but also for those men and women she had known, or of whom she had been told, who dwelt here, and created, through a period of many generations, the town wherein she herself was privileged to dwell. . . . She never lost this personal feeling for the spirit, as well as the body, of Charleston.[5]

Her initial real-estate venture was the purchase (1909) of two unpretentious frame houses on a little triangle of land near the marshes at the west end of Tradd Street. She soon sold these houses to the city at a good profit. Had she chosen to remain active where development was certain (in North Charleston, which experienced a building boom in the World War I era), her business career might have had a different ending. But Susan Frost was hardly conventional and rarely predictable. She was soon borrowing heavily, despite a temporary recession, and seeking her fortune in a most unlikely place—amid the blight and tarnish at the east end of Tradd, on the lower east side of the peninsula.

Old Charlestonians had lived in their mansions and great houses in genteel poverty for decades after the Civil War. They were joined in that condition by thousands of freedmen who flocked into the waterfront alleyways and lanes in the 1860s and 1870s. Poor health and sanitation conditions affected all; Charleston lagged far behind other cities in municipal improvements. In writing of the neighborhood around

St. Michael's Alley, ca. 1910, Charleston, South Carolina. Once the location of offices of Charleston's most noted antebellum attorneys, it became a seedy neighborhood by the early twentieth century. Photograph courtesy of South Carolina Historical Society

Cabbage Row (the area made famous as Catfish Row in Dubose Heyward's classic *Porgy*), Elizabeth O'Neill Verner told what it was like when the old grandeur had slipped away:

[when the area was] seething with vermin, the great wharf rats were crossing the street in broad daylight, and many of the houses were without water except for a spigot in the yard; when there were no bathrooms or electric lights, and other sanitary conditions were unbelievably dangerous; when typhoid fever was prevalent and bedbugs a curse.[6]

Restoring Tradd Street was indeed a business for Frost. But even more, it was a labor of love, and part of a responsibility she felt to help preserve a portion of the fine old fabric that numerous generations before her had helped to weave. Tradd's history was rich; its stucco and brick buildings were Charleston's oldest. The first postmaster lived there; so did bankers and important colonial officials. Tradd's history was also Miss Frost's history. Her roots were traceable to a palatial brick Georgian dwelling (now No. 61 Tradd) built by Jacob Motte, wealthy merchant, banker, and treasurer of colonial Charleston. Descended from Motte's daughter-in-law (Rebecca Brewton), "Miss Sue" was born in the Brewton mansion on King Street.

Susan Frost called the Tradd Street process "pyramiding." Each of the nine houses she had purchased in the blighted area underwent, by 1919, a similar restoration—cleaning, painting, addition of old Charleston artifacts (a mantel or a balcony or an iron gate), and general reconditioning. The building that served as the town's first post office was rehabilitated, as were former colonial shops and stores.

Miss Frost continued a long tradition of the Low Country aristocracy, that of utilizing the skills of black artisans to maintain the brilliance of the old homeplaces.[7] An essential component of her program to resurrect Tradd Street and the surrounding environs included "turning out" black residents. She blamed landlords, however, not the residents, for allowing much of the lower peninsula to deteriorate; and once she and her sisters established total ownership of the Miles Brewton house, she frequently allowed homeless blacks temporary residence in the former slave quarters. But "Miss Sue" desired only the "best" people on Tradd, as was true in the colonial period, and blacks were displaced, just as they would be again with the celebrated Ansonborough renewal in the 1950s.

Another component of her program was the paving of streets; Charleston's streets were ill-paved, if they were paved at all, in the early part of the century. Getting petitions through property owners and city council did not ensure speedy results and ultimately she went deeper in debt, independently contracting with the city to repair roadways and sidewalks. Finding her financially hard-pressed in the mid-thirties, the mayor eased Frost's tax obligations in recognition of her "significant development of real estate, her restoration of many old buildings, and her sacrifice of much time and energy in the city's interest."[8]

Susan Frost's reach quickly exceeded her grasp. Few responded to her pleas to "pioneer" by living in still run-down neighborhoods. Rising construction costs following the outbreak of war left several Tradd houses idle, awaiting repairs. Undeterred, and dreaming more dreams

("Life has only so many years, and I want to do so much"), she continued pyramiding into the streets and alleyways surrounding Tradd Street.

The combined burden of second and third mortgages, of paving
taxes, and of the large loan incurred by buying relatives' shares of her
ancestral home (the Miles Brewton House) did not prevent Susan Frost
from her most ambitious preservation undertaking—the purchase of
an entire block on the eastern waterfront. Little more than saloons and
decaying tenements, the old buildings of East Bay (now the famous Rain-
bow Row section) once housed the most prominent of Revolutionary
Era merchants and politicians. Miss Frost wagered that the heavy influx
of war personnel (many employed at the Charleston Navy Yard), coupled with some noticeable expansion of the business district northward
and her own reclamation work nearby, would insure revitalization of
East Bay and, in turn, her own future. Writing to Irénée DuPont, president of the chemical company, to request a loan, she relayed her optimism: "It is quite the most important and best thing I have yet

*St. Michael's Alley in the 1980s. Susan Frost spent large sums of money refurbishing the office of
famed antisecessionist lawyer James L. Pettigru (the building with the gabled roof and balcony
partially shaded by the tree). Photograph by Sidney R. Bland*

handled . . . if I can now take hold of this East Bay block, I will be satisfied with what I have been able to accomplish for Charleston and incidentally for myself."9 DuPont had been an earlier Frost benefactor, and his generosity made possible her six East Bay Street acquisitions in 1920.

Now overwhelmingly encumbered, and with no new lenders in sight, Susan Frost had little recourse but to rally others when the Joseph Manigault house was earmarked for demolition. To save the 1803 structure, one of the finest late Adam-style residences in the country, she spearheaded formation of the Society for the Preservation of Old Dwellings (now the Preservation Society of Charleston). Originally a band of thirty-two in 1920, the Preservation Society now has a voting membership of some 3,500.

Susan Frost served as president of the Preservation Society for its first seven years. New members were few and money even scarcer, and the thirteen years of hard work to save the Manigault structure (now one of Charleston's major house museums) was largely a one-family effort. The Society lost its meager funds in a bank failure. Sound by-laws came only with the second president. Frost's own energies were further dissipated by the necessity of opening the Miles Brewton to tourists for over a decade, to meet tax and loan obligations. But the name of Susan Pringle Frost is writ large in the early history of the Preservation Society. She was its chief publicist, its constant promoter, its "moving spirit," its visionary. She stubbornly insisted that the word "dwelling" be included in the title of the organization in order to denote the permanence, stability, and continuity of generations of Charlestonians living and working together, yet she defined the mission of the group in much broader terms than merely safeguarding the buildings of the old gentility. "Miss Sue" saw Charleston as a whole, an entire canvas of wood and stone and iron, of walls and gardens and churchyards. She told one audience:

No tiny bit of this beauty in any remote section of our city is too insignificant, or too unimportant in its integral part of the whole setting, to be worth saving, first in its surroundings, and if those surroundings are jeopardized, then in some other section of our city, where they can be saved for future generations of our own people.10

Susan Frost was well ahead of most preservationists of her day in her vision to save more than just the buildings in which great men lived or historic events took place.

The 1920s and 1930s witnessed a bitter miscarrying of the personal dreams of Susan Frost. Several years of postwar depression undercut the real estate market. Her intemperate financial management and her penchant for overextension, exacerbated by the Miles Brewton obligations, brought a staggering indebtedness.

Sentimentality clouded whatever business sense she possessed. Some Tradd Street properties remained unsold in the thirties, and blacks stayed on as tenants in East Bay buildings through most the Depression to provide needed rental monies. One by one her row of treasures slipped, unrestored, into the hands of others.

Despite her business failures and despite the emergence of a group of professionals who propelled Charleston into the forefront of the nationwide preservation movement by the 1930s, Susan Frost remained a preservation propagandist and a highly visible force on the local scene for another generation. Her social clout ensured that the political establishment would hear her views; she was appointed to two city commissions, and she served nine years (until her mid-seventies) on the Zoning Commission.

Susan Pringle Frost stood astride two ages. Deep within her were inherited ideals and reverence for the golden era of the South that had passed. Yet her activism, her independence, and her challenge to the traditional role of the southern woman made her part of that new phenomenon in the New South—a generation of women who exerted a significant influence in the public sector. She helped shape new conceptions of the proper role for women in southern society in the twentieth century while, paradoxically, she achieved her greatest fame preserving the visible remainders of a culture that afforded women little opportunity for independent development and accomplishment.

Riches never came to Susan Frost, yet she provided the avenue for new fame and fortune for her beloved Charleston. Others soon dared to settle in the once-dingy alleyways and decaying streets of the old city, because of her courage. Generations would benefit from her energy and purpose.

Preservation historians would do well to note the career of Susan Frost. Private restoration programs by real estate agents are now commonplace on the urban scene, but such was hardly the case in the early twentieth century. Few women were in real estate at all, fewer still in the South. Many cities today have historic district zoning, some simply copying the ordinance that Charleston enacted in 1931. (Several years before his city made history as the historic-district zoning pioneer, the mayor

of Charleston was already advising his corporation counsel to pay special heed to the "new line of thought" being advocated by Susan Frost
in her "commendable work," that of enacting an ordinance prohibiting removal of old iron work and woodwork from the city.[11])

In "seeding" the neighborhood preservation concept, an idea that
would bear rich fruit in the work of the Historic Charleston Foundation, "Miss Sue" was also well ahead of her day. It was only in the fifties
and early sixties, when urban renewal projects and interstate highway
systems were rapidly destroying historic buildings and neighborhoods,
that the tack of preserving communities for continued use, rather than
as historic showpieces, enjoyed a wider following. In her celebrated 1920s
debate with New England preservation pioneer William Sumner
Appleton over the wisdom of selling a redeemed building back into private ownership, Frost has been vindicated.[12] Countless restored neighborhoods and proud homeowners across the country offer testimony
to the wisdom of Susan Pringle Frost.

Notes

This work was supported by grants from the Penrose Fund of the American Philosophical Society and the James Madison University Program of Grants
for Faculty Research.

1. Anne Firor Scott, "Historians Construct the Southern Woman," in *Sex,
Race and the Role of Women in the South*, ed. Joanne V. Hawks and Sheila L. Skemp
(Jackson: University Press of Mississippi, 1983), 108. See also: Scott, *The Southern
Lady: From Pedestal to Politics 1830–1930* (Chicago: University of Chicago Press,
1970); Scott, "The 'New Woman' in the New South," *South Atlantic Quarterly* 61
(Autumn 1962): 417–83; Martha Swain, "Organized Southern Women as a Force
in the Community" (Paper read at A Symposium on Women in Southern Soci-
ety, University of Richmond, 1984, copy in possession of author).

2. Letter, Susan Frost to Mrs. M. T. Coleman, 15 July 1915, Reel 33, National
Woman's Party Papers, Library of Congress.

3. Marjorie Uzzell, "I Bought My House From Miss Sue," *Preservation
Progress* 7 (March 1962): 1–2. "Miss Frost appeared behind the wheel of a large
and ancient vehicle. She drove rapidly, never bothering to slow down at corners. Miss Sue talked all the while at top speed, occasionally turning about to
my husband on the rear seat. Miraculously we arrived safely at the first house."

4. Frost was related to Louise DuPont Crowninshield, wealthy society
matron affiliated with numerous preservation projects. Frost's cousins spearheaded the drive of the South Carolina Society of Colonial Dames to save the

oldest public building in Charleston (the Powder Magazine, built in 1713 and used as an arms storehouse throughout the conflict with England).

5. Alston Deas, "They Shall See Your Good Works," *Preservation Progress* 7 (May 1962): 1.

6. From a tribute to Susan Pringle Frost by Elizabeth O'Neill Verner in *Preservation Progress* 5 (November 1960): 5.

7. Letter, Susan Frost to *News and Courier*, 13 December 1952. For insights into Charleston's debts to its black artisans and, particularly, the work of one of the last practicing blacksmiths, see John M. Vlack, "Phillip Simmons: Afro-American Blacksmith," *Black People and their Culture: Selected Writings from the African Diaspora* (Washington: Smithsonian Institution Press, 1976), 37–40; and Vlach, *Charleston Blacksmith: The Work of Phillip Simmons* (Athens: University of Georgia Press, 1981).

8. Letter, Burnet Maybank to L. F. Ostendorff (Abutment Clerk), 23 November 1936, Charleston City Archives.

9. Letters, Susan Frost to Irénée DuPont, 8 March 1920; 12 March 1920; 27 March 1920; Irénée DuPont Papers, Eleutherian Mills Historical Library.

10. Letter, Susan Frost to *News and Courier*, 9 March 1928(?), as cited in *Preservation Progress* 7 (March 1962): 3.

11. Letter, Thomas Stoney to John I. Cosgrove, 27 May 1925; Stoney Papers, Charleston City Archives.

12. Appleton, founder and moving force of the Society for the Preservation of New England Antiquities, repeatedly warned Frost that selling a property back into private ownership would subject it to the dangers from which she had so recently rescued it. Frost just as firmly insisted that her society could accomplish more by buying old houses, renovating them and then renting or selling them to "desirable people." This was a debate in correspondence only, although each undoubtedly debated this question with others. Appleton ultimately learned that admission fees and periodic appeals for public donations could never pay for the vital work of preserving architectural monuments.

PART II.

RECOUNTING

PERSONAL

INVOLVEMENT

Introduction

If a first-person account is less than
a carefully balanced essay by a seasoned scholar, it is also more: a privileged glimpse of what it was like to be there. From the perspective of
the 1980s, the writers on the following pages take us back through sixty
years of women working in architecture, adding the wisdom of years of
reflection to these personal stories.

Louise Hall shows us the Class of 1930 at MIT's School of Architecture, full of spirit and promise, and boasting a higher number of women
students than ever before, as they faced graduation after the Crash. Men
in architecture were affected by the Depression, too, but it is a telling
fact that after the unusually high enrollment of women architecture students in 1930 at MIT, the numbers dropped back again for many years
afterward.

More heartening, but with its own tale of a vision thwarted, is the
story of the extraordinary Cambridge School, open only to women.
Dorothy May Anderson recalls the school and its closing early in World
War II, followed immediately by the admission of women to Harvard's

Graduate School of Design. Even today, a GSD newsletter states only that women have been allowed since 1942 but makes no mention of the school that provided the first female students when the men went off to war.

Not all women who cared about the design of their surroundings were trained professionals, of course. Adele Chatfield-Taylor draws memorable portraits of two skilled amateurs for whom architecture was "a sort of calling"; they knew instinctively what many architects take years to learn. These gifted designers seem part of a bygone day. Who is responsible for design in the busy households of today?

Those of us who are not historians tend to take for granted the product, unmindful of the process by which masses of data are unearthed, probed, and interpreted. Sara Holmes Boutelle describes her introduction to Julia Morgan in the early 1970s and her continuing search for this elusive architect. We owe much of our knowledge of Morgan to this historian's enterprise and energy.

Stamina of many kinds must have been required in the 1970s by those who pressed the establishment about the small but increasing presence of women architects. Judith Edelman, first chairwoman of the AIA's Task Force on Women, writes candidly about the trials and achievements of the Task Force and the AIA's often reluctant response to the work.

The Women's School of Planning and Architecture arose in the mid-1970s from the awareness of women in architecture that their needs and strengths alike required a new approach. Leslie Kanes Weisman, one of WSPA's seven founders, discusses this unique experiment and its purpose of providing a feminist education. Although the school failed to continue beyond six years, Weisman points out that it should not be considered a failure.

7

A Pivotal

Group in

Architecture

The Fourteen Women of

MIT, Class of 1930

LOUISE HALL

Nobody knows why more women than ever before—or, indeed, for many years thereafter—enrolled during the late 1920s to study architecture at the Massachusetts Institute of Technology, familiarly known as "Boston Tech."

Was it something about MIT? Precedent, perhaps? Vassar graduate Ellen H. Swallow, earned her S.B. in 1873 at MIT, became widely known as a food chemist, and was the first woman to teach at the Institute. Or was it something about the times? We were children standing on the brink of war in 1916; but war was a mere word to us. Even when the press in 1916 heralded the election of the first Congresswoman, Jeanette Rankin (R—Montana), we were not yet serious newspaper readers. And most probably we never knew that on 13 June 1916, "Boston Tech" floated its official treasures across the Charles River Basin on a gaily decorated barge to the "New Technology" (built since 1913) in Cambridge.[1]

Pageants, band concerts, and parades to honor all manner of causes and occasions stirred the air more frequently in those days than after broadcasting began. A Cambridge class member, earlier in the Girl Scouts (founded in 1912), recalls how hard the wind gusted when she donned her khaki uniform to bear aloft the Colors—whipping and snapping—in a Liberty Loan parade from North Cambridge all the miles down Massachusetts Avenue to MIT's starkly new Great Court. Embellished later, that special place became a favorite landmark.

Off the ships in the Port of Boston came young men marching home after the 1918 Armistice, and in 1919 President Woodrow Wilson, standing precariously in a black touring car during the triumphal procession welcoming him back from Versailles. It was a time of Suffragette parades before the good old gals won us the vote with the Nineteenth Amendment in 1920; and of the battalion of little Yeomen (F)—for female—without their typewriters but identifiable by their flat straw boaters as the work force from the Charlestown Navy Yard. Perhaps we were seeing larger groups of women on display than had our forebears. Still, possessing no comparative data we very truly took for granted the potential we shared with these numerous and interesting creatures: Ellen Swallow, Jeanette Rankin, and all the nameless paraders. None of us sent up a shout either for or against Women. By then we were too busy with Architecture.

The programs of men and women candidates for admission to MIT were divided not by gender but by preparation.[2] Two in our group of fourteen girls went out for the master in architecture degree: one a graduate of Vassar and of Columbia University School of Architecture; the other progressing from bachelor to master within MIT.

Nine more of the fourteen girls presented earned degrees and could expect to have certain courses "written off," thus promoting expeditious passage toward our architectural goal. Two of the nine will never forget dancing away the night of our Wellesley senior prom, 20 May 1927, and waking up next morning to learn that Capt. Charles A. Lindbergh had improved the same hours by completing his pioneer flight across the Atlantic alone. Life at MIT soon grew equally earnest. The two dancers labored through the first ten days of MIT summer session before hastening back to Wellesley commencement to receive their diplomas. Only then could they submerge themselves altogether in Architecture.

The last three of the fourteen girls enrolled as regular undergraduates, like most students, and followed the full curriculum for the four years then prescribed. Two of them arrived firm in their belief that they had come to "Boston Tech." As it turned out, in a way they had. The great move by barge in 1916 had left behind at "Boston Tech" one solitary Department of Architecture. Until that became the School of Architecture in 1938, and itself crossed the river to Cambridge, the student body's home remained in Boston. The monumental and capacious Rogers Building, at 491 Boylston Street, embraced the best part of our world. We seldom left it before ten o'clock at night. Indeed, we almost resented having to go off to a class across the river where young males, less accustomed than our counterparts to seeing girls around, delighted in clapping sharply to enhance every footfall of a hapless maiden until she could reach the farthest end of a seemingly mile-long corridor.

The fourteen girls who began with, or finished with, the Class of 1930 must be thought of relative to the one or two or three girls among perhaps seventy-five architect men in neighboring classes. To be sure we were not the 40 percent of today, but we were enough to make a splash. Who were we? Considerable variation in age resulted from the range of birthdates between 1901 and 1908. Our nationalities were equally diverse. The member characterized by her peers as "the most talented" came from Bucharest, Romania. Not even the one from Santurce, Puerto Rico, could compete with that.[3]

Were we related to any architects? Had we ever met a woman architect? Did we work for any architects while still at MIT? Well, yes to all three. One of the master's candidates was a daughter of John V. Van Pelt, FAIA; the bachelor's candidate from Barnard was daughter to a general contractor engaged in many large-scale projects; and one of the full-curriculum girls sprang from the journalist-inventor of a machine used before 1918 to send line drawings by telegraph. It has been whispered that the persons most influential in the girls' choice of architecture as a profession seem to have been the fathers with more daughters than sons, who perhaps tended toward conversion of the former into the latter. Women architects did attract the young to the profession. At least two of us sought the advice of a woman who would now be known as a "role model"—a term then not yet heard. Mrs. Eliza Jacobus Newkirk Rogers, Wellesley 1900, MIT 1905, taught at Wellesley part-time, and it was she who found a place in her Boston office for summer learners. So did Miss Mary Almy, AIA, MIT 1920.

As participants know, though every reader may not, our progress through the Beaux-Arts system came to be measured by the points accumulated on juried design problems—each of several weeks' duration— from The Orders to Analytiques to Class B and Class A Planning. Intermittently, a six- or nine- or twelve-hour Sketch Problem flashed by. Nine

hours a week went into Life Drawing in charcoal from the trained figures engaged to pose. Whatever hours in the week could be spared were
used for clay modeling. Oh, and two students—a man and a woman—
found time to sing with the Handel and Haydn Society, who rehearsed
weekly in our own Rogers Building.

We no longer ground our own Chinese ink for monotones, favoring color. But across the street at Spaulding-Moss, we could buy the mak-
ings of a stretch—a huge sheet of Whatman paper to be dampened, and
the requisite vegetable glue to hold it down on the board until it dried
taut. Since when has anybody seen a stretch? In our day it connoted
genuine athletic accomplishment.

We were always having to cross the river to take an elective or two,
such as acoustics; to push our mathematics through differential and integral calculus; and to shove our mechanics hardly farther than early warehouse construction. Some few of us in the best of times might have been
able eventually to sign "Architect and Engineer." Most of us would probably have followed the quaint custom of the day by farming out our
structural dilemmas to an engineering firm; otherwise, a large enough
architecture office often kept what was known as "a tame engineer."
Disgraceful, in retrospect, and yet eloquent of differing emphases.

We studied avidly the mounted plates from Paris, some of which
already reflected the Exposition des Arts Decoratifs. Decades later some
voice unknown christened the Exposition product "Art Deco." To us, it
was just the 1925 Show. Of course we were a little vague about Darmstadt,
and the Bauhaus transfer from Weimar to Dessau. Nevertheless, we tentatively squared away planes, wiped off ornament, and tried to tidy up
our compositions. Perhaps we felt a bit guilty about undermining the
Beaux-Arts tradition; it did seem rather like leveling a gun at mother.
Anyway, we believed we were the first class to break away toward the
future, and, by contrast, we were the last class to finish in four-only jam-
packed years. Five years were required of those who came after, with a
sixth for the master's degree.

Even if we must say it ourselves, this group of fourteen girls contained no dummies and held considerable promise of delivering a fresh
approach. Alas! That which pride preceded was a fall, and we fell with a
quite unnerving thud. On 28 October 1929, half-way through our next-
to-last term, the market's house of cards collapsed. Family fortunes followed suit. So did the monies essential to managing architecture firms
and their building projects. And the first Social Security check was still
eight years away.

One of us, who had her priorities straight, decided to forego her S.B. in Architecture and return home to pick up her share of the load. Later she served in the Naval Reserve, and spent all of her life at work with architects in Virginia and Maryland. Another, lacking only a single course before graduation, was enabled by a kindly professor to double up classes and clear the record quickly by midyear, while a job was still open with a former flyer in the Lafayette Escadrille. In June 1930, that firm's office still supported a chief draftsman and thirty men on the boards. Nobody could imagine four months later that the chief and four men would be doing what little work there was. The boss, a humane man, devised small jobs to be done at home, such as lettering the names of donors upon panels destined for display in a large and distant church. Even one Master in Architecture, retreating from the fray to work for her father, found him—like everybody else—devoid of work for either of them.

Like digging out after an earthquake, we had to come to terms with what people were beginning to call the Depression.

In the final term our beloved Dean William Emerson furnished us with sheaves of letters of recommendation and advised us, if we could possibly scrape up $200, to become Life Members of the American Institute of Architects. That had to be a bargain without takers. (Even thirty years after graduation, only three of the fourteen belonged to the AIA.) At commencement all but three received either the master in architecture degree or the S.B.—the B.Arch. belonged to the next generation. As for professional registration, that depended on the whims of the states. One member sailed through the registration examinations in Pennsylvania; another left Massachusetts before the Commonwealth registered architects and arrived in North Carolina after expiration of their grandfather clause. Variations of these grim inconsistencies still color the recollections of our few survivors.

Some fortunate girls availed themselves of private funds or scholarship aid to ride out the crisis abroad. Studying especially in Paris, but also farther afield, they brought home reams of spontaneous watercolor paintings. At least two later engaged in archaeological digs: one in Antioch, Syria, the other at Winchester in southern England.

Other girls seized a chance to sharpen their academic skills. Rewarding these efforts were a master's degree in art history, another in the teaching of modern math, and a Ph.D. in architecture. Two taught math in high school for many years, a third became an actuarial clerk for the insurance company in her home town, and a fourth "supervised fifty or so men and a woman or two" for the New York City Housing Authority. A fifth, having founded an art department in a university, called upon a lifetime in architecture for the design of double-projector lectures intended to transform men and women students in various fields into intelligent and perceptive clients for architects.

A number of us contributed a quite contrary set of nonacademic talents during World War II, when we sent only one member into uniform. Civilian service expanded as different dialects of the visual language proved to be interchangeable. One civilian served in the U. S. Office of Scientific Research and Development, representing the parts of a then-secret instrument at four times actual size. In Washington, when the uniformed officers of the U. S. Coast and Geodetic Survey left for posts overseas, we were ready with a second-generation group of women students—this time from Duke—to pinch-hit with limited training in cartography and photogrammetry. Engineering drawing, then needed by the U. S. Naval ROTC and V-12, had to be taught by a dozen men and one woman in four two-hour shifts per day, six days a week, to most of the thousand new men who arrived every four months at Duke—other thousands at other institutions. In 1942, when the nation lacked some 192,000 high school teachers of math and physics, the U.S. Office of Education offered Engineering, Science, Management War Training courses to civilian war workers, and the acronym ESMWT was listed on our service records.

So far as our survivors can tell today, only one of the fourteen girls could support an independent office, not so much because all were women as because all, men and women alike, were grappling with economics. Drawings by that select member—an MIT Master in Architecture, licensed to sign "Architect and Engineer"—attracted attention in 1978 as part of a show on Chicago Women Architects.[4]

The other MIT Master in Architecture, who specialized in rendering, turned her hand to visual presentation of hospitals, sewage plants, and like ample projects. And the member judged by her peers to be "the most talented," who completed a graduate problem or two in her senior year, became an architectural designer for a New York firm.[5]

Grand projects and comfortable domestic units are not to be judged by size. Rather, their common denominator lies in the degree of creative imagination implicit in their differing scale, texture, color, and so on. One of us alert to preservation cleverly rescued two eighteenth-century Newport houses from oncoming fate as tenements. Attractive summer homes have been designed by frustrated class members; one such is described today as "weathering with more grace than I am."

Detached as we must remain in our memories of those no longer with us to answer our questions, we can be cheered by recording the eventual marriage of all but five of the fourteen girls (only two to architects), and a covey of descendants unto the fourth generation. It is likewise cheering to discover the renewed public interest in "Our Times." Wellesley, for example, in 1987 held a three-day symposium entitled "The Great Depression and All That Jazz: America in Transition 1929–39."

Our impersonal story could have been better rounded if called for twenty years earlier, when all but one were still living to testify. Now, half of us have died and an eighth is unlocated. To the six survivors, therefore, we are grateful for filling out the story with phone calls, written recollections, clippings, and moral support. Several of the "old boys" have also corroborated our story as being like theirs. We are particularly grateful to persons identified in the text who helped us weather the storm, and to MIT officials who have checked documents for us.

To this day, nobody knows why so many girls suddenly converged on MIT, though we understand well enough the later silent decades. Like it or not, we felt at home in MIT without fighting for anything but Architecture. Let others repeatedly rediscover Women. The eleven of us already armed with undergraduate degrees before admission obviously had an easier time of it than did the three who carried harder schedules. As the last class in the four-year course, we could all see the wisdom of expansion to five years, plus Master. Right down to the Crash, we were leaning toward the future as we envisioned the future at that time. There we were, poised on our pivot, only to tumble off. That was not in the script. But somehow, each of the fourteen girls succeeded in turning a lost class into a class lost in amazement over our freedom and capacity to design ways around life's dicey situations—as architects do.[6]

Notes

1. Positioned on board in his role as Merlin stood the director of the colorful extravaganza: medievalist Ralph Adams Cram, architect, MIT professor 1914–22.

2. Diversity prevailed among the preparatory institutions: The University of Illinois, Urbana; in New York City, Columbia University School of Architec-

ture, Columbia University, and Barnard College; the College of New Rochelle, New Rochelle, N.Y.; Vassar College, Poughkeepsie, N.Y.; Smith College, Northamption, Mass., Radcliffe College, Cambridge, Mass., and three from Wellesley College, Wellesley, Mass. The group who entered the full curriculum had been trained, respectively, at the American High School in Paris; the Agnes Irwin School in Rosemont, Pa.; and Girls' Latin School in Boston. Even among the three entrants from Wellesley, none had a clue that any other planned to attend MIT.

3. Aside from the girls born in Romania and Puerto Rico, and those from Chicago, Ill. and Erie, Pa., the rest outlined the Atlantic Coast northward from Suffolk, Va.; Wilmington, Del.; Montclair, N.J.; New York, N.Y.; Mount Vernon, N.Y.; Newport, R.I.; and the Massachusetts girls, one each from Pittsfield and Cambridge, and two from Boston. Obviously no committee dictated the gathering of such an assortment.

4. Two years later, exhibition by a local gallery netted sales in three figures. Her work is represented in the permanent collection of the Art Institute of Chicago.

5. She was credited with work on the New York State Building at the World's Fair of 1939, on the rebuilding of the New York subway system, and on the community colleges of New York City.

6. Our half-dozen survivors beg leave to point out that our collaborative illustration of what happened to the profession of architecture, at the onset of The Depression and later, far exceeds in importance our identity as individuals.

8

The

Cambridge

School

An Extraordinary

Professional Education

DOROTHY MAY ANDERSON

The Cambridge School exists today only as an idea and a memory. Started early in World War I, the Cambridge School was closed abruptly when the United States entered World War II. During its brief lifetime, it operated at five locations on or near Harvard Square in Cambridge—always outside the Yard. This was not quite so derogatory as living beyond the Pale, but the location underscored the fact that Harvard did not admit women, and of course the Cambridge School existed only for women.

Surviving four moves before finally settling into permanent quarters at 53 Church Street, the school also endured repeated changes in its name. In the beginning, students called it the Little School, and Harvard men dubbed it the Frost & Pond Day Nursery. Soon it became known as the Cambridge School—the fine, simple name that could never be used officially because it belonged to a well-established day school in Cambridge. By the 1930s, along with getting the affiliation necessary to grant degrees, it became the jaw-breaking Smith College Graduate

Henry Atherton Frost, 1883–1952, the one and only highly respected director of the school so many women can never forget. Photograph courtesy of William A. Frost and PDA Publishers Corporation

School of Architecture and Landscape Architecture in Cambridge; parents complained when writing tuition checks.

The school was started in 1915 when a Radcliffe graduate, who wanted to become a landscape architect, found she could not enter the Lowthorpe School in Groton[1] until the following year. She approached Professor Pray, head of Harvard's Graduate School of Landscape Architecture. Could she study there for one year? No, she could not. It was completely, almost shockingly, against the rules. Professor Pray was sympathetic, however, and persuaded a young instructor in the Graduate School of Architecture, Henry Atherton Frost, to tutor her in architectural design.

Within a short time, several other women turned up at the office of Henry Frost and his partner Bremer Pond, a landscape architect. In a few more months, the group of eager women had doubled. The young Harvard professors realized that their very crowded office had turned into a school, and they set about devising a curriculum, increasing their modest tuition fee by a small amount, and looking for larger quarters.

Harvard's President Lowell was less than enthusiastic about the experiment on his doorstep. He said it could not succeed; it had "no basis for
continuity." Mr. Frost interpreted this as Bostonese for no money and
no tradition, which was certainly true. Nevertheless, the Little School
went merrily on its way, enrolling almost five hundred women before
the short-sighted administrative decision by Smith College ended the
school twenty-six years later.

I came into the picture in 1929 as a Cambridge School student and
remained closely in touch from then until the school was closed in 1942.
Without exception, all of us who passed through the school found Mr.
Frost an inspiration to us as students and a strong influence on our
lives afterward. One alumna speaks of "the dominant reality of Mr. Frost.
He didn't just lend a flavor to the school. He *was* the Cambridge School."
I believe the relationship between teacher and learner at the school was
unique, and indeed the most influential teacher by far was the director
himself.

"What did the Cambridge School do for me?" asks one woman. "It
made me grow up in a hurry." Another remembers her class in graph-
ics: "Mr. Frost lectured so fast. Being ambidextrous, he drew on the board
with both hands at once. We all gasped for breath." She lived through
it, as did many others, and finally learned to draw "an improbable line
of intersection of a sphere pierced by a cone at some crazy angle." Did
that discourage her? No. "I'd love to do it all over again—anytime." One
former student sums up her memories by saying, "It was where we
learned to learn."

Mr. Frost stretched us to our limits. One of the first graduates recalls,
"Over the years I've had many excellent teachers but never anyone like
Henry A. Frost! After his criticism of a problem I would be left on top
of the world, sure I could do anything. Only later did I realize he had
torn my design all apart but with such constructive criticism that I was
inspired and not depressed."

When Mr. Frost saw signs of tension or hostility, or perhaps immi-
nent tears, he would usually offer one quick bit of advice on how to
attack the problem more constructively and then disappear—for hours
or even days. When he returned, he restored the student's self-
confidence with encouraging criticism, bringing out all the good points
of her new solution. Sometimes faint praise worked just as well. I remember his coming to my drafting table just after I'd finished a problem.
"You are an intellectual designer," he said. "You do things because you

know they are right. Nothing much wrong with that, only why don't you try just once to be a little creative?" Off he went.

The magic of the director's eager enthusiasm and his New England sense of discipline and hard work rubbed off on his well-chosen faculty.[2] No Cambridge School student ever took a course because she thought it would be easy. Actually, we had little choice. Demands were clearly laid out and, with encouragement and help, we met them. Period.

We appreciated our teachers for their professional criticism and also for their personal interest in our efforts. When one solid and sound instructor of architectural construction found that a student of his was planning to be in New York when he was, he invited her to join him for a walk on the last day of December. They walked from Wall Street to Ninety-second Street, going into what she recalls as "every building along the way," including the brand new Bonwit Teller building where they went down the fire escape from roof to street. She skipped a New Year's Eve party that night, but she learned a lot about architecture.

One day Mr. Frost called me into his office and asked why I had not signed up for a four-day field trip. I told him the truth—I had no money. I was earning my way through graduate school doing odd jobs, and every nickel was allocated. He said "I thought so. Well, I know of a small fund that will cover your expenses. You can have the money as a loan or a gift." Years later I learned that the mysterious fund came from the pocket of one of the faculty.

We put in very long hours, spurred on by the expectations we had for ourselves and the expectations our faculty had for us. We often arrived with the janitor at 6 a.m. and were always pushed out by him at 10 p.m., with homework still awaiting us. The ten-hour day was the short

Vehicles from another era. The Cambridge School acquired a new home at 53 Church Street in 1928 and remained here until the school was closed in 1942. Photograph by Mrs. Neil Macneale, Jr., courtesy of PDA Publishers Corporation

The rarely empty drafting room. This may have been a posed photograph, as the drafting room looks neater to the author than she remembers it. Photograph courtesy of Smith College Archives, Smith College

Surveying. Students of the Cambridge School did everything with determination—and with style. Photograph by Acme Newspictures, courtesy of Smith College Archives, Smith College

kind. Meals were snatched on Harvard Square or eaten at our desks. When the school became an integral part of Smith, the college treasurer was appalled at our light bills. Mr. Frost had to assure him that, yes, live bodies occupied the drafting rooms during the dark hours.

All Cambridge School students went through the same basic training whether to become architects or landscape architects; at other graduate schools, students were generally trained in separate departments. In most schools, training in pencil drawing and color work focused on drafting and rendering of finished problems. At the Cambridge School we had plenty of that, but we also sketched buildings and landscapes outdoors and splashed watercolors all over the place, indoors and out. The Cambridge School differed, too, in that juries for our assigned problems were chosen not from the faculty but from professional men and women practicing in Boston and elsewhere.

Other ways in which the Cambridge School differed from professional schools of the time? I think the Cambridge School students were more highly motivated, more intensely interested, than those of other graduate schools, but that is a matter of degree, not difference. The basic difference, above and beyond all else, was that the Cambridge School existed exclusively for women.[3]

Design and construction were taught on an individual basis. The dual emphasis in our studio training was on learning to see and on keeping things in scale. We looked at everything inside, outside, through, behind, and under—always asked "why?" We criticized each other's work ruthlessly, and surprisingly we remained friends.

We struggled through short classroom courses in physics, math, and office practice, as well as the history of art, architecture, and landscape architecture. Field trips took care of other necessary training. Wind, bitter cold, frying heat, chilblains, or sunburn were of no consequence when learning the difference between a Red Oak and a Scarlet Oak. We were lucky if we did not babble Latin names in our sleep. We learned well the design value of one plant over another in terms of size, structure, texture, and color. I remember, though, that on one of our Study Trips Abroad we clambered over the top of dusty cathedral vaulting in the dark and climbed down to devour wild strawberries and cream in the sun at a nearby inn. It was this disciplined professional investigation relieved occasionally by sympathetic personal indulgence that made the Cambridge School unique.

In retrospect, it seems that everyone worked with and for the students. I remember our handsome librarian with his longish white hair

Education indoors and outdoors. Mr. Frost discusses a fine point of brickwork with students in 1940; the Cambridge School stressed theory and practical application equally, with the aim here of learning to recognize quality workmanship. Photograph by Jane Pearson, courtesy of PDA Publishers Corporation

and glasses worn on a black ribbon. He not only knew what was inside his treasured books, he also made models for us with the skill of a well-trained cabinet maker. And our jack-of-all-trades janitor, our mender of all broken objects! I never saw him without a disreputable hat on his head and a cigar in his mouth, indoors or out. We know he would do anything for us—except keep the building open just a little after 10 p.m. so we could draw just a little more. But he was a soft-hearted keeper of pets and miscellaneous treasures and we loved him.

By 1941 the Cambridge School had become fairly well known for its excellence. Students were winning more than their share of honors in national competitions, the school's traveling exhibition was well received in many states, enrollment had increased to the point where larger quarters were again being considered, and alumnae were proving their competence as active professionals.⁴ Although students were generally unaware of financial problems, the need for more money was of much concern to the director, as it was to the new president who arrived at Smith in 1940. The abrupt closing of the Smith College Graduate School of Architecture and Landscape Architecture in Cambridge immediately after Pearl Harbor, however, came as a surprise to everyone. Eleanor Raymond (perhaps the most distinguished alumna of the Cambridge School) was the only member of the Smith College Board of Trustees who voted against closing its graduate school in Cambridge. She was not alone among Cambridge School alumnae in deploring the board's decision.

The sadness of personal loss still lingers among us. We had such fun! We worked so hard! It had not occurred to us that our school would not go on forever—by a miracle, if necessary, but it would survive. However, I think our anger at the news of closing and our frustration at being unable to alter the decision were not entirely personal nostalgia. We thought also of the future and of the missed opportunity to maintain a prestigious graduate school for women interested in our professions. The early 1940s were very uncertain and worrisome times, and everywhere decisions were made that later seemed to have been too hasty.

Harvard was stunned by the exodus of students and young professors to military service immediately after Pearl Harbor. Reluctantly, it opened its Graduate School of Design to women "for the duration of the war." A few displaced Cambridge School students applied and eventually were graduated from Harvard. Most of them, however, chose other institutions or found war jobs.

By fall 1942 the tiring details of transferring academic records and disposing of the property and equipment at 53 Church Street were finally finished. The Cambridge School was no longer vibrant proof that women could be taught the design of buildings and landscapes but became a memory, a casualty of World War II.

Notes

1. Lowthorpe, like the Cambridge School, had an unwieldy official name: The Lowthorpe School of Landscape Architecture, Gardening, and Horticulture for Women. It was founded in 1901 by Mrs. Edward Gilchrist Low, who had

studied horticulture at Swanley College in England and wanted to make similar training available to American women.

2. Most of the faculty taught at Harvard, too. Also on the faculty were a few professors from nearby institutions and a few early graduates of the Cambridge School (notably, Mary P. Cunningham and Edith Cochran, who were regular course teachers, and Eleanor Raymond, who came in as a special critic).

3. Henry A. Frost said many times that men and women approached problems differently though they found approximately the same solutions. After his initial resistance to the first tutoring assignment in 1915, he became a truly ardent believer in teaching men and women separately. He thought women were more sensitive and more serious about their future than men (perhaps because at that time a professional future for women was more uncertain). He told me once that women at the Cambridge School were more thorough and worked more steadily than his students at Harvard. (The men usually goofed off until the last minute; Mr. Frost remarked that the men may have been *thinking* about the assignment more than he realized, because they came through in the end, but he knew that the Cambridge School women were working steadily because he saw us every day.)

4. The sins of omission weigh heavily on my conscience. I mention the seven architects listed below because I know them or know of them through close associates. Other Cambridge School graduates have undoubtedly done fine work, but I have lost all contact with them. What few Cambridge School records are available in the Smith College Archives are mostly minutes of trustees' meetings and official correspondence. They include very little personal information. Because students at the Cambridge School studied both architecture and landscape architecture, records seldom separated them and it is difficult to determine who became architects. Unfortunately, the Alumnae Association of the Cambridge School, which for several years kept track of graduates, did not survive the closing of the school in 1942. My apologies to all colleagues I have overlooked.

Helen Douglass French, in partnership with her landscape architect husband Prentiss, in San Francisco, designed Hacienda del Gato, the large residence and gardens of William S. Rosecrans in Indio, Calif. Included in her designs for other large estate houses is the Procter Place (Orelton Farm) in Stockbridge, Mass. She also remodeled one of Daniel Chester French's studios in Stockbridge. Among her hundreds of jobs are many smaller residences in Sarasota and Venice, Florida. Her drawings are in the hands of the University of California at Berkeley.

Ruth Hovey was a brilliant designer and a whiz at advanced mathematics. She worked for Beatrix Farrand in New York for many years, designing much of the architectural detail in her gardens. Probably she will be remembered longest for her spectacular pebble parterre at Dumbarton Oaks, D.C., kept under a film of water to bring out the pattern and color of her complicated Baroque design.

Sarah Pillsbury Harkness is the vice president and principal of The Architects Collaborative in Cambridge, Mass. From a long list of buildings she has designed, I mention the headquarters of the Tennessee Valley Authority in Chattanooga, Tenn.; the library and several other campus buildings at Bates College, Lewiston, Maine; and the art school addition to the Worcester Art Museum, Worcester, Mass.

Victorine duPont Homsey, of Victorine and Samuel Homsey, Inc. in Wilmington, Del., designed many outstanding buildings in that area, including an office building, a garden tours' pavilion, and a lecture hall for the Winterthur Museum, as well as the Lamont duPont Copeland residence and the William W. H. Henry Comprehensive High School. Victorine designed the American Embassy in Teheran and was the AIA Chairman for the Restoration of the Octagon House in Washington, D.C.

Eleanor Raymond, our most distinguished alumna, was one of the first students at the Cambridge School and was connected with it on an almost daily basis as advisor, critic, trustee, and founder of the Alumnae Association. She has just celebrated her one hundredth birthday, as I write. Her significant contribution to American architecture is discussed in Doris Cole's comprehensive book *Eleanor Raymond, Architect* (Cranbury, N.J.: Associated University Presses, 1981).

Gertrude Sawyer designed many distinguished residences in and near Washington, D.C. Among the most interesting are the homes of Judge J. Edgar Murdock and of Nathan Scott, now the official residence of the president of American University. Her largest and most diversified project is Point Farm on the Patuxent River. From a stately mansion and guest houses to a farmer's house with numerous outbuildings, as well as the famous show barn for Black Angus cattle, Point Farm runs the gamut of different types of domestic buildings. In 1983, the estate was deeded to the State of Maryland and is now the Jefferson Patterson Historical Park and Museum.

Nathalia Ulman Williams studied at Fontainebleau as well as the Cambridge School. She did research on the White House while her landscape architect husband, Morley, was doing similar research on the grounds. At Mount Vernon they restored George Washington's fruit and vegetable garden, and Nathalia designed a new director's house. They worked together for several years on the restoration of the old North Carolina capital at New Bern, which included among other historic buildings Tryon Palace and its many outbuildings and gardens. Nathalia also designed the houses for a development near Wilmington, N.C.

Many other architects from the Cambridge School did fine work in various fields. Whether they practiced under their own names, worked in other offices, or did part-time consultation while raising a family, virtually all alumnae gave much professional time to the community—lecturing, writing, and serving on advisory boards. Readers may recognize their neighbors among the following:

Geneva Bacon, Dorothea Breed Bates, Anita Rathbun Bucknell (worked for Cross & Cross and for Dwight James Baum in New York), *Ruth Bemis Burke* (worked for Willard Gulick and for Frazier, Forman & Peter in the Boston area), *Frances Whitmore Burgess* (scientific laboratories and other buildings at California Institute of Technology), *Wenonah Sibley Chamberlin* (residences in Louisville, Ky., and work for the city in neighborhood conservation and community development), *Mary Craver, Lucile Council* (practiced with Florence Yoch in Pasadena, Calif.), *Laura Cox* (after working for Eleanor Raymond, maintained own practice in Boston), *Margaret Fisher* (worked for Holabird & Root in Chicago; then, with the encouragement of Alfred Stieglitz, turned to painting; major shows at the Fogg Museum at Harvard and the Art Institute of Chicago), *Elizabeth Fleisher* (worked for James Bush-Brown in Philadelphia), *Linda Smith Hines, Priscilla Callan Houle* (worked for Charles Cole and for Jasinsky Architects Associated on residential and commercial buildings throughout New England; designed residences in Georgia and New Mexico), *Franziska Porges Hosken, Frances Jackson, Esther Kilton, Louise Leland* (administrative assistant to Henry A. Frost, residences in Louisville, Ky.), *Florence Smith Lindstrom, Anne Halle Little* (practiced in Cleveland), *Harriet Gilbert McPherson* (residences in Connecticut), *Bertha Mather McPherson* (residences in Connecticut), *Henrietta Marquis Pope, Eleanor Kew Przybylska, Esther Schwink* (worked for Macomber & Francis, Saginaw, Mich.), *Elizabeth Taylor, Deborah Gilbert Von Rosenvinge, Miriam Woodbridge* (various jobs in Detroit), *Sarah Owen Wund* (after further study at Fontainebleau, worked at Cranbrook School, Birmingham, Mich. and in the Boston area.)

I add the names of three colleagues who do not fit easily into categories. Basic training in two professions made all graduates of the Cambridge School very flexible in their approach to the project at hand. *Eunice Hull Campbell* received her master's degree in landscape architecture and now practices in Spokane, but she designed a hospital wing in Yellowknife, British Columbia. *Eleanor Jones Eastman* practiced landscape architecture for a while before taking a Civil Service examination in planning and placing second in a group of one hundred. She now has a very successful planning practice in Texas. *Cornelia Hahn Oberlander* had intended to enter the Cambridge School in the fall of 1942, but after the school was closed she decided to go to the Harvard Graduate School of Design to study under Henry A. Frost. After receiving her master's degree in landscape architecture from Harvard, she worked with architects in Philadelphia and Washington, and subsequently she opened her own landscape office in Vancouver, British Columbia. In 1986 she was elected president of the Canadian Society of Landscape Architects.

Had it not been for the Amherst Angel, whose real name is Jean Kavanagh, this footnote would have lacked much detail. Though she had no connection with either the Cambridge School or Smith College, she went to Northhampton and dug out needed information from the college archives. Had it not been for Gertrude Sawyer, whose memory and patience are phenomenal, this chapter could not have been written.

9

The Essence

of Design

Lessons from

Two Amateurs

ADELE CHATFIELD-TAYLOR

In my house, design has always been the domain of women. All the architects I knew as a child were men and my mother's father was trained as an engineer, but their design worlds were remote. Our world was shaped by women.

In my youth, what the women were doing was not called design; it was called "running the house." Like being a mayor and running a town, this could mean something modest or something grand depending on the size, population, and resources of the place. It often involved the well-established design disciplines of architecture and landscape architecture. It always involved the design activities that only now exult in their own titles: interior design, industrial design, graphic design, and fashion design.

Wisdom leap-frogs a generation at a time, in our family. My mother, Mary Owen Lyon Chatfield-Taylor, was most impressionable with her grandmother, and I was the same. Although my mother had (and has) a highly developed design sense, which dominates my idea of how to make valentines and birthday cakes, she was fully occupied during my formative years in raising six children, and I probably owe my particular design sense to my grandmothers, Marie Constance Bentley Lyon (called GM) and Adele Blow Chatfield-Taylor (called Grandmother). I spent a good deal of time with them, at a time when each was occupied with design as a sort of calling.

I am sure they never thought they were transmitting lessons about design or womanhood. But it seemed to me that design was a central part of their lives, even though as people they were very different.

GM was a tyrannical, magnetically attractive matriarch, thought of by us and everyone else in the county as a Rock of Gibraltar. I grew up in Virginia, and our enormous family of grandparents, aunts and uncles and cousins lived in Virginia, or in the neighboring Greenspring Valley of Maryland. GM was the epitome of Virginia, where the idea of building a house *new*, or buying a set of china *new*, or acquiring a piece of jewelry *new* was like an idea from outer space. Virginians think that everything you need in life can be found in the attic. So to Virginians design is merely a matter of elegantly pairing up the existing things with the current generations of people.

When I was a child, the people and animals—though apparently permanent, because all the characters seemed so fixed then—were ephemeral compared to the things. The things were an amazing assortment of houses, furniture, pictures, silver, jewelry, wooden jigsaw puzzles, rotating birthday presents, smocked baby clothes, archaic kitchen equipment, and cars—modern additions that were absorbed without fanfare or explanation into the otherwise ancient inventory. The things seemed to have existed forever, destined to move on endlessly through time.

This was the way it was, no matter how inconvenient or staggeringly impractical never to be able to discard anything old. My memory of it is, of course, a fantasy. But in retrospect, it had three definite effects: first, it gave me the impression that the pool of stuff was finite and had to be handled with extreme care so it could last through eternity; second, that the things had value far exceeding their worth in the outside world (be they gems, chairs, or potato peelers), and third, that good design was a matter of ingenious fit—the opposite of intrusion—a matter of a thing having an elegance and inevitability that made it seem always to have been there.

GM lived, until her death at ninety-seven, at Black Oak Ridge, a 1930s house in the rolling Blue Ridge foothills of Loudoun County. The house is a picturesque, fieldstone pile with lots of fireplaces, cupboards, shutters, and white trim—a dream environment for the comings and goings of six families of grandchildren, slowly expanding and circulating through the Christmases and christenings that punctuated the years. The genius of the place is its site plan, thanks to which the house sits serenely at the highest and flattest part of Black Oak Ridge, and from which point it confers with the neighboring Blue Ridge Mountains— the fading, floating, calling presence to the west—the ravishing *raison d' etre*. The key is that the house faces north and is perpendicular to the mountains. It easily could have faced west, parallel to the mountains, but that would have been wrong. As it is, you burst through a small woods and see the house and mountains at the same moment: a single composition, like a couple in a portrait. The house is almost coy in not looking directly at the Blue Ridge, but the Blue Ridge stand ever by. It is the most tantalizing design relationship I have ever seen.

Black Oak was not solely GM's work of art; my grandfather—GP— had had everything to do with its design. But by the time my association with the place began, the whole thing was in its maturity, and the design work consisted primarily of gardening—both of the house and the grounds—and this, clearly, was GM's pleasure and calling.

To me, the house always seemed to want to be a land mass more than a work of architecture. Even from within, it seemed to be a series of caves and grottoes and interlocking pools rather than a sequence of rooms. GP once told me that as a concession to the '29 crash they had decided on lower ceilings, and this in part accounts for the cavernous feeling. But the house also has thick stone walls, numerous niches and jogs, and a southern coolness even in the height of August. It seems not so much built as hollowed out of a huge rock.

The senses most engaged by GM's design instincts were those of the nose, the ear, and the palate—the antennae most engaged in the subtle monitoring of a house that is apparently unchanging to the eye and the hand.

The scent of the house was an unmistakable combination of lavender, ancient rose potpourri, pipe ashes, books, recently fluffed sofas, and a cloud of whatever was in bloom. GM was a brilliant gardener; still, indoors, her flowers were not meant to be overpowering displays, only spare reminders of the season, and for some reason, this heightened their scent. This fragrant air was real, but miragelike if you tried to focus on it, and the moment she died it vanished.

The sounds of the house varied, and defined its different zones. The front hall was the public part of the house, and a grandfather clock languidly ticked, chimed, and struck the times of arrivals and departures. In the study, there was bookish silence or the sound of the *National Geographic*'s or the *New Yorker*'s pages being turned, as some exhausted cousin retreated from the din. In the sitting rooms, a dozen conversations in the family accent, and crackling fires; at times cards snapping in an ongoing bridge game that GM usually won, or the sound of intense concentration as the group did the puzzle and GM occasionally muttered the word "absurd." Upstairs, the intimate hush that comes from the obligatory tiptoe to guard against waking a sleeping child or weary adult, the latter coming in all ages and conditions.

GM's taste was encountered in ritualized food—old-fashioned "receipts" and old-fashioned menus. Sunday breakfast was kidney stew and fried tomatoes, summer lunch was cucumber, aspic, and homemade mayonnaise, and Christmas was a never-ending procession of popcorn and bloody Marys, baked oysters, Smithfield ham, a turkey in a cranberry necklace, creamed celery, sauerkraut, baking powder biscuits, gravy, plum pudding and wine gelatin, and, once or twice a decanter of bad dandelion wine.

These details may appear to be no more than the carrying on of tradition, but to me they were part of a definite design, as GM deftly arranged the chairs, sent for the silver, or commanded the appearance of whomever would galvanize an otherwise random event into a ritual.

Grandmother also had Virginia roots. But because of a globetrotting upbringing that broke the cycle, she turned out to be opposite of GM— a rebel.

Like all rebels, Grandmother partly yearned to be conventional, to belong absolutely to the thing she was going against. But her soul was that of an artist, and she lived to experiment. She was an amateur architect who designed and "did over" many houses in Virginia and Lake Forest, and on Nantucket Island. She would put a whole house under construction, move in and get it settled down, and then, suddenly, just as people thought she had finally found what she was looking for, she would get rid of it, as though it were a lover who had let her down in some way. For this behavior, there seem to be two possible explanations: either her lifelong disappointment over not, as a young matron, winning the Nelson House, the Virginia homestead that had gone to a younger brother in a family lottery after her mother died—she adored the house and missed it for the rest of her life—or simply that she was a perfectionist who, like many people obsessed with design, would get a piece of architecture as far as it would go, see the flaws, and want to put new insights into effect on the next project. She lived to be eighty-five and in the process got good—if never economical—at designing and bringing houses to life.

She came by her obsession honestly. Her own mother, Adele Matthiessen Blow, had been a rather good painter who, at any time later than the nineteenth century, might have been able to make this the central event of her life. As it was, she was obliged to marry and bear four children, and although she led a privileged life, she had to steal the time to paint. It was Grandmother's unlucky task as a child to have to find her mother in the garden at the end of every afternoon, wherever she had set up her easel, and call her back to dinner and her obligations. I think Grandmother always felt herself to be a messenger over-associated with this mission—returning this woman to earth—and she vowed to have a life where she would have to answer to nobody. For her part, Adele Matthiessen never made her peace with the situation, apparently felt that her work did not really develop, and specified that all her paintings be destroyed at her death. By chance, one canvas survives: a landscape rendered with great skill and a magical light.

The gift carried over to Grandmother, who mastered a life of somewhat more independence, and who thought a more satisfactory venue for self-expression was the design problem of the domestic environment. She considered this a high calling and a full-fledged artform. As an unlicensed amateur, however, no matter how skillful, she was obliged to work within the system, and so she had numerous associations with trained architects. Reams of drawings and papers survive to indicate that these were solid collaborations. She did several projects with George Howe in Washington, D.C., and in the 1920s a Georgian manor house from scratch in Lake Forest with a European architect whose name is long since forgotten.

She had a fabulous eye, and a passion for risk. She knew and loved the classics and insisted on "good bones." But she was a modernist, too, a sort of Isadora Duncan of design. She even behaved a bit like the pioneering dancer; she understood color and line and the *essence* of what she was after, in the modern sense. She would come streaming into a room in a cloud of gauzy material, or a garland of flowers, or a truly odd hat. She had a high ringing voice that was less a communication device than a sound effect. She was a great beauty and a real wit. Her rooms, in fact, were stage sets for characters like herself.

In other words, she understood effect. She was interested in ideas, in dogs, and in style. She perfected three artforms: the house, the letter, and the euphemism. You never had the slightest idea what she was driv-ing at until she had created the *atmosphere* for her point, be it architec-tural, literary, or parental. But once she did, you knew you had been addressed by a pro.

If GM made Black Oak convey the feeling that it would never change, Grandmother made her houses seem to *belong* wherever they were, and this had a parallel effect—it made permanence unimportant. She always made her own statement, but signaled that she knew the native language, too. This was a skill that also stood her in good stead as an inveterate traveler. By the time she was old and traveling light, she could unpack a few fragments from her suitcase—a photograph, the mail, an alarm clock, a book open to a certain place—and arrange them in her room so that she was at home and looked it.

She also, of course, thought that a work-in-progress quality was a necessary aspect of the designed environment. On one level, she may have thought (like many designers) that it was death to finish something; so no room was without a swatch of material being sized up, a canvas sparkling with wet paint, or a desk stacked with papers. The only use she had for a kitchen was as a habitat for the glorious natural design of the tomato, eggplant, or seasonal fowl, which she took pleasure in arrang-ing on the kitchen table (and then leaving for someone else to cook). Wherever she left this evidence of her hand, this small sign that she con-sidered everyday living a design problem, it electrified the room. You could tell she had been there, but it was a subtle enhancement rather than a grand gesture.

Grandmother's genius had to do with the eye and the hand. She attuned herself to the landscape and the town and the house where she was, to stake her claim. She seemed to pull her ideas out of the turf and the sky. On Nantucket, she opened her houses to the light, making all the rooms seem as pale, speckled, and opaque as the clouds and dunes to which they would report. To the touch, the design was clean and sim-ple. At Mantua, on the other hand, a great Georgian house in the north-ern neck of Virginia, she caught the faint light, the yellowish sand, and the mustiness of the Rappahannock landscape; this house looked west through ponderous curtains, walls of books, and deep *chaise longues* in which you could lose yourself forever. To the touch, this place was fuzzy, private, and plush.

Before I could read, Grandmother taught me to draw plans for houses, availing herself of the damp sand of the Nantucket beaches. And the minute she taught me this language, I knew that I was home. I knew that design was for me.

This was a perfect pair of grandmothers, I think—GM an eagle, guarding our standards, and Grandmother an artist, breaking new ground. GM imparted a love of continuity and gravity, and Grandmother a yen for the beautiful and untried; but they both understood the lure of the direct hit. And they liked each other, to everyone's astonishment, because in spite of being so different, they had something vast in common, and it was an unspoken agreement about their job, which was to mind the design—the idea, the history, the underpinning, the function, and the decor of every single thing that went on—so that life could happen without calling too much attention to itself, but at the same time so that it could have the rush of a special occasion. They knew this combination came when things were properly planned and made and maintained, which is to say when things were properly designed.

10

An Elusive

Pioneer

Tracing the Work of

Julia Morgan

SARA HOLMES BOUTELLE

My interest in Julia Morgan was
evoked exactly one hundred years after her birth by something millions
had shared: a tour of San Simeon on California's central coast. As a
teacher of history of art and architecture, my honor was at stake. How
could I, in 1972, have been ignorant about this early woman architect,
even if she had never designed anything other than this one commission for William Randolph Hearst? She lived not too long ago (1872–
1957). How had she managed to hide herself so successfully from history? I was determined to find out about her and her work, unaware
that the quest would become an obsession requiring a cross-continental
move and a dozen years of monomaniacal research.

When I returned to the East Coast that fall, I asked the librarian at
my school for a book on this amazing woman architect. But there were
no books on Julia Morgan—in or out of print. Even the biographies of
Hearst gave scant attention to his lifelong architect.[1]

Research in traditional architectural sources was no more fruitful.
Esther McCoy effectively excluded Morgan from her landmark book,

Julia Morgan, 1872–1957, from her carte d'identité. Ecole des Beaux-Arts, 1899, given to the author by the late Morgan North, nephew of Julia Morgan. Photograph courtesy of Sara Holmes Boutelle

Gothic Study, 1927, San Simeon, California, Julia Morgan, architect. From this grand room on the third floor, Hearst directed his publishing and motion-picture empires. Photograph by Richard D. Barnes

Entrance, Berkeley Women's City Club, 1930, Berkeley, California, Julia Morgan, architect. Still in use by the original owner (now calling itself the Berkeley City Club), this building is one of Morgan's relatively few buildings on the National Register for Historic Places. Photograph by James H. Edelen, courtesy of Sara Holmes Boutelle

Five California Architects. Lewis Mumford, who gave the name to "Bay Region" architecture, had omitted Morgan. Vincent Scully, who made the Bay Area and Shingle Style the focus of several publications, had failed to mention Morgan. Clouded in the mists of *Citizen Kane* and the rest of the anti-Hearst mythology, San Simeon was derided by puritans of the modern movement and not considered architecture in any serious sense. Julia Morgan's obscurity began to be comprehensible. I looked further afield. In one university, I found a listing for *Julia Morgan, Rebel* and seized upon the publication excitedly, only to discover that a Tennessee historical society was honoring a Civil War heroine who had taken up her fallen husband's gun to fight the Yankees. I should confess, too, that I read a lot about Justin Morgan, the horse-breeder, hoping in vain that he might be a relative. As for J. P. Morgan, another dead end.

Since it seemed possible that although Julia Morgan had not reached national prominence, she might be heralded in California, I returned there for a summer of research. Beginning in Berkeley, where

YWCA, 1930, San Francisco, California, Julia Morgan, architect. Many of the materials in this building (for instance, the roof tiles) were imported from China. Julia Morgan loved all things Chinese; she was studying Chinese characters when she died. This building, in San Francisco's Chinatown, is still in use as a community center. Photograph courtesy of American Institute of Architects Archives, Washington, D.C.

the young Julia came in 1890 from her Oakland home and high school to study engineering at the university, I found traces of her career. There she met Bernard Maybeck, teacher of descriptive geometry and alumnus of the Ecole des Beaux-Arts; it was Maybeck, as well as her cousin Pierre LeBrun, who inspired her to go to Paris and pursue a career in architecture.[2] Frustrated by the scant material even in the famous Bancroft Library at Berkeley, I determined to trace Morgan's own footsteps. The deeper I went, the more challenging the project became and the more important it seemed that Julia Morgan's rightful place in architectural history be established.

The first challenge was the architect herself. She granted few interviews and wrote nothing for publication; she was quoted as saying she was not "a talking architect." Worse yet, in 1951, she saw to the destruction of many of her office files and drawings; she had no room for them at retirement.[3] There were no lists of her buildings, no books, and only one 1918 article on her work.[4] A woman pursuing a librarianship degree in 1964 had compiled a Julia Morgan "bibliography" that was in the Berkeley architecture library.[5] It was a pathetically short list, mostly news articles and obituaries from local newspapers. Nevertheless, it was a start. In 1974, Morgan had been the subject of a paper by a graduate student in architectural history, later published,[6] but I discovered that several doctoral candidates had rejected Morgan as a dissertation topic because of the difficulty in finding information.[7]

The task I set for myself was to locate her hundreds of buildings, have them photographed, and identify them by client and date of construction.[8] Even biographical material was sparse. Morgan never married, her four siblings were dead, and her heir, the son of her lawyer sister, would give no interviews. Almost all clients had died or moved away. My request to the Hearst family came just as Patty Hearst made the headlines, thus closing off material that might otherwise have been available. When I applied to the Hearst Foundation for funds for travel and photography, and was told they could give grants only to nonprofit corporations, I decided to incorporate the Julia Morgan Association. And when the Hearst Foundation lawyers said they could not approve a grant for a new, small corporation, I arranged to have funds channeled through the University of California at Santa Cruz. Finally by 1976 I had a nonprofit association, a university affiliation, and a grant from a

Hockenbeamer House, 1913, Berkeley, California, Julia Morgan, architect. Morgan did at least one hundred redwood shingle houses in Berkeley alone, but many were destroyed in the disastrous Berkeley fire of 1923. Only a score or so of these houses remain; Etna and Derby Streets in Berkeley are living museums of Morgan's skill with the cheap and available materials of the Bay Area. Photograph courtesy of Sara Holmes Boutelle

national foundation. Julia Morgan, Architect, had grown from a casual interest into a full-time occupation.

Luckily, people were still in the Bay Area who had worked for Morgan; Walter Steilberg, author of the 1918 article, a Santa Claus of a man in his late eighties, was full of recall about the Morgan office he had joined in 1910. It was a critical loss when he was run over and killed on an afternoon walk. I also found a contractor who had been with Morgan on a dozen projects, a tilemaker in his mid-nineties, a woman who made stained glass, another who painted murals, two woodcarvers, two retired practitioners of the extinct trade of ornamental plastering, an artist who worked in cast stone, and tapestry weavers and gardeners from San Simeon. These rare craftspeople were ripe with anecdotal material.[9]

For me, it was hurry, hurry to discover and interview aged respondents, then hurry to prevent destruction of old buildings. Demolition was occurring just ahead of me. The building for the *Oakland Enquirer* was replaced by a parking garage; the San Jose YWCA was demolished for a parking lot; banks, schools, and community buildings in Marysville and Vallejo met similar fates. In the midst of destruction, it became urgent to lobby for preservation. I pushed for exhibition of Morgan's Ecole drawings, a bequest stored literally in garbage cans in the College of Environmental Design at Berkeley.

When the Berkeley City Club (designed by Morgan) and then the Oakland Museum agreed to my exhibition proposals, even Morgan's nephew unbent and loaned drawings from his collection. The tide was turning. The landmark Museum of Modern Art show of Ecole drawings in New York helped reexamine architectural pieties, and at the same time scholars began to notice that women existed in history. Material on Julia Morgan was sought for a book chapter, an oral-history project, articles, and a college credit course.[10]

Valuable leads came from every lecture and article; new information and wonderful memories came to light from unlikely sources. Morgan's life and character were emerging from the wood and concrete. But she remained her own private self. To people who ask me about "Julia," I say they may first-name her only if they refer to Frank Lloyd Wright as "Frank."

In 1978, Morgan's nephew decided I was her "legitimate biographer" and granted me access to the basement where his aunt's papers and memorabilia were stored. At last I had the resources for a definitive book, but after three weeks of intensive study, when I called to check the next

Living room, YWCA Hostess House, 1918, Camp Fremont, Menlo Park, California, Julia Morgan, architect. When the War Department asked the National YWCA to construct Hostess Houses (where relatives and friends could meet with soldiers at some forty training camps), Julia Morgan had already done distinguished work for the YWCA. She was invited to serve as national architect for the entire program but consented only to an appointment for the West because she did not want to leave her San Francisco office for Washington or New York. Tight budgets, limited labor, and war restrictions on materials tested her experience in creating an inviting place from inexpensive designs and materials. Photograph courtesy of National Board YWCA Archives

appointment, I was told that her nephew had died the night before. Another door shut tight. It was two years before the material was released to Cal Poly and I could see it again.[11] During the tantalizing period when I knew what existed but could not get at it, I sought to spread the word about Julia Morgan beyond the West Coast. A grant from the National Endowment for the Arts made possible a visit to two Hawaiian sites with a photographer, and the creation of a modest slide show introducing Morgan to schools.[12] This led to speaking engagements at Yale, MIT, Smith, and Princeton, and the privilege of giving the opening address at the Exposition of the International Union of Women Architects at the Pompidou Center in Paris (where I was billed as the Secretary

General of the Julia Morgan Association!).

But there are disappointments. No one has yet been willing to do a full television documentary on Morgan; the Post Office has resisted efforts to award her a place on a stamp. In 1986, Robert A. M. Stern's series on architecture ("Pride of Place") introduced a brief section on Morgan with material from *Citizen Kane* (which was entirely irrelevant to Morgan's work) and misrepresented both client and commission. Those few moments on public television were a setback for architectural history and for Julia Morgan. People find it difficult to believe that she enjoyed Hearst's imagination and vigor, and that he admired her and deferred to her throughout (even though he was emotionally centered on Marion Davies and the Hollywood world).

There are other disappointments. Research on monuments such as San Simeon and Asilomar proved relatively easy.[13] But many of Morgan's private residences and smaller structures were very difficult to find and authenticate. It was a formidable task just making a list of the nearly eight hundred projects attributed to her office. Even after ten years of research, the number of "mysteries" remains distressingly high as I continue to track down disappeared families, changed street numbers, and lost documents. In addition to the files burned upon her instructions, other records have gone—the city deeds in Berkeley were accidentally destroyed by fire, and the records in Piedmont were intentionally destroyed rather than moved to a new location. Facts about each commission have been pieced together from family records, newspapers, archives, social registers, and rumors. Even those who appreciate Morgan structures—like the YWCAs and women's clubs that made up a formidable part of her practice—have overlooked important commissions.

Although I agree with Morgan that her buildings speak for her, I also realize that they do not speak until they have been introduced. It has seemed both necessary and worthwhile to make this introduction for an architect who is of importance for her part in the development of the Bay Area regional style, and is of universal interest for her combination of the symmetry of Ecole teaching (balanced but never inviolable) with the client-centered environmentalism of her native region. Her own passionate response to the medieval crafts ideal (with its meticulous devotion to detail and to the total building at the same time), her love of history, and her close relations with other design disciplines from engineering to crafts work and gardening give Morgan's buildings a lot to say.

The Mills campus tower and library (1904 and 1906), an early reinforced-concrete house in Berkeley (1906), the Asilomar Conference Center of about twenty crafts-style public buildings (1913–1929), churches, clubs, schools, hospitals, gymnasiums, and hundreds of residences (including about twenty-five for the Hearsts alone), all amount to a body of work that resists classification while it commands interest and respect. Her sensitive relationships with clients and employees, her sharing of profits, her personal warmth and humor, all combine to make this woman a compelling figure in American architecture.

Notes

1. In 1969, to commemorate the fiftieth anniversary of the start of the ever-unfinished "Hearst Castle," Hollywood folklorist Ken Murray compiled a film called *The Golden Days of San Simeon* and a book of the same name (New York: Doubleday & Co., 1971). He identified shots of client and architect, however, as "Mr. Hearst and his secretary." The film is still shown, but at my insistence the guides explain that the small woman in the porkpie hat was his architect, Julia Morgan.

2. After a year's work for Maybeck in Berkeley, Morgan set off in March 1896 for Paris and the architecture section of the Ecole des Beaux-Arts. Two years later, after her third try at the entrance examination, she was the first woman accepted in the course; in 1902, she was the first woman granted a certificate.

3. Her secretary, Lillian Forney, saved some drawings, which were later given to Berkeley by Forney's daughter. Other material was stored in Morgan's basement until her death, when her nephew took charge.

4. Walter Steilberg, "Some Examples of the Work of Julia Morgan," *Architect and Engineer of California* 55 (November 1918): 39–107. Steilberg had worked in her office from 1910, when he graduated from Berkeley.

5. Charlotte Tyler assembled the material from a librarianship course at Berkeley taught by Flora Elizabeth Reynolds, who was Mills College librarian, 1955–1976. "An Annotated Bibliography of Julia Morgan, California Architect and her Works," College of Environmental Design, Berkeley (unpublished) also cited two additional articles from *Architect and Engineer of California*, each about one Morgan commission: "Woman Architect Who Helped Build the Fairmont Hotel," Jane Armstrong, 7 (October 1907): 69–71; and "Berkeley Women's City Club," by Morgan staff member Julian C. Mesic, 105 (April 1931): 25–34; as well as "The Early Domestic Architecture of the San Francisco Bay Region," by Elizabeth Kendall Thompson, *Journal of the Society of Architectural Historians* 10 (October 1951): 15–21.

6. Richard W. Longstreth, "Julia Morgan: Some Introductory Notes," *Perspecta 15, Yale Papers on Architecture* (1976), 3–24. This was later published as a booklet by the Berkeley Architectural Heritage Association, in 1977 and 1987.

7. There is a chapter in a book by Elinor Richey, *Eminent Women of the West* (Berkeley: Howell-North Books, 1975), lively but not reliable as to facts.

8. The Morgan office followed the usual pattern of numbering commissions chronologically; work from the year 1907 in the Bancroft Library was numbered in 200s, Asilomar (1913) began with number 380, the Hearst San Simeon commission (1919–1938) all counted as job number 503, and the Pope house in Carmel (1940) was number 785.

9. A problem of what could be called "filial piety syndrome" arose among some of my sources. Sons, daughters, and nephews of Morgan's staff made conflicting claims of the importance of their respective relatives' contributions to her oeuvre. I had to reassure them that they were all significant parts of the whole (as indeed they were) and that their reminiscences should be preserved, with other records, in the library of their choice rather than in a carton at home.

10. Sara Boutelle, "Julia Morgan," in *Women in American Architecture: A Historic and Contemporary Perspective*, ed. Susana Torre (New York: Whitney Library of Design, 1977), 79–87; Sara Holmes Boutelle, "The Julia Morgan Architectural History Project," ed. Suzanne B. Riess, Bancroft Library Regional Oral History Office, Berkeley, 1976; extension courses on Julia Morgan given by Sara Holmes Boutelle, University of California at Santa Cruz, 1975 and 1981; Sara Boutelle, "Julia Morgan," in *Macmillan Encyclopedia of Architects*, ed. Adolf K. Placzek (New York: Macmillan Co., 1982), vol. 3, 238–39; Sara Boutelle, "Julia Morgan," in *The Master Builders: A Guide to Famous American Architects*, ed. Diane Maddex (Washington, D.C.: Preservation Press, 1985), 132–35. On this last, Morgan shares the cover with William Thornton, Henry Hobson Richardson, and Frank Lloyd Wright!

11. The Julia Morgan material is housed in the Special Collections Department, Robert E. Kennedy Library, California Polytechnic State University, San Luis Obispo, Calif. 93407 (telephone 805-546-2305). The library has published a 103-page *Descriptive Guide to the Julia Morgan Collection*.

12. Slides are available from Budek Films & Slides, Newport, R.I. The slide show received special commendation from the NEA in 1980 in its first grants recognition program (looking back at the best Design Arts projects of NEA's first fifteen years).

13. The California State Parks and Recreation Department has the category of "state monument" under its jurisdiction, and both of these building complexes are officially protected and administered as state monuments. Asilomar, which was built as the YWCA Conference Center, is now known as the Asilomar Conference Center. The Hearst State Historical Monument is the official name for what visitors continue to call the "Hearst Castle."

11

Task Force

on Women

The AIA Responds to

a Growing Presence

JUDITH EDELMAN

Considering the tremendous fer-
ment over women's status and rights in the late sixties and early seventies, the response of the American Institute of Architects, the major professional society, would seem to have been tardy. But women were only
a tiny segment of the profession at that time—somewhere between
1 percent and 3 percent according to the meager statistics then available—and although we were concentrated in the northeast and California we felt a severe sense of isolation from each other.

Small as our population was, an even smaller part of it belonged to
the AIA, and it is not surprising that women began to find their collective voice outside the AIA. In 1972, when the time was apparently ripe,
three organizations arose independently of each other: Women Architects, Landscape Architects, and Planners (WALAP) in Boston, Alliance
of Women in Architecture (AWA) in New York, and Organization of
Women Architects (OWA) in San Francisco.

Those of us involved felt a tremendous urgency. Speaking up in
our own behalf at last, we felt that we could demonstrate genuine griev-

ances and would soon see great changes. We wanted to press the effort on all possible fronts. It did not take long to start putting pressure on the AIA.

I was in a good position vis-à-vis the AIA. In 1971 I became the first woman elected to the executive committee of the New York chapter. With the formation of the AWA, I became part of its first coordinating committee. The very existence of the AWA was reinforcement for me, ending my long-standing isolation as a professional and enabling me to work more effectively within the AIA.

One of the AWA's most pressing concerns was, of course, discriminatory employment practices, and one of its earliest efforts was a salary survey. Although disappointingly small, the response showed clearly that salary discrimination was a real issue. The experience proved valuable for what was to follow.

Then surprisingly, in 1973, came a burst of activity in the New York State Association of Architects/AIA (not to be confused with the New York chapter). A survey was disseminated in two newsletters to all members, and by separate mailing to all registered women architects in the state and all AWA members. Again results pointed up the inequities between women and men. National AIA had yet to be heard from.

In early 1973, I served on the NYC/AIA's committee to formulate resolutions for the national convention in May, and we submitted a resolution on the status of women in the profession. Two other chapters, Boston and New Jersey, submitted similar resolutions; the three were consolidated by the national resolutions committee into the form presented for convention vote in San Francisco.

RESOLVED, That the AIA take action to integrate women into all aspects of the profession as full participants.

RESOLVED, That The Institute conduct a study on the status of women in the profession and report the results to the Board of Directors in December and to the 1974 Convention. The study should include a survey of present statistics and employment practices relative to women in architecture and consider the formulation of policies in the following areas:

1. The encouragement of women to become architects.

2. The involvement of more women in AIA activities and structure.

3. ~~The elimination of sexist wording in all AIA documents and publications.~~ (deleted by Convention)

4. The initiation of an affirmative action program to implement the Equal Opportunity Section of the "Manual of Personnel Practices" AIA.

Despite stiff opposition the resolution passed by 996 to 627; now came a period of false starts and road blocks, cooperation and intransigence, frustration and exhilaration.

In September 1973 I was asked to chair the new "Subcommittee on Women and Other Minorities" of the Personnel Practices Committee. I was taken aback that a subcommittee was proposed, that its charge included "other minorities," and that the entire subject was relegated to a minor arm of a committee dealing with many other issues. We had supposed that an independent committee or task force would be the appropriate entity. (The term "task force" was later used loosely to apply to the subcommittee, and I will use it here for simplicity.) I accepted the assignment in spite of misgivings.

In October when I met with the AIA staff member assigned to the Commission on Professional Practice, I insisted that the entire intent of the resolution must be addressed. It was agreed that the scope would be limited to women since a full AIA department was already devoted to minorities. I would submit a written program and budget. The man from Washington said, "You're funded!" I began to feel that the problems could be worked out.

Then something so peculiar happened I am still puzzled by it. In mid-November our staff man in Washington told me that a survey questionnaire could be included in the December *Memo* (the AIA's national newsletter), if we could prepare it in time. The task force hadn't been formed yet; I had been working with a small group in New York, none of whom would be appointed to the task force. We had two weeks! But we were so charged up to get something rolling that we actually produced a responsible questionnaire capable of being analyzed by the then most appropriate computer program. On 10 December, I was informed that the questionnaire could not appear in *Memo* because it would conflict with the impending and very official "AIA 1973 Survey of the Profession." To this day I do not know whether our staff person made a stupid mistake or was deliberately misleading us. It was not a good beginning, but postponing the survey ultimately was advantageous. Had the questionnaire appeared in *Memo*, only AIA members would have been polled, and already we had a much broader list of women in the profession.

David Bowen, chairman of the Personnel Practices Committee, was in New York in early January, and we discussed the need to supplement the AIA survey because of its absurdly small sampling of women. He believed that if our questionnaire were reviewed by the Personnel Practices Committee during the February meeting it could be mailed by March. I was advised to submit a new budget request for the task force. However, no one had informed me about the timing of funding allocations or, in fact, about any of the usual procedures. As I later discovered, basic budget allocations for 1974 had been made in December 1973. Much later I learned that our staff man had passed along neither my original program and budget nor the January budget and in fact had misrepresented both requests.

On 7 February, off I went to Washington to take my seat on the Personnel Practices Committee and to meet the members of my subcommittee/task force: Marie Laleyan, San Francisco; Patricia Schiffelbein, Washington, D.C.; Joan Sprague, Boston; and Jean Young, Seattle.

Early on that first day I was called out of the meeting by the deputy executive director of the AIA and the chairman of the Commission of Professional Practice. They told me very brusquely that there was no funding for the task force other than travel expenses; we were not authorized to do any research whatsoever; and we were to limit our work to formulating an equal opportunities statement for the 1974 convention. When I reported back to the Personnel Practices Committee, Bowen was hearteningly outraged. The committee consensus was that this did not constitute adequate implementation of the resolution; the committee would review the questionnaire for distribution as soon as possible.

In mid-March the deputy executive director wrote me an astonishing letter. He was happy to give the go-ahead for our survey, but he sternly told us we must "do the impossible": an analysis of the survey results and a draft report must be ready for review by the Personnel Practices Committee on 2 May; a printed report must be ready for the preconvention board of directors meeting a few weeks later. We had the report ready on 2 May, including a computer analysis of responses. Some copies were printed for the board meeting along with an interim affirmative action proposal. But the board failed to act on the report so it was not printed for distribution at the convention. This was both embarrassing and disappointing.

I was scheduled to speak to the convention about the task force and was able to summarize the survey findings. Serious problems were compellingly documented in three major problem areas: 1) underrepresentation in the profession; 2) discrimination in employment; and 3) alienation of women architects from the AIA.

Although this convention did not take formal action relative to the task force work, a great deal of interest was expressed and the atmosphere seemed to bode well for continuing efforts. Major tasks remaining for the balance of 1974 were: completion of the study on the status of women with expanded analysis of the survey data and completion of a statement on equal employment opportunity and a guide to lawful employment practices, all to be published as AIA documents. We requested a change in status to an independent task force for 1975 and submitted an outline of our goals, purposes, and activities. The essential goal was the integration of women as full and equal participants in all aspects of the architectural profession. The tools would be affirmative action programs for the AIA both national and local. In the feminist ferment of the early seventies, coming not long after the peak of the civil rights movement, we had high hopes that once equal rights and affirmative action concepts were defined and codified then specific goals could and would be enforced.

I appeared before the board of directors in September to give an update on our work and took the opportunity to describe the obstructions with which we had been beset. Although this caused some furor, it was effective: we were authorized to complete the 1974 program and to become an independent task force in 1975. However, it was not until March 1975, after intervention by William Marshall and Louis DeMoll, president and first vice president, that the board approved the report for publication and directed the task force to develop an affirmative action plan. I asked Marie Laleyan to co-chair the task force because of her proven leadership capabilities and because of her knowledge of affirmative action laws and documents. Joan Sprague dropped out and Natalie DeBlois joined our group.

The change from subcommittee to independent task force brought some beneficial changes in attitude at AIA headquarters. James A. Scheeler, deputy executive director, was assigned to expedite our work, and we even received some clerical help.

The 1975 *Affirmative Action Plan for the Integration of Women in the Architectural Profession* consisted of three sections: (a) *Affirmative Action Commitment* dealt with AIA policy and its dissemination; (b) *Administration* dealt with implementation of the AAP, including monitoring and evaluation; and (c) *Objectives, Goals, Programs*—the real guts of the document—stated numerical goals. Very specific assignments of responsibility were made to various departments, commissions, and committees of the AIA. Specific actions were proposed.[1]

We completed the plan in late 1975, the board approved it, and the task force disbanded. In spite of the odds against us, we had produced a very thorough document with great potential for accelerating improvement in the status of women architects.

And nothing much happened. The AAP was not distributed within the AIA. Requests for the *Task Force Report* and AAP (bound together as a 73-page document) were not filled. It is hard to say whether this was an attempt to ignore the whole effort or was typical bureaucratic failure. However, in 1976, Scheeler presented the AAP at a "Grassroots" session in San Francisco; some chapters responded by developing their own AAPs. Also, before resigning as AAP coordinator, Scheeler made one or two progress reports on its implementation.

But the task force work could not simply be forgotten. A lot of people, some inside the AIA, were interested in following the results. Enough questions were asked to provoke the 1978–79 AIA president, Elmer Botsai, to appoint a new Women in Architecture Task Group to look into the implementation of the AAP and update it, but the members chose to ignore the AAP and develop other programs. In the years since then there has consistently been some task group or committee dedicated to women's issues. They have met with varying degrees of acceptance and cooperation, but they were responsible for two additional surveys in 1981 and 1983 (using questionnaires similar to the one used in 1974) and a brief update in 1985.

Undoubtedly we did something of value. The initial report was the first statistical study of national scope describing the status of women in the profession. The affirmative action plan could have had a significant impact, and to some extent the AIA wanted to support the effort, but seeing it succeed was another matter. Perhaps the AIA would have been more responsive if numerical and percentage goals had not been such an important part of the plan; there has, of course, been wide opposition to the use of anything that could be construed as a "quota." In hindsight, I think that some of the goals and programs should not have been tied to numbers at all, particularly where these goals seemingly accepted continuing inequities. But without any quantified goals, the AAP would have been little more than a vague statement of good intentions and, I believe, would have been shelved anyway. Without doubt, we changed the consciousness of quite a few male architects who had some contact with the task force work, but for the majority our very presence was an irritant. Today, when many more women are taking leading roles in the AIA, the discomfort is still evident.

Yet the significant increase in the number of women architects in the last dozen years is hardly, if at all, a result of the task force work.

And in spite of increased numbers, full acceptance and true equity may still be a long way off. Fundamental attitudes are slow to change.

Notes

1. Space prevents my reiterating these proposals here. Readers who want a copy of the 1975 affirmative action plan may write to the Women in Architecture Committee, the American Institute of Architects, 1735 New York Avenue, N.W., Washington, D.C. 20006.

12

A Feminist

Experiment

Learning from WSPA,

Then and Now

LESLIE KANES WEISMAN

For many of us, the institution of higher education is embodied in the formal quadrangles of Oxford, Cambridge, Harvard, and Princeton—architecture that symbolizes the dignity and ceremony of the collegiate tradition. What we cannot easily imagine are the ways in which power is maintained and transferred behind the walls and inside the chambers: the unspoken agreements that determine who will get certain privileges and information and who will not.

In my twenty-four years in architectural education, the fact that I am a woman has never been given as the reason why I have been held back, paid less, told that my "commitment to architecture" was questionable, or continually assigned to teach introductory courses (denied the special challenge of teaching at higher levels and doing research in my areas of special expertise). Yet I have no doubt that sex discrimination has profoundly shaped the quality of my own education and has led me to define my life and my work as an educator by its imperatives.

*Intensive design courses.
Many workshops at WSPA,
over the years, explored the
possibilities of a woman-made
environment. Photograph
courtesy of Noel Phyllis Birkby*

In undergraduate school I was advised to study the suitably female subjects of fine arts and interior design; I accepted the former but refused the latter in favor of architecture. When I landed my first teaching job, in a midwestern university, I became the only woman faculty member in their department of architecture—a position I was perfectly pleased to hold until I became a "card-carrying" feminist in the late 1960s.

By 1974, the year I attended the first conference on women in architecture held in America (at Washington University in St. Louis), I was deeply disturbed by the seeming contradiction between my politics and my paycheck. I began to ask myself, "What is the relevance of architecture to the social change needed to improve the quality of women's lives?" I had no answers. Neither did six other women—architects and planners, teachers and practitioners—I met that year, at or through the St. Louis conference.

Guided by the mutual belief that we had something important to offer to our professions and to each other, we decided to create a forum in which we could discover the particular qualities, concerns, and values that we, as women, bring to the practice and teaching of architecture and planning. We would found a "school" of our own where we could learn from each other—all of us teachers and students, exchanging questions, challenging convention, inventing new areas of inquiry and research, and sharing knowledge in a supportive atmosphere where women's accomplishments would be visible, their skills respected, and their differences valued.

Our experiment, the Women's School of Planning and Architecture (WSPA), was to become the only school of its kind to be completely conceived of, founded, financed, and run by women for women. During its years of operation, 1975–1981, it was known and highly regarded internationally both by feminists and by establishment schools of architecture and planning.[1]

When the cofounders signed the simple partnership agreement that established WSPA in 1974, most of us hardly knew each other. Some of us had never even met, since we lived in four different cities: San Francisco, Detroit, New York, and Boston.[2] Yet the personal bonds we shared even then were far more compelling than the legal and professional ones we created later. Our group was not formed by individuals who all believed in a common, explicit political position. What each did believe in was the others' desire to collaborate with women and to struggle to make greater sense of her own life and life's work through this process.

Creating the events of the day.
The wall calendar at WSPA's
first session was 7 feet tall and
20 feet long. Field trips,
picnics, parties, presentations,
spontaneous discussions, and
all-school meetings could be
scheduled by any participant
during any time not taken by
core courses. Photograph
courtesy of Leslie Kanes
Weisman

Sharing information. A 20-
foot-long display was produced
by Katrin Adam to bring some
of the material of her core
course to the entire school.
Photograph courtesy of Noel
Phyllis Birkby

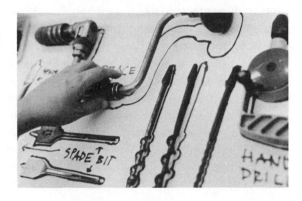

From the very beginning, WSPA was to be for women only. Each two-week session was scheduled in August and designed to bring together about sixty women from across North America—women with diverse interests, educations, experiences, incomes, ages, and ethnic and racial backgrounds. The only admissions "requirement" was an acknowledged interest in architecture, planning, and environmental design. In keeping with our philosophy of inclusiveness, children were welcome, child care was provided, and campus facilities were wheelchair accessible.[3]

WSPA's first brochure described a curriculum taught by experienced professionals whose extensive credentials—university degrees, teaching positions, research, publications, practice—were listed jointly "to express the cooperative and nonhierarchical spirit of WSPA." For the same reasons, courses were often team-taught and were scheduled to allow us to meet once with each of the others; in addition, every course organized one event or presentation for the entire school.[4]

The emotional and intellectual intensity, the constant stimulation by the enthusiastic presence of others, was sometimes exhausting. I was grateful that we had had the foresight to seek campus facilities in naturally beautiful settings—on the Atlantic and Pacific Oceans, in the mountains and woods, and near picturesque cities of historical and cultural interest—environments in which to escape, be alone, relax, and restore our balance as needed.

WSPA's curriculum changed yearly to incorporate the interests and expertise of new members of the coordinating group—participants from previous WSPA sessions replacing cofounders who were voluntarily "retiring" from administration on a temporary or permanent basis.[5]

After our first session in Maine (1975), we held two-week sessions in California (1976),[6] Rhode Island (1978),[7] and Colorado.[8] The last WSPA session, in Washington, D.C. (1981) could hardly be called a WSPA session at all. Structured like a traditional, three-day weekend conference, it had every workshop scheduled opposite many others, with panels of "experts" lecturing to a passive audience. Nevertheless, the theme and intention of the session, "A National Symposium: Community-Based Alternatives and Women in the Eighties," was well conceived and timely. Many of us were adamant that our WSPA network must expand to include more nonprofessional women, women of color, women active in shaping their own communities as housing advocates, leaders in tenant management, economic developers, founders of shelters, and so on.[9] But the "real" content of a WSPA session was missing—the shared lives, activities, time, and space that engender lasting personal and professional relationships, the lessons of tolerance, collaboration, and celebration that generate the motivation and momentum needed to organize future sessions and sustain us in the interim.

If we cofounders erred at all in our long-range planning, it was in believing that each new coordinating group would find its own creative way of organizing and operating within the framework of WSPA's philosophy. This was certainly true for some time. But as time passed, although the WSPA coordinators were well-intentioned and skillful, they were increasingly drawn to familiar convention. They began to function more as administrators implementing the basic tenets and procedures authored by others and less as innovators responsible for delivering their own framework and curriculum.

After the symposium in Washington, D.C., there were those who believed WSPA had finally "failed." I did not agree, then or now. Longevity is, in my mind, not the ultimate measure of success for a feminist educational "institution." The primary value of such an education is its ability to create social change through the personal transformation of those it educates. The point of feminist education is not so much the delivery and understanding of academic subject matter, but rather the collective process through which each woman is better able to define life and change it. Feminist education is based on the morality of political responsibility, accountability, empathy, and rigorous self-examination, and begins with defining the self and the community to which the self belongs. Feminist education means searching to fully understand the social forces that have shaped our individuality, and then locating that self in the world, understanding the true nature of the "we" that each self feels herself a part of.

In this sense, a feminist education is not inherently related to an educational institution at all, but to its participants, and must be evaluated in terms of its effect on them. Accordingly, although WSPA failed to continue, it succeeded in many ways, at the time, and for those who participated in it, well beyond the years of our participation.

WSPA helped many of us gain the confidence and sense of direction necessary to take responsibility for shaping our own futures. For some women this meant entering accredited schools of architecture and planning; for others it meant leaving old jobs and creating new ones. For all of us, WSPA was an experience that enhanced our self-esteem as women and strengthened our identification with each other.

Over the years, WSPA touched the lives of more than three hundred participants. Many have gone on to found construction compa-

A group of WSPA "Sistas" at the third seesion, August 1978, Bristol, Rhode Island. Photograph by Tequila Minsky

nies and development corporations, to design and build housing for low-income and single-parent women, to develop new areas of scholarship and feminist theory on women and environments, to write books, give lectures, teach new courses, and create new organizations and task forces directed toward improving the built and planned environment for all women.

The burden of a feminist consciousness can fall heavily upon those who struggle to live with integrity in a society that feeds its children on a diet of prejudice and social injustice. Although the kind of writing, teaching, and lecturing that WSPA has led me to do—interdisciplinary, controversial, oriented toward women's needs—has been scorned and devalued by some of my colleagues and students, it has brought me the admiration and respect of others.

Collaborating with women enabled me to find my own place within my male-dominated profession and the world at large. And although it is not always a comfortable place, each time I hear my voice raised in challenge or protest, I also hear the affirming voices of hundreds of WSPA sisters reverberating in my words—amplifying and strengthening their resonance and veracity.

I am surprised, even now, that I am often asked whether WSPA might happen again. When I reply, "I doubt it" (although we are still legally incorporated), I feel the disappointment. But I do not feel responsible for or interested in resurrecting a school whose energy and imagination was derived from the authentic and propitious needs of its cofounders and coordinators over a decade ago. That was then; this is now. Feminists have moved beyond the consciousness-raising task of defining problems to the current task of designing and implementing solutions.

In the last few years, housing has become a particularly compelling arena of feminist activism, bringing together designers, academicians, women in the building trades, and community women, in alliances that cross the boundaries of race, class, and educational privilege. And in the process, women have acquired an impressive array of skills: from grant writing and administration to financing, construction, and tenant management. These "lessons" should be shared with all women and women's organizations interested in designing, building, rehabilitating, and owning transitional and permanent housing that includes support services essential to women (such as child care, health care, family planning, job counseling, job training, employment, and access to transportation). I think that the WSPA of the next decade, if there is to be one, should be a school devoted to this task. For what women must teach each other now, like the education WSPA provided, cannot be found in textbooks, in design schemes taped to drafting boards, or in independent work, but rather in the empowering and transforming lessons of our collective experiences, needs, wisdom, and aspirations as women.

Notes

1. Between 1975 and 1981, WSPA cofounders and coordinators ran four successful summer programs in rented college campus facilities—in Biddeford, Maine (1975), Santa Cruz, Calif. (1976), Bristol, R.I. (1978), Denver, Colo. (1979)—and a fifth session, a weekend, in Washington, D.C. (1981). For a thorough discussion of WSPA's history, philosophy, organizational and financial structure, curricula, and pedagogy, see Leslie Kanes Weisman and Noel Phyllis Birkby, "The Women's School of Planning and Architecture" in *Learning Our Way: Essays In Feminist Education*, ed. Charlotte Bunch and Sandra Pollack (Trumansburg, N.Y.: The Crossing Press, 1983).

2. Founding coordinators of WSPA were Katrin Adam, Ellen Perry Berkeley, Noel Phyllis Birkby, Bobbie Sue Hood, Marie Kennedy, Joan Forrester Sprague, and Leslie Kanes Weisman.

3. To remain independent from other institutions or funding sources, we agreed to finance WSPA entirely through student fees. The total cost of room, board, and tuition for our first two-week session was $380. To provide financial assistance to women unable to afford the whole amount, we created a work/study program; these participants had their tuition waived for doing some sort of work, from videotaping our classes to operating our library. The work/study concept allowed us to subsidize about one-third of the participants and helped diminish the differences in roles and responsibilities between them and us.

4. Five courses were offered: "The Community Context of Town Development" (Ellen Perry Berkeley), "Demystification of Tools in Relation to Design" (Katrin Adam), "Professionalism Redefined" (Marie Kennedy and Joan Forrester Sprague), "Urban Design: The Outside of Inside" (Bobbie Sue Hood), and "Women and the Built Environment: Personal, Social, and Professional Perceptions" (Noel Phyllis Birkby and Leslie Kanes Weisman).

5. In addition to the original founding coordinators, WSPA coordinators over its history included the following: Susan Aitcheson, Nancy Baker, Jilliene F. Bolker, Elizabeth Chase, Harriet Cohen, Polly Cooper, Gail Frese, Amy Freundlich, Patti Glazer, Marian Cyril Haviland, Helen Helfer, Charlotte Hitchcock, Marjorie Hoog, Nan Ellen Jackson, Anne Laird-Blanton, Mary Ann McCarthy, Wendy Sarkissian, Cathy Simon, Marilyn Mason Sommer, Charlotte Strem, and Mary Vogel.

6. The second session, in California, added courses in the design and construction of architectural scale tapestry (including the building of portable looms in our tool shop); energy-conscious design; the application of ecological principles to architecture and landscape architecture; the politics and ideology of the urban planning process; a designer's approach to the writing process; and basic woodworking techniques.

7. The third session, in Rhode Island, recalled many aspects of core courses of previous years but was also structured thematically around the special meanings to women of workplaces and dwellings—historically, cross-culturally, and based on differences in race and socio-economic class.

8. The theme for the fourth session, in Denver, "Transitions: Designing the Future as if Women Mattered," focused on the global role that women architects, planners, and designers could play in the transition from a resource-consumptive industrial society to a postindustrial conserver society characterized by an evolving social, physical, and spiritual order. Courses discussed environments for life transitions: hospices and natural-childbirth centers, child-care facilities, shelters for battered women, and housing for the aged and disabled. Special attention was given to recycling old communities and buildings, and to self-help and low-cost construction.

9. WSPA coordinators had obtained a grant from the United States Department of Housing and Urban Development to permit the participation of these

groups through scholarships. Among those represented were American Indian National Bank, National Congress of Neighborhood Women, National Council of Negro Women, National Hispanic Housing Coalition, Rural American Women, and Southeast Women's Employment Coalition.

PART III.

SUGGESTING

VARIOUS

POSSIBILITIES

Introduction

Wanting the future to take various new directions, each of the following essayists draws from the past and present in a different way. Mimi Lobell, believing that ancient female-centered societies have much to bring to women, to architects, and to society at large, goes back thousands of years to the "buried treasure" of female imagery from these prehistoric cultures.

Gail Lee Dubrow's essay looks at the landmarks-preservation movement, which has been led by women since its beginning in the nineteenth century. Dubrow writes that feminists today are trying to uncover not only the homes and gravesites of exceptional women but also those places speaking to the ordinary experience of women throughout history, and not only the places women occupied in the male-defined world but also those elements of the environment that were "created, defined, and used" by women themselves.

Anne Griswold Tyng is concerned with the process by which women can shed the role of muse to the heroic creator and assume the creative role themselves. She writes about remarkable women in the past who served as muse. Her focus is on women of the present and future and on their struggle to achieve their own visible creative identity "without guilt, apology, or misplaced modesty."

Women architects have a growing visibility in popular magazines as "ad-architects." Misleading as these advertising images may be—idealized concepts of beautifully groomed women in hard hats or leaning over blueprints—this approach may accomplish more than many affirmative action plans, suggests Diane Favro, because the public is becoming more comfortable with women architects. How long, we can wonder, will it take for the professional journals to show so many women architects, and for the popular magazines to show women architects in the same ways that men are depicted.

Karen A. Franck, hoping for a future in which the designed environment is more closely matched to human needs, wonders how women might approach this challenge. She draws on recent feminist writings in psychiatry, psychology, philosophy, and the philosophy of science to suggest a list of ways in which women know the world and act upon this knowledge. Citing the appearance of these same characteristics in women's architectural research, design, and proposals for alternative communities, she cautiously offers "part of a fledging effort to outline a feminist approach to architecture."

13

The Buried

Treasure

Women's Ancient

Architectural Heritage

MIMI LOBELL

In the summer of 1984, I received an envelope of material on women and architecture from Pauline Fowler, who was then finishing architecture school at the University of Toronto. The material included design projects she and other women had done for a Women's Cultural Building, a research paper she had done under George Baird analyzing the various ideological approaches to the Cultural Building program,[1] and an article she had written critiquing Kenneth Frampton's work.[2]

I was impressed with the brilliant intellectual rigor of Fowler's work, and the design projects were ideologically stimulating, displaying both a rich sense of irony and a serious search for an inspiring female heritage in architecture. Because the project was a Women's Cultural Building and the designers were women, I hoped to see in the designs something of the archetype of the feminine principle in architecture, that deep psychological reservoir of forms and meanings culled from eons of female experience, sensibilities, and ways of knowing the world.[3] There were ancient cultures whose architecture was largely generated from this archetype, and in recent decades archaeologists have been excavating their remains and bringing more information about them to light.[4]

Ten years earlier, when several women architects in New York began planning what was to become the exhibit and book *Women in American Architecture*,[5] two very different approaches were apparent. One group wanted to show that women can design as well as men; the other, that women have something different to offer. This is a fundamental split in feminist theory, but I believe that people are increasingly adopting the second attitude. In addition to insuring that women have equal opportunities to succeed in the "man's world," we need to recognize the differences between men and women. We need to value what women have to offer and allow women to transform this world to make it more balanced, more life-affirming, psychologically richer, and more fully human. In order to do this, however, women must be able to draw strength and vision from a well-developed inner reservoir of women's cultural heritage that is at once archetypal and historical, mythic and psychological.

The women designing the Women's Cultural Building addressed a broad range of theoretical issues, and they clearly aspired to expressing something uniquely female. Although they did not tap this inner reservoir, they ingeniously sought other sources of inspiration: some designers overtly reacted against masculinist architecture (Fowler's project, for example, was an excellent deconstruction and reformation of the traditional men's club); one or two focused on gardens rather than buildings as inspiration; another drew a free-form *tabula rasa*; and another presented an image-montage rather than a building design. Some designs incorporated kitchens, laundries, and day-care facilities as evocations of women's culture. The women may have emphasized these domestic facilities for their present-day irony or for their symbolic meaning (ovens, for instance, suggest the magical retort of women's highest "alchemical" powers: the womb), but I feared the women used them mainly because they had not been exposed to the extensive body of ancient sites, buildings, and works of art that would have given them access to the rich reservoir of archetypal female imagery in architecture. Alison McKenzie, designer of one of the garden projects, summed up the problem: "Lacking a visible mythology, women's culture therefore lacks a symbolic language."[6]

This cultural impoverishment of women can, in part, be traced to the way architectural history is taught. Most architecture schools, as well

Paleolithic goddess, the so-called "Venus" of Laussel, France; Gravettian, ca. 25,000 B.C.; 21 inches x 14.5 inches. Originally covered in red ochre, she holds in her right hand a lunar-crescent-shaped cornucopia with thirteen marks; her left hand points to her womb. Drawing by Mimi Lobell

as art and architecture history texts, ignore the huge body of archaeological data that has become available in the last forty years. Perpetuating the nineteenth-century assumption that history begins with the "high" civilizations of Egypt, Mesopotamia, and Greece, they convey the impression that nothing worth mentioning was built by the cultures that preceded the male-dominated, hierarchical, warlike states of the ancient world.[7] They virtually ignore the Paleolithic and Neolithic cultures whose art and architecture abound in female imagery, and who also *invented* architecture and urbanism. This neglected aspect of history (namely, *prehistory*) constitutes what I call a "buried treasure" of women's ancient heritage in architecture. The response I sent to Pauline Fowler outlining this observation was the genesis of this essay.

There *is* a women's cultural heritage in architecture (it is, of course, also a men's heritage in that men, too, need to reconnect with the feminine principle). It dates back to at least 25,000 B.C., the Gravettian period in the Upper Paleolithic, when people began to carve sculptures of female figures such as the so-called "Venus" of Laussel in their rock-shelters. This figure announces some of the major symbolic motifs that continued through nearly thirty thousand years, making feminine imagery in art and architecture far older and longer-lived than masculine. The Venus of Laussel was originally covered in red ochre, which has a color affinity with blood and often was used in prehistory to indicate the sacred mysteries of life and death. An ample, pregnant woman, the Venus carries in her right hand a horn of lunar crescent shape, the earliest representation of the Cornucopia and the Horns of Consecration. The horn has thirteen marks of the type Alexander Marshack has correlated with Paleolithic lunar records.[8] Her left hand rests over her womb, as if to point to the connection between the cycles of the moon and her menstrual cycle, within the overall matrix of fertility suggested by the Horn of Plenty.[9]

Later, the Horns of Consecration reappear in association with female deities in every part of the world that had domesticated cattle[10]: in Çatal Hüyük shrines in 5500 B.C., in Sumerian cattle byres sacred to the Goddess Inanna in 3500 B.C., in the Palace at Knossos in Crete in 1500 B.C., and in an Egyptian image of the Temple of Hathor at Dendura dating from the first few centuries B.C., to name just a few. In the more general form of gateways to sacred precincts, this symbol appears in much of the world's religious architecture including the pylons of Egyptian temples, the Jachin and Boaz columns in Solomon's Temple, and even the tripartite entrances to Gothic cathedrals.

Three important criteria determine whether a work contributes to women's ancient heritage in architecture: 1) The work is the product of a culture that revered the feminine principle (shown, for instance, by goddess worship and by the expression in the culture of feminine values such as peacefulness); 2) Women in the culture enjoyed equality, independence, and respect (discernible in art, burial practices, dwelling layouts, and other material remains, as well as in ethnographic parallels); and 3) The work is *gynecomorphic*, that is, shaped like the female body or symbolizing it in some way (often subtly).

Based on these criteria, a distinction can be made between primary and secondary works. A primary work is one that meets all the above criteria. A secondary work is gynecomorphic in form, may be dedicated to a goddess, but was not built by a female-centered civilization. For instance, the apse of the Gothic cathedral has its archetypal origins in such Neolithic structures as Newgrange and the Maltese temples. Although the Gothic apse is gynecomorphic and is associated with a "goddess" (the Virgin Mary), we would consider it secondary because it was built by a patriarchal civilization.

Secondary works are important, however, because they greatly expand the manifestations of women's cultural heritage in the world. Most of the world's sacred architecture is modeled on Neolithic proto-types or on the archetype of the feminine principle: not only the apse and crypt of the Gothic cathedral, but also the *garbha-griha* or "womb-house" of the Hindu temple, the *anda* or "cosmic womb" of the Buddhist stupa, the "Great Womb Store" of the Japanese Shingon sect, the *kiva* or "womb of Mother Earth" of the Pueblo Indians, and the dome of the Islamic mosque (the dome is considered feminine while the minaret is masculine).

The unifying image is the "womb-cavern," which has attracted countless seekers, pilgrims, heroes, ascetics, mystics, prophets, and sages in their quest to reunite with their origins in the primal darkness in order to attain the highest illumination. The world's mythologies and religions are full of accounts of those who failed in the encounter and came out mad, as well as those who succeeded—from Mohammed to Milarepa—and emerged with the holy books, oracles, treasures, and visions that inspire the human spirit. Because the journey into the cavern of the underworld is the central human quest, the "womb-cavern" is the archetype of every holy-of-holies. It is as though architecture has recorded for eternity the forgotten goal of religion—to reunite with the feminine principle in order to transcend duality and attain wholeness, oneness, and enlightenment.[11]

The works of art and architecture of the Buried Treasure are not anomalies isolated from meaningful or widespread cultural contexts. On the contrary, these works span the Upper Paleolithic, Neolithic, Chalcolithic (Copper), and early Bronze Ages, with the majority representing the Neolithic way of life that spread across the earth as people began to develop agriculture and domesticate animals.[12] The female-centeredness of prehistoric cultures is typically indicated by evidence of the following:

1. The worship of goddesses—usually represented by small, sacred figurines found in homes, small shrines, tombs, or granaries, which contrast markedly to the large, impersonal, hieratic sculptures of the later male-oriented religions.
2. Marked and prolonged peacefulness—seen for example in the absence in art and architecture of signs of war such as weapons,

armor, fortifications, scenes of battle, and burials of people killed in war.

3. Egalitarian social structures—demonstrated by burial practices, which are usually communal, and by relatively little status differentiation in dwellings.

4. Matrilineal descent and inheritance patterns, where evidence is available.

5. The prevalence of female imagery in art and architecture, combined with the lack of dominant male figures in art and architecture—for instance, female-centered cultures do not have princely burials, heroic commemorative art, or powerful chieftains and kings.

Because these cultures subscribed to a world view so different from our own, they are not well understood in the male-dominated fields of archaeology and anthropology,[13] and they are even less known to the public. Yet they have much to teach us because they are not simply reversals of patriarchal cultures (thus the term "female-centered" is preferred over "matriarchal," which suggests a simple role reversal with powerful queens and women warriors oppressing men.) The values and institutions of female-centered cultures emanate from and reify the feminine principle, and thus are vastly different from the values and institutions of patriarchal cultures, which emanate from and reify the masculine principle. One gift of the Buried Treasure is the revelation that war is not inherent in human nature and that people were able to thrive for thousands of years without it. Certainly the fact that these cultures flourished in simpler times and in a less crowded world contributed to their peacefulness, inventiveness, and general prosperity; but the veneration of women and feminine values was important also.

What then are the primary works of architecture in women's cultural heritage? There are many types. Below is a listing of some of the more important ones.

Megalithic structures—Including long barrows, passage mounds, stone circles, dolmen, and temples (ca. 4000–2500 B.C.). Some examples are Newgrange and Knowth passage mounds in Ireland;[14] Avebury,[15] West Kennet Long Barrow, and Merry Maidens in England;[16] Gavrinis and Carnac in France;[17] and the temples and rock-cut tombs of Malta.[18] Most of these structures are *gynecomorphic*. For instance, West Kennet Long Barrow and several Maltese temples have plans in the shape of an amply bodied Mother Goddess. Newgrange, Knowth, and Gavrinis have dark,

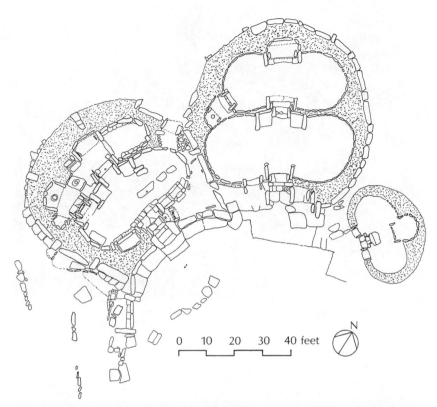

Plan of Mnajdra (Mn-eye'-dra) Temple, Malta; Neolithic, 3500–3000 B.C. This complex has three goddess-shaped megalithic temples. Drawing by Oriel Mor after J. D. Evans

Goddess from Hagar Qim (Ha'-jar Heem', pronounced with a soft "j"), a temple group a few hundred yards from the Mnajdra temples, Malta; Neolithic, 3500–3000 B.C.; 19 inches high. The plan of the largest Mnajdra temple, which has an oracle chamber, is very similar to the shape of this statue: to enter the temple was to reenter the goddess for spiritual rebirth. A separate head, attached to the figure by cords through neck holes, was probably manipulated by priestess-oracles in answer to devotees' questions. Drawing by Mimi Lobell

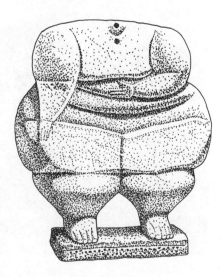

Hagar Qim Temple, Malta; 3500–3000 B.C. Photograph by Mimi Lobell

Spinsters' Rock, Devon, England; Neolithic. A typical dolmen, thought to have been a burial chamber originally covered with an earthen mound. Local legend fancies that three spinsters erected these stones one day before breakfast. The capstone alone weighs 16 tons. Photograph by Mimi Lobell

Silbury Hill, Wiltshire, England; Neolithic, ca. 2700 B.C.; 130 feet high. The largest prehistoric earthwork in Europe, Silbury was long thought to contain a rich king's tomb, but none has ever been found. Michael Dames believes the mound was a lunar-oriented effigy of the Great Goddess used in ancient celebrations of the First Fruits Festival on Lammas Eve. Photograph by Mimi Lobell

womblike chambers with entrances and passageways resembling the birth canal. They also have engravings of eye goddesses.

Earthworks—Windmill Hill, Silbury Hill, Maiden Castle (Neolithic phase), and Knowlton Circles in England (3000–2700 B.C.)[19] and Hopewell and Adena mounds in Ohio (1000 B.C. to A.D. 400), such as the Great Serpent Mound.[20]

Shrines—Çatal Hüyük in Anatolia (ca. 5500 B.C.), a Neolithic town with shrines rich in female imagery, including a relief sculpture of a goddess giving birth to bulls;[21] Lepenski Vir in Yugoslavia (6500–5500 B.C.), a village consisting of buildings with vulva-shaped arrangements of stones in their centers;[22] and Sabatinovka II in Soviet Moldavia (ca. 4200 B.C.), a shrine with sixteen small, clay, serpent-headed goddesses seated on horned thrones and one large throne, probably used by a presiding priestess. Grindstones and a large round oven suggest the baking of sacred bread.[23]

Beehive dwellings and tholoi—Khirokitea in Cyprus;[24] and Arpachiyeh in Mesopotamia (ca. 5500 B.C.)[25] had small, domed, undifferentiated,

Cliff Palace, Mesa Verde, Colorado; A.D. *1200–1300. Both Anasazi and contemporary Pueblo cultures have many characteristics in common with ancient female-centered civilizations: peacefulness, egalitarian social structures, consensus decision-making, reverence for the earth, matrilineal families, farming, pottery, a cyclical sense of time, solstice and equinox alignments, serpent veneration (in the rain-making Hopi Snake Dance, for instance), spirals and labyrinths. The round, subterranean, sacred kiva is a Womb-Cavern where spiritual birth occurs: the mythical emergence from the underworld and the ceremonial birth of ordinary humans into kachinas. Photograph by Mimi Lobell*

"uterine" dwellings typical of Neolithic Near Eastern cultures, which also produced a multitude of goddess figurines.

Kivas—Pueblos and cliff-dwellings in the southwestern United States (ca. A.D. 1100 to the present). As the transformative womb of Mother Earth, the sacred *kiva* is the mythical Place of Emergence where dancers enter as humans to be reborn as *kachinas*.[26]

Sacred caves—France and Spain (Upper Paleolithic), where the veneration of bulls was first expressed (e.g., the "Hall of Bulls" at Lascaux), as well as the sculpting of female figurines; Crete (ca. 6000–1500 B.C.), a Bronze Age civilization that did not build temples, but instead worshipped goddesses in sacred caves in mountains.[27]

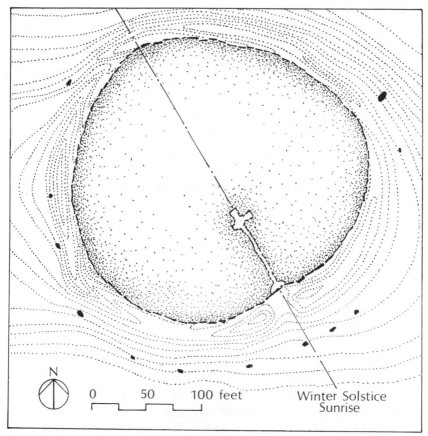

Plan of Newgrange Passage Mound, showing the remains of the stone circle surrounding the mound, the curbstones defining the mound's perimeter, the interior passage and cruciform chamber, and the axis of the Winter Solstice sunrise. Drawing by Mimi Lobell after Michael J. O'Kelly

Sacred springs and wells—Various shrines in the Mediterranean, the Near East, the British Isles, the Aegean, etc.[28] The association of water with goddesses is one of the earliest forms of religious symbolism. Many rivers, such as the Danube, Boyne, and Ganges, were named for goddesses; and Bath and Chartres were located at healing springs sacred to pre-Roman and pre-Christian goddesses, respectively.

Ritual baths—Mohenjo-Daro in Pakistan (2500–1800 B.C.), a sophisticated Bronze Age city with an elaborate ritual bath that may have been used for menstrual purification much in the manner of the Jewish *mikvah*.[29]

Clay female figurines were the most abundant finds in Mohenjo-Daro's Indus Valley civilization.

Early villages and towns—The villages of Mesopotamia up to the Ubaid period and those of Egypt up to the Gerzean period;[30] Çatal Hüyük and Hacilar in Anatolia; Khirokitea in Cyprus (ca. 5500 B.C.); Mohenjo-Daro in Pakistan (2500–1800 B.C.);[31] Banpo in China (Yang Shao culture, ca. 2000 B.C.).[32] These towns and villages and others mentioned above exhibit most of the characteristics of female-centered cultures.

Art and artifacts—The non-architectural record of female-centered cultures includes bas reliefs and sculptures (Paleolithic "Venuses" and Neolithic goddess figures); petroglyphs and stone engravings as at Newgrange and Malta; pottery and textile designs; tools; toiletries, clothing, and jewelry; paintings and frescoes as at Çatal Hüyük and Knossos.

The last category also embraces artifacts from prehistoric female-centered cultures that left little architecture, such as the Paleolithic rock-shelter dwellers of Laussel, or whose architecture has disappeared or is too fragmentary or insufficiently excavated to be conclusive, such as the Valdivia culture of Peru (with its many fine female figurines);[33] the Neolithic Amur culture of Siberia,[34] and the Jomon of Japan.[35] In *The Goddesses and Gods of Old Europe*, Marija Gimbutas presents abundant evidence of goddess-worship in Neolithic European civilization.[36] Though comprehensively excavated architectural sites may be rare for these cultures, their pottery and sculpture are rich in symbolic meaning.

Taken together, the architecture, enhanced natural sites, art, and artifacts of women's cultural heritage build a complex vocabulary of feminine forms, symbols, and psychological principles. Recurring motifs include: the "womb-cavern" (seen in sacred caves, passage graves, tholoi, and kivas); sacred springs and wells; female-shaped buildings such as the Maltese temples; and shrines ornamented with water signs, spirals and labyrinths,[37] fish symbols, serpents, oculi, ovens, grain grinders, stylized vulvas, lunar crescents, bulls and the Horns of Consecration, and other symbols traditionally associated with women and with goddess worship. Contrary to common belief, not all the motifs have to do with fertility. The composite feminine principle that emerges from the Buried Treasure embraces astronomy and the rhythms of the stars as well as the earth and its agricultural seasons. Many megalithic structures, for instance, were aligned to the solstices, equinoxes, and significant extremes in the moon's orbit.

The feminine principle includes not only the physical powers of fertility, birth, nurturance, and sexuality, but also the spiritual and intellectual powers of prophecy, divination, death, transformation, and resurrection.[38] The Great Goddess shown in prehistoric art was the sun as well as the moon, heaven as well as earth, spirit as well as body. It was only under the dualistic metaphysics of the later male-dominated cultures that women and the feminine principle came to be equated solely with the earth, fertility, sexuality, nature, matter, and the unconscious. (Even ostensibly balanced schema such as China's yin/yang symbol, India's Siva/Sakti principles, and various concepts of androgyny are products of this later thinking.)

The recurring motifs offer a rich and satisfying treasury of new/old forms to draw upon in design, but they are more than a mere stylistic repository. Because they originate in our deep past, dating to thousands of years ago, these forms activate a deeply buried archetypal stratum in our psyches, a powerful, potentiating inner Buried Treasure waiting to be discovered to enrich our understanding and practice of architecture.

On art historical and technological grounds alone, however, the architecture of the Buried Treasure is important and should be known to every architect. The Newgrange passage mound, built in 3200 B.C., is 280 feet in diameter and was once entirely covered with white quartz. It contains a megalithic, corbel-vaulted, cruciform chamber, 20 feet high, which can be seen as the dome of the Treasury of Atreus in primitive form and as the primordial cathedral plan. The mound is precisely oriented so that on the winter solstice the rays of the rising sun penetrate the chamber—an architectural enactment of the birth of the pre-Christian Divine Child (the sun) from its winter nadir. In the Boyne Valley surrounding Newgrange, several other structures are oriented to the sun at other times of the year, so that the whole landscape cradles an extensive system of megalithic calendars predating Stonehenge by a thousand years. Unlike Stonehenge, which has no art to speak of, Newgrange and its neighbors have stones engraved with a full symbolic language of abstract art: spirals, meanders, zig-zags, lozenges, solar disks, lunar crescents, and astronomical and calendrical notations.[39]

In many of the works, we can find precedents and origins for more familiar historical motifs and architectural achievements. The city of Mohenjo-Daro in the Indus Valley of Pakistan had sophisticated plumbing and drainage systems predating those of Rome by two thousand years.[40] The impressive megalithic temple at Tarxien in Malta is ornamented with highly refined spirals and with the first known egg-and-

Newgrange Passage Mound, Ireland; Neolithic, ca. 3200 B.C. In its reconstructed state, the mound is only partially faced with the white, high-quartz-content rocks that once covered the whole mound, making it an architectural "white goddess." Photograph by Mimi Lobell

Entrance to Newgrange Passage Mound. The rich spirals engraved on the "hymen stone" are found universally in Neolithic art and pottery. Above the entrance is the "roof box," a carefully positioned rectangular opening that allows the sun's rays to penetrate the inner chamber at dawn on the Winter Solstice. Photograph by Mimi Lobell

Stonehenge, Wiltshire, England; Neolithic through Bronze Age, ca. 3100–1550 B.C. The earliest, most astronomically significant phase of Stonehenge was laid out by a typical egalitarian Neolithic culture that built many stone circles. The monumental central stones, shown here, were added mainly for ceremonial purposes by the increasingly hierarchical, warlike, and patriarchal Beaker people and Wessex chieftains of the Bronze Age, who eclipsed the earlier, more female-centered and peaceful civilization. Photograph by Mimi Lobell

Knowlton Circles, Dorset, England; Neolithic; 200–800 feet in diameter. Knowlton's well-preserved Central Circle, 348 feet in diameter, is an excellent example of a prehistoric sacred site that was taken over and built upon in the Christian era. The ruined church dates from the twelfth century, and its tower was added in the sixteenth. Photograph by Mimi Lobell

dart motif. The concave entrances to passage mounds such as at Los Millares in Spain prefigure similar entrances in baroque architecture. The motif of flanking, protective lions (such as those in the Lion Gate at Mycenae and outside the New York Public Library) appears for the first time in a sculpture from a Çatal Hüyük granary showing the Great Goddess giving birth while seated between two leopards.[41]

Greek and Roman temples and medieval cathedrals often were superimposed on ancient structures. This is obvious at sites such as Maiden Castle and Knowlton Circles in England where a Romano-Celtic temple and a Norman church, respectively, sit within Neolithic henge monuments. The asymmetry of Canterbury Cathedral's Trinity Chapel indicates that its foundations were laid directly upon an egg-shaped prehistoric stone circle.[42] When Alexander Thom surveyed thousands of stone circles, he found that the egg was a common shape.[43]

Wells Cathedral is sited near natural springs, from which the town and the cathedral take their names, and one spring is an ancient holy well.[44] Like the waters of nearby Bath, the site drew worshippers and pilgrims from the earliest times and may have originally been presided over by a female water deity similar to the goddess at Bath, whom the Romans renamed Sulis Minerva. Although the Christians dedicated the well to St. Andrew, their building of the nearby St. Mary's Chapel in the early tenth century restored the tradition of associating wells with female divinities. By superimposing temples, baths, and churches on preexisting sacred sites, later cultures drew on their energy and inspiration while channeling the devotion of the old sites' worshippers into the new religious and social order. Thus, another meaning of the Buried Treasure is that often it literally lies buried beneath some of the most important monuments of the later classical and Christian cultures, just as in the metaphor of the mind, it lies buried beneath the patriarchal cultural superstructure under which we currently live.

For what it can do for women, for architecture, and for society at large, the Buried Treasure of women's cultural heritage in architecture needs to be unearthed. This will mean much more than simply adding a few new structures to those that architecture students must memorize. It will mean recognizing an entirely different model of culture, consciousness, and gender. It will mean giving women the imagery we need to gain confidence and independence *through* our womanhood, not in spite of it. For women and men alike, it will mean reentering that deep, dark, womb-cavern in the psyche from which we create, from which we are spiritually reborn, and in which we find that eternal, peaceful, still center allowing us to *listen* to our work, to approach it as oracles and seers rather than as heroes.

Notes

An asterisk (*) indicates that the writer has some awareness of female-centered cultural contexts and interpretations or has an interest in issues concerning women and architecture.

1. Pauline Fowler,* "Architecture for a Women's Cultural Building," paper for Professor George Baird (University of Toronto, 29 February 1984). Fowler is now a university teacher in Cardiff, Wales.

2. Pauline Fowler,* "Shaking the Foundations," *Fuse* (February 1984): 199–204.

3. Erich Neumann,* *The Great Mother: An Analysis of the Archetype* (Princeton: Princeton University Press, 1955).

4. Jacquetta Hawkes, *Atlas of Ancient Archaeology* (New York: McGraw-Hill, 1974), a good introduction to many of the sites under discussion, and James Mellaart,* *The Neolithic of the Near East* (New York: Charles Scribner's Sons, 1975), a valuable summary of the ancient Near East by the archaeologist who excavated Çatal Hüyük.

5. Susana Torre,* ed., *Women in American Architecture: A Historic and Contemporary Perspective* (New York: Whitney Library of Design, 1977).

6. Alison McKenzie,* quoted in Fowler, "Architecture": 24.

7. Colin Renfrew, "Ancient Europe Is Older Than We Thought," *National Geographic* 152 (November 1977): 615–23. Corrected radiocarbon dates have revealed that prehistoric Western European sites are up to 1800 years older than traditionally estimated; these sites were therefore not subject to cultural influences from Crete, Egypt, or the Near East as was long assumed. See also Merlin Stone,* *When God Was a Woman* (New York: The Dial Press, 1976). Stone analyzes the origin of the suppression of pre-existing female-centered cultures and religions in the Biblically based, male-dominated cultures of the Near East.

8. Alexander Marshack,* *The Roots of Civilization: The Cognitive Beginnings of Man's First Art, Symbol and Notation* (London: Weidenfeld and Nicolson, 1972).

9. Joseph Campbell,* *The Masks of God: Primitive Mythology* (New York: Viking Press, 1970). Campbell has also discussed the meaning of the Venus of Laussel in several lectures.

10. Gertrude Rachel Levy,* *The Gate of Horn* (London: Faber, 1963).

11. José and Miriam Arguelles,* *The Feminine: As Spacious as the Sky* (Boston: Shambhala Publications, 1977).

12. Mimi Lobell,* "Ancient Religions in the Context of Cultural Types," in *Archaeology and Fertility Cult in the Ancient Mediterranean: Papers Presented at the First*

International Conference on Archaeology of the Ancient Mediterranean ed. Anthony Bonanno (Amsterdam: B. R. Grüner Publishing Co., 1986), 43–54. See also Mimi Lobell,* "Spatial Archetypes," *ReVISION*, 6 (Fall 1983): 69–82.

13. Mimi Lobell,* "Male-Biased Paradigms in Archaeology" (Paper presented at the World Archaeological Congress, session on "History of Pre and Proto-Historic Archaeology," 1986).

14. Martin Brennan, *The Stars and the Stones: Ancient Art and Astronomy in Ireland* (London: Thames and Hudson, 1983). See also Michael J O'Kelly, *Newgrange: Archaeology, Art and Legend* (London: Thames and Hudson, 1982).

15. Aubrey Burl, *Prehistoric Avebury* (New Haven and London: Yale University Press, 1979). See also Michael Dames,* *The Avebury Cycle* (London: Thames and Hudson, 1977).

16. Richard Cavendish, *Prehistoric England* (New York: British Heritage Press, 1983).

17. Aubrey Burl, *Megalithic Brittany* (London: Thames and Hudson, 1985).

18. J. D. Evans, *The Prehistoric Antiquities of the Maltese Islands* (London: Athlone Press, University of London, 1971); Renfrew, "Ancient Europe"; Sibylle von Cles-Redon,* *The Realm of the Great Goddess: The Story of the Megalith Builders* (London: Thames and Hudson, 1961), written before corrected radiocarbon dating eliminated the possibility of Near Eastern cultural diffusion to prehistoric Europe; and Robert Wernick and the editors of Time-Life Books,* *The Monument Builders*, The Emergence of Man series (New York: Time-Life Books, 1973).

19. Cavendish, *Prehistoric England*; Michael Dames,* *The Silbury Treasure: The Great Goddess Rediscovered* (London: Thames and Hudson, 1976); and Mimi Lobell,* "Temples of the Great Goddess," *Heresies 5: The Great Goddess* (Spring 1978): 32–39.

20. Robert Claiborne and the editors of Time-Life Books, *The First Americans*, The Emergence of Man series (New York: Time-Life Books, 1973), 126–35; and Robert Silverberg, *Moundbuilders of Ancient America: The Archaeology of a Myth* (Greenwich, CT: New York Graphic Society, 1968).

21. Dora Jane Hamblin and the editors of Time-Life Books,* *The First Cities*, The Emergence of Man series (New York: Time-Life Books, 1973), 42–67; Lobell,* "Temples," and Mellaart,* *Neolithic*.

22. Marija Gimbutas,* *The Gods and Goddesses of Old Europe: 7000 to 3500 B.C.* (Berkeley and Los Angeles: University of California Press, 1974). Gimbutas wanted her book to be titled *The Goddesses and Gods of Old Europe* . . . , but the publisher refused to put "goddesses" first in the title; in 1982, however, the book was reissued under Gimbutas's original title. See also Dragoslav Srejovic, *Europe's First Monumental Sculpture: New Discoveries at Lepenski Vir* (New York: Stein and Day, 1972).

23. Gimbutas,* *Gods*, 72–73.

24. Vassos Karageorghis,* *The Civilization of Prehistoric Cyprus* (Athens: Ekdotike Athenon S.A., 1976), 19–57.

25. Mellaart*, *Neolithic*.

26. Frank Waters,* *Pumpkin Seed Point* (Chicago: The Swallow Press/Sage Books, 1969) and *Book of the Hopi* (New York: Viking Press, 1972).

27. Lobell,* "Temples." See also Vincent Scully, Jr.,* *The Earth, the Temple, and the Gods: Greek Sacred Architecture*, Revised Edition (New York: Praeger Publishers, 1969).

28. von Cles-Redon,* *Realm*; and Janet and Colin Bord,* *Sacred Waters: Holy Wells and Water Lore in Britain and Ireland* (London: Granada, 1985).

29. Rosemary J. Dudley,* "She Who Bleeds, Yet Does not Die," *Heresies 5: The Great Goddess* (Spring 1978): 112–15.

30. Mellaart,* *Neolithic*.

31. Hamblin,* *First Cities*. See also Sir Mortimer Wheeler, *Civilizations of the Indus Valley and Beyond* (London: Thames & Hudson/McGraw-Hill, 1966).

32. Kwang-Chih Chang, *The Archaeology of Ancient China*, Third Edition (New Haven and London: Yale University Press, 1977), 80–143.

33. Henri Stierlin, *Art of the Incas* (New York: Rizzoli, 1984), 17–40.

34. Alexei Okladnikov, *Art of the Amur: Ancient Art of the Russian Far East* (New York: Harry N. Abrams, 1981).

35. Namio Egami, *The Beginnings of Japanese Art* (New York and Tokyo: Weatherhill/Heibonsha, 1973), 13–36.

36. Gimbutas,* *Gods*.

37. Janet Bord,* *Mazes and Labyrinths of the World* (New York: E. P. Dutton, 1975).

38. Gimbutas,* *Gods*; and Neumann,* *Great Mother*.

39. Brennan, *Stars*.

40. Hamblin,* *First Cities*; and Wheeler, *Indus Valley*.

41. Hamblin,* *First Cities*; and Mellaart,* *Neolithic*.

42. Lyle B. Borst and B. M. Borst, *Megalithic Software* (Williamsville, NY: Twin Bridge Press, 1975).

43. Alexander Thom, *Megalithic Sites in Britain* (London: Oxford University Press, 1967).

44. L. S. Colchester, *Wells Cathedral: A History* (Shepton Mallet, Somerset: Open Books, 1982), 3–14.

14

Restoring a

Female

Presence

New Goals in

Historic Preservation

GAIL LEE DUBROW

Although women have led the historic preservation movement, the history of women has not been adequately preserved. This situation is changing now, with diverse recent efforts by feminists to increase the visibility of women at the nation's historic sites and buildings. To understand these efforts, it is useful to review the impressive—but until now limited—participation and focus of women in the preservation movement.

Women were at the forefront of the historic preservation movement from the earliest efforts to commemorate the nation's origins. When the economic depression of 1830 slowed progress on Boston's Bunker Hill Memorial, a women's committee led by Sarah Josepha Hale urged female support for the monument's completion. The women of New England responded to the call. Their grandmothers had sacrificed husbands and sons to war. Now, in the midst of a business depression, housewives were encouraged through their "industry, economy or self-denial" to honor the memory of the Bunker Hill martyrs.[1] Mothers in the young Republic were offered an opportunity to instill in their children patriotic sentiment, "fervent gratitude toward those who laboured to secure our Independence and Liberty."[2] Leadership in fundraising was consistent with the supposed feminine virtues of self-sacrifice, devotion, and charity. Denied the direct expressions of national loyalty that military service and public office offered to men, women found surrogate means for patriotic expression in this activity. In the words of one observer, "the monument which was begun by men, was finished by women."[3]

Women assumed leadership in many early preservation battles. George Washington's home at Mt. Vernon was rescued from neglect in 1853 by Ann Pamela Cunningham who founded the Mt. Vernon Ladies' Association of the Union. The Old South Meeting House in Boston was saved in 1876 by Mary Hemenway. The survival of Fraunces Tavern in New York City is credited to Melusina Peirce. Women were responsible for preserving the Alamo, lobbying for the establishment of the National Park Service, opening the Mesa Verde Cliff Dwellings to the public, and more.[4]

Female discontent with the historic preservation movement was one aspect of the emergence of feminist consciousness in mid-nineteenth-

Women as leaders in many early preservation battles. George Washington's home was rescued from neglect in 1853 by Ann Pamela Cunningham (seated beside the bust of Washington) and the Mt. Vernon Ladies' Association of the Union. Photograph (ca. 1873) courtesy of Mt. Vernon Ladies' Association of the Union

A new focus in preservation. Women's groups such as the Daughters of the American Revolution were formed in response to the "one-sided" masculine view of patriotism and history in preservation activities at the time. One of the DAR's many commemorative projects was fundraising for this monument (in Fredericksburg, Virginia) to Mary Washington, mother of the nation's first President. Photograph courtesy of Library of Congress

century America. Pioneering physician Harriot Hunt reflected on the gender symbolism of the effort to complete the Bunker Hill memorial, to which she had contributed some years earlier. Hunt viewed the half-completed monument as symbolic of a culture that exalted the accomplishments of men over women. "Half a people make only half a monument," she wrote; "the other half the feminine makes it whole."[5] Hunt lamented the fact that the memorial commemorated only male contributions to the American Revolution, having been designed for "John and Peter, not for Mary and Deborah." Optimistically she added, "[i]t will not always be so."[6]

Discontent with the predominantly masculine focus of the preservation activities undertaken by fraternal organizations such as the Sons of the American Revolution led women to carve out a place of their own. In 1890, the Daughters of the American Revolution was formed in response to what founder Mary S. Lockwood termed "one-sided patriotism" on the part of the Sons of the American Revolution.[7] Incensed with the traditional view of women as men's helpmates, both in history and historic preservation, and determined to win recognition for the men *and* women who had achieved American Independence, the DAR embarked on an ambitious program of commemorative and preservation activity.

In addition to erecting shrines, monuments, and memorials throughout the original thirteen states, and saving the headquarters of

Washington and other Revolutionary leaders, the DAR preserved the homes and marked the graves of many American "Marys and Deborahs." The society raised funds for the Mary Washington Monument Association, erected a memorial in Arlington Cemetery to the nurses of the Spanish-American War, marked the birthplace of Benjamin Franklin's mother, and honored Revolutionary War heroine Deborah Sampson, who had disguised herself as a man in order to fight.[8] These preservation activities were defined in rather masculine terms (favoring the sisters and mothers of notable men and women engaged in male-specific activities such as the military), and reflected a narrow preoccupation with the Anglo-American heritage of the DAR, Colonial Dames, United Daughters of the Confederacy, and Native Daughters of the Golden West. Still, these activities were the first organized efforts to preserve the built environment associated with women's history.

While women's clubs worked closely with the DAR on many preservation projects at the turn of the century, the more explicitly feminist agenda of club women influenced not only their choice of heroines but ultimately the kinds of places they saved. Rhode Island women's clubs spearheaded efforts to erect a statue to Anne Hutchinson, the Puritan religious dissenter.[9] Elsewhere and through innumerable commemorative schemes, clubwomen sought to elevate feminist leader Susan B. Anthony to the level of Washington and Lincoln in the national consciousness. (In 1942, the effort by the Rochester Federation of Women's Clubs to place a tablet at the house where Anthony had lived and worked for forty years, ultimately resulted in the complete restoration of the building.[10])

The organizational strength and financial resources of middle- and upper-class women in the late nineteenth and early twentieth century gave them power and prestige in the historic preservation movement. However, women's organizations suffered declining influence after 1920, and then the Depression dealt a staggering blow to women's clubs by reducing their membership and depleting their resources. So too, in the eyes of many, there were far more pressing causes. As the president of the National American Woman Suffrage Association, Carrie Chapman Catt, remarked about the battle during the Depression to add Susan B. Anthony to the carvings at Mt. Rushmore, "I am inclined to think that women are never going to get their full share of monuments in this world, but I do not think that that is important,"[11] later adding that memorials seemed superfluous when "the people of our land are in such need."[12]

If economic and political conditions combined to constrict women's influence, developments within the architectural profession and the field of preservation itself completed the process by which women were relegated to the periphery. Women's status in preservation hinged on the outcome of a schism that emerged in the movement during the first two decades of the twentieth century. Andrew Green and Edward Hall of the American Scenic and Historic Preservation Society, on the one hand, viewed their mission in lofty terms to "quicken the spirit of patriotism" by preserving historically significant places. William Sumner Appleton, of the Society for the Preservation of New England Antiquities, on the other, focused strictly on preserving architecturally distinguished historic buildings.[13] As long as historic and patriotic values prevailed, the field of preservation had ample room for amateurs. However, the gradual ascendency of Appleton and his allies in the architectural profession signalled declining influence for women in the historic preservation movement, as new standards were set for professionalism and, for the first time, technical expertise was required.

Evaluating the architectural significance of buildings, and then carrying out technically accurate restoration, required skills that architects

Cooperative efforts to save a landmark building. The house in Rochester, New York, where Susan B. Anthony worked and lived was purchased and restored in the 1940s by local women's groups. Photograph courtesy of Library of Congress

alone claimed to possess. Yet for the most part, women found formal architectural education denied to them. A few determined individuals secured such training; there is evidence, for example, of women architects as measurers and delineators in the Historic American Buildings Survey.[14] But the goals of federal documentation projects and preservation programs alike tended to reinforce the exclusion of female preservationists and women's history. The Historic American Buildings Survey and the Historic American Engineering Record (two New Deal programs designed to relieve unemployment among architects, engineers, photographers, and draftsmen) contributed directly to the professionalization of preservation and, indirectly, to the field's masculinization. The National Park Service's limited resources were primarily devoted to saving sites significant in American military and political history, and thus offered only limited opportunities for commemorating women's history given the historic exclusion of women from the rights and responsibilities of citizenship. As the architectural profession gained hegemony over historic preservation, formal and aesthetic values prevailed. By the 1930s, women had lost the organizational power that once had allowed them to define the content of preservation. Women in the preservation movement underwent much the same experience as women in medicine, law, and other fields in the process of professionalization. Institutional barriers effectively marginalized and eventually disempowered them.[15]

With the 1976 Bicentennial, public concern about the status of women at historic sites and buildings reemerged. Against the background of the Second Wave of feminism and the explosive growth in the field of American women's history, new questions arose. In a 1976 article, Marion Tinling and Linda Ruffner-Russell first called attention to the dearth of places associated with women's history on the National Register of Historic Places. They also criticized the stereotypical and distorted images at state landmarks that commemorate "women whose fame rests on slim historical evidence ... the Pioneer Mothers, the Madonna of the Trail, [and] the Indian Maiden."[16] More recently, Heather Huyck has pointed to vast opportunities for interpreting women's history within the historical parks managed by the National Park Service; to date, these opportunities remain largely unexplored.[17]

My own analysis of selected landmark registers lends credence to the contentions by these authors that womens history is poorly represented at the nation's historic sites and buildings. In a review of the 1985 register of National Historic Landmarks, I found that less than 3 percent of sites and buildings incorporated women's contributions to history among the explicit reasons for landmark designation.[18] A similar pattern appeared in my review of selected state and local landmark listings. As of 1982 in California, women's contributions to history were recognized at only 3.3 percent of designated sites and buildings.[19] In Los Angeles, as of 1986, 5.2 percent of Historical-Cultural Monuments marked women's contributions to the development of the city.[20] Yet as historian Gerda Lerner has pointed out, women have always been at least half of human history.[21]

If the preservation movement has been slow to respond to calls to enhance the visibility of women at the nation's historic sites and buildings, pressure for change is likely to mount as grassroots projects appear with increasing frequency. Walking tours of women's history landmarks have been developed in a number of U.S. cities. These tours include the New Orleans Women's History Tour; Domer, Hunt, Johnson, and Wheeler's *Walking with Women through Chicago History*; Lacy and Mason's *Women's History Tour of the Twin Cities*; and the Los Angeles Women's History Project developed by Gail Lee Dubrow, Carolyn Flynn and Sherry Katz.[22] Two national guides to women's history landmarks have been published (Lynn Sherr and Jurate Kazickas's bicentennial *The American Woman's Gazetteer*, and Marion Tinling's encyclopedic *Women Remembered*[23]); these guides give the visitor knowledge of hundreds of sites and buildings associated with women, from the Daytona Beach home and college named for black educator Mary McLeod Bethune, to the Alaska homestead and town named for roadhouse operator Nellie Neal Lawing.

Still, there remains a pressing need to link new-found knowledge of U.S. women's history with the skills and resources of the preservation community. The recent commitment by the National Park Service to establish a Women's Rights National Historical Park in Seneca Falls, N.Y., and to cooperate with historical associations in a survey of nationally significant women's history landmarks are the first steps in the right direction.[24] However, the National Park Service and state historic preservation offices have not made major commitments of staff and fiscal resources to support the identification, preservation, and interpretation of women's history landmarks. Additional state and local surveys are needed to fill gaps in existing knowledge about the status of tangible resources associated with women's history.[25]

As we begin to review the landmarks of women's history, it is essential to recognize that the conception of women's history has changed

A growing interest in the everyday history of women. Efforts to preserve women's history are reaching beyond the homes of notable women to the spaces created and used by ordinary women. Here, for example, women gather in the poorly lighted room (BOTTOM) behind the undistinguished storefront (TOP) that housed the 1920s Negro branch of the YWCA in Los Angeles. Photographs courtesy of Urban Archives Center, California State University, Northridge

considerably since the Daughters of the American Revolution first set out to preserve it in 1890. The past emphasis on notable women has given way to a wider view. Equal emphasis is now given to the collective struggles and accomplishments of women and to their daily lives; new importance is assigned to women's history in the household, workplace, and community. The conception of women's history has expanded to include the historical experience of working class and minority women.[26] A wider range of tangible resources becomes visible from this perspective. Not only can we see homes and gravesites of exceptional women, but also elements of the built environment that speak to shared and ordinary historical experience. Not only must we look at the woman's place in a male-defined world, but also the places that women themselves created, defined, and used: hospitals, kindergartens, social settlements, schools, women's club buildings, women's residences, and the sites of strikes, protests, and public speeches.

Protecting the landmarks of women's history will require the cooperative efforts of women in the architectural profession, the academy, and the preservation community. Beyond that, it will require support from an even wider constituency. But if there is a lesson to be learned from our foremothers in the historic preservation movement, it is that organized women hold the power to ensure a female presence at historic sites and buildings.

Notes

1. "Bunker Hill Ladies Appeal" (3 April 1830), Schlesinger Library, Radcliffe College.

2. Ibid.

3. Harriot K. Hunt, *Glances and Glimpses or Fifty Years Social, including Twenty Years Professional Life* (Boston: John P. Jewett and Co., 1856), 163.

4. For a brief account of women's early contributions to historic preservation, see Marion Tinling and Linda Ruffner-Russell, "Famous and Forgotten Women," *Historic Preservation 28*: 3 (July–September 1976): 18. Also see Elswyth Thane, *Mount Vernon is Ours: The Story of its Preservation* (New York: Duell, Sloan and Pearce, 1966); Larkin Dunkin, ed., *Memorial Services in Honor of Mrs. Mary Hemenway by the Boston Public Schoolteachers* (Boston: G.H. Ellis, Printer, 1894); and Jack C. Butterfield, *Women of the Alamo* (San Antonio: Daughters of the Republic of Texas, 1960).

5. Hunt, 163.

6. Ibid.

7. Mary S. Lockwood and Emily Lee Sherwood, *Story of the Records, DAR* (Washington, D.C.: George E. Howard, 1906), 21.

8. Lockwood and Sherwood, 115, 122, 176.

9. Karen J. Blair, *The Clubwoman as Feminist: True Womanhood Redefined* (London and New York: Holmes & Meier, 1980), 107.

10. The preservation strategy employed by clubwomen at the Anthony house took advantage of their wide social network. Local groups assumed responsibility for restoring individual rooms according to an overall plan: the League of Women Voters sponsored the study; the University of Rochester alumnae supported the back parlor; and the Women's Alliance of the Unitarian Church that Anthony had attended made the front parlor its project. Martha Taylor Howard to Rose Arnold Powell (2 December 1946). Rose Arnold Powell (RAP) Papers, Schlesinger Library, Radcliffe College.

11. Carrie Chapman Catt to Rose Arnold Powell (2 February 1935), RAP Papers, Schlesinger Library.

12. Carrie Chapman Catt to Rose Arnold Powell (21 June 1938), RAP Papers, Schlesinger Library.

13. Charles B. Hosmer, Jr., *Presence of the Past: A History of the Preservation Movement in the United States before Williamsburg* (New York: G. P. Putnam's Sons, 1965), 261–63.

14. Laura S. Nelson's unpublished paper, "In the Beginning: Women in HABS" (1986), documents the work of women in nine states in the Historic American Buildings Survey. [Archives of the American Institute of Architects. 1735 New York Avenue, N.W., Washington, D.C. 20006].

15. Hosmer, 300. Hosmer correctly observes that "women were predominant in the preservation movement as long as it stressed history and patriotic inspiration. When architectural preservation began toward the end of World War I, men became equally active." However, Hosmer wrongly attributes women's declining influence to the supposition that "women apparently were not so enthusiastic about the field of architecture." Here he overlooks the structural barriers faced by women seeking an architectural education, and wrongly assumes that a balance of power was struck between men and women in the preservation movement.

16. Tinling and Ruffner-Russell, "Famous and Forgotten Women": 18.

17. Heather Huyck, "Beyond John Wayne: Using Historic Sites to Interpret Women's History," in Lillian Schlissel, Vicki L. Ruiz and Janice Monk, eds., *Western Women: Their Land, Their Lives* (Albuquerque: University of New Mexico Press, 1988), 303–330.

18. Analysis based on U.S. Department of the Interior, National Park Service, History Division, *Catalogue of National Historic Landmarks* (Washington, D.C.: United States Government Printing Office, 1985). A closer look at the composition of women's history sites on landmark registers reveals three further problems: (1) the inadequate protection of cultural resources associated with ethnic

and minority women; (2) the limited variety of tangible resources preserved (most are houses); and (3) the uneven regional distribution of National Historic Landmarks incorporating women's history themes (most are located on the eastern seaboard between Maine and Virginia). It should be mentioned, concerning the theme surveys carried out by the National Park Service, that the long-standing NPS themes of Exploration and Settlement, the War for Independence, the Civil War, and Westward Expansion have traditionally focused on male achievements; recently added thematic categories such as Social and Humanitarian Movements, however, to the credit of the NPS, have left wider room for women.

19. Analysis based on California Department of Parks and Recreation, *California Historical Landmarks* (Sacramento: California Department of Parks and Recreation, 1979; rev. 1982).

20. Analysis based on records of the Los Angeles Cultural Heritage Commission.

21. Gerda Lerner, *The Majority Finds Its Past: Placing Women in History* (New York: Oxford University Press, 1979).

22. Gehman and Ries, *Women and New Orleans: A History* (New Orleans: Margaret Media, Inc. 1985); Domer, Hunt, Johnson, and Wheeler, *Walking With Women Through Chicago History* (Chicago: Salsedo Press, 1981); Lacy and Mason, *Women's History Tour of the Twin Cities* (Minneapolis: Nodin Press, 1982) [out of print]; and the Los Angeles Women's History Project, whose findings were reported in the *California Historical Courier* 37: (February 1985): 11.

23. Lynn Sherr and Jurate Kazickas, *The American Woman's Gazetteer* (New York: Bantam, 1976) and Marion Tinling, *Women Remembered: A Guide to Landmarks of Women's History in the United States* (Westport, Conn.: Greenwood Press, 1986).

24. "Reclaiming Our Past: Landmark Sites of Women's History" is a three-year project begun in May 1986, cooperatively sponsored by the Organization of American Historians, Coordinating Committee for the Promotion of History, and National Park Service. [Page Putnam Miller, Director, National Coordinating Committee for the Promotion of History, 400 A Street, S.E., Washington, D.C. 20003.] The purpose of the project is to identify existing sites on the National Register of Historic Places for nomination to the National Historic Landmark Program, and to fill gaps in the coverage of women's history by identifying new sites and reinterpreting female historical experience at currently designated landmarks.

25. Rich finds await surveyors. Hidden in a Boston alley I discovered the former headquarters of the Boston Women's Trade Union League. Across the street from Copley Square are the one-time offices of the *Woman's Journal* and the Massachusetts Woman Suffrage Association. In Los Angeles, with Sherry Katz and Carolyn Flynn, I discovered a cluster of buildings known in the 1920s as the "Civic Center of Women's Activities," and residences for black women

founded by the Sojourner Truth Industrial Club. State and local preservation officials know little about such sites.

26. Few landmarks currently speak to women's labor history. Preservation efforts could rescue from invisibility such significant sites of female labor militancy as the scene of the 1910 garment workers' strike in Chicago and many others.

15

From Muse

to Heroine

Toward a Visible

Creative Identity

ANNE GRISWOLD TYNG

Understanding the role of muse is a step in the psychic development of women and men. When Louise Blanchard Bethune became the first woman accepted by her peers in the AIA, it was far more likely for an unusually intelligent and stimulating woman to have a salon. Playing the role of hostess, she would aspire to the role of muse, providing the spark for a man's creativity. In this role she became the man's anima or feminine soul (as described by the Swiss psychologist Carl Jung[1]); the man for whom she was anima became for her a masculine soul or animus. Just as she functioned as his generator of creative potential, he functioned as her unrealized capacity for creative production in the outer world.

The greatest remaining hurdle for a woman in architecture today is the psychological development necessary to free her creative potential. To own one's own ideas without guilt, apology, or misplaced modesty involves understanding the creative process and the so-called "masculine" and "feminine" principles as they function in creativity and in male-female relationships.

Two unusual women of our century played the role of muse—Alma Maria Schindler for Mahler, Kokoschka, Gropius, and Werfel; Lou Salomé for Nietzsche, Rilke, and Freud. Their stories will illuminate the difficulty that women have had in attaining a visible creative identity. Examples of women architects from more recent times will suggest the stages by which women have attained first a modest and then a fully independent creative image.

Alma Schindler (1879–1964), "the most beautiful girl in Vienna," had ability she might have developed as a composer; at twenty-two she married Gustav Mahler, who was forty-one and already a famous composer-conductor. On the eve of their marriage, Mahler wrote to Alma:

How do you picture the married life of a husband and wife who are both composers? Have you any idea how ridiculous and, in time, how degrading for both of us such a peculiarly competitive relationship would inevitably become? What will happen if, just when you're 'in the mood,' you're obliged to attend to the house or to something I might happen to need? . . . You must become 'what I need' if we are to be happy together, i.e., my wife, not my colleague.[2]

Alma agreed to Mahler's demands. But, married three years, she wrote in her diary. "It came to me suddenly that I am living what only appears to be a life. I hold so much inside of me, I am not free—I suffer—but I don't know why or what for." For his part, Mahler was unable to compose without her presence to nourish and inspire him.

At thirty-one, Alma met the twenty-seven-year-old architect Walter Gropius. He asked Mahler's permission to marry her but she chose to stay with Mahler, who died a year later. She soon became the lover of the painter Oskar Kokoschka, strengthening and encouraging him, while stifling her own development. After an evening with Gustav Klimt and others, she wrote,"I was actually happy. After the isolation with Oskar of the last few years this evening was a cure for me." Alma never transcended the role of muse. When she and Kokoschka drifted apart, she quickly filled the emptiness in her life by rekindling Gropius's love and marrying him in 1915.

Although Gropius saw Alma as his muse, she was not excited by his views on architecture, experiencing in their relationship an unfamiliar and uncomfortable autonomy. But by this time the role of muse had become more appealing than developing her own creative energy. In 1918 (still married to Gropius), Alma fell in love with Franz Werfel, the poet, novelist, and playwright. She divorced Gropius.

One of Alma's two daughters by Mahler lived. Her daughter by Gropius died at eighteen and a son by Werfel at ten months. But these deaths did not throw Alma onto her own creative resources; she had never fully confronted suffering, but had quickly escaped it with a new relationship. Alma eventually married Werfel and they escaped to the United States in 1940. Werfel died in 1945.

As a muse, Alma had affairs with other noted men. Her lack of self-realization seems evident in her quick shifts of allegiance, her turn-abouts to previous lovers, her one-time enthusiasm for Fascism and Nazism, and (although married to two Jews) her sweeping anti-Semitism. Nine published songs remain as fruits of her own creativity.

Lou Andreas-Salomé (1861–1937) was muse to many brilliant men, but transcended the role to develop a strong identity and productive creativity. Known principally for her friendships with Nietzsche, Rilke, and Freud, she was the author of 20 books, 119 articles, 4 unpublished manuscripts, and numerous journals.[3]

She had been a remarkable child, with a vivid fantasy life and a rigorous mind. At seventeen, with the death of her father and of her belief in God, she focused her love on her teacher, Hendrik Gillot, minister of the Dutch Reformed Church in St. Petersburg. Her notebooks indicate the depth and breadth of her work with him. She was shocked by his passionate proposal of marriage (he was twice her age and had a wife and children) and refused, but felt she would always love him. The intensity of her early intellectual development provided an independence of spirit and a psychic identity not easily lost in sexual submission.

Lou and her mother travelled to Zurich to continue her studies; Gillot had told her mother that Lou was a genius. In Zurich a distinguished theologian wrote, "Your daughter is a very unusual woman: she has a childlike purity and integrity of character and, at the same time, a quite unchildlike, almost unfeminine, direction of her mind and independence of will. She is a diamond." But her fainting spells, which had begun while she was working intensely with Gillot, became so frequent that doctors ordered her to a warmer climate. In Rome she met philosophers Paul Ree and Friedrich Nietzsche (she was twenty-one, Nietzsche thirty-eight) and conceived of the idea of a platonic threesome living together to study and work.

From the start both men had trouble with Lou's concept of a "holy trinity." Nietzsche wanted a trial marriage with Lou, but she was both attracted and repelled by him and definitely not interested in marriage. About their intellectual rapport, Nietzsche wrote,

The most useful experiences I have had this summer were my conversations with Lou. . . . I have never known anyone who could gain so much objective knowledge from experience, no one who obtained so much insight from what she learned. . . . I wonder if there ever existed such a philosophic candor as exists between us.

Lou's rejection of Nietzsche as lover and husband (or Nietzsche's rejection of Lou as friend and sister) brought him despair, but in his suicidal misery he began writing *Thus Spoke Zarathustra*. (One of Lou's admirers said, "Lou would form a passionate attachment to a man and nine months later the man gave birth to a book.") On her part, Lou's escape from the powerful attraction of playing muse freed her to develop her own creative identity.

Her only marriage was to Friedrich Andreas, forced by his attempted suicide in her presence. She was twenty-six; he, forty-three, a linguist, historian, and naturalist. From all accounts, the marriage was never consummated. Lou agreed that he should have a "substitute wife" (who became their housekeeper), and they maintained separate apartments in the same house until Andreas died four decades later.

Lou continued to travel and maintain friendships with brilliant men. She was described as having an "extreme readiness toward life, a humble and courageous holding-herself-open to the joys and woes, a fascinating mixture of masculine earnestness, childlike light-heartedness and feminine ardor." Yet she maintained her virginity until she was thirty-three or thirty-four.

At thirty-six, Lou met the poet Rilke, then twenty-one. On reading her *Jesus the Jew*, Rilke felt she had written what he had been trying to say in his *Visions of Christ*. He wrote to her:

The transforming experience which then seized me at a hundred places at once emanated from the great reality of your being. . . . Slowly, and with great difficulty I learned how simple everything is and I matured and learned to say simple things. All this happened because I was fortunate enough to meet you at a time when I was in danger of losing myself in formlessness. . . . [And later] You magnificent one, how vast you have made me.

Their intense involvement was also expressed by Lou.

I was your wife for years because you were the first reality, body and man undistinguishably one, the incontestable fact of life itself. . . . Our surprised unity recognized a preordained unit. We were brother and sister, but as in the remote past, before marriage between brother and sister had become sacrilegious.

She ended the affair four years later; to her, Rilke showed "dangerous signs of mental sickness."

At Martin Buber's suggestion, Lou wrote her book *Eroticism*, published the year before she met Freud.

Sexual love, artistic creativity and religious fervor [she wrote] are but three different aspects of the same life force. . . . Symbolic of this threefold aspect of the life force is a woman's threefold function as mistress, mother and madonna.

Interestingly, Lou correlates artistic creativity with the mother function (as nourishing muse?) rather than identifying a fourth function as woman's own creative identity.

Lou was introduced to Freud by the Swedish psychotherapist Poul Bjerre, who fell in love with her although he was fifteen years younger and married. Years later he said of Lou,

She had the gift of entering completely into the mind of the man she loved. Her enormous concentration fanned, as it were, her partner's intellectual fire. I have never met anyone else in my long life who understood me so quickly, so well, and so completely. . . . When I met her I was working on the foundations of my psychotherapy which is based, in contrast to Freud's, on the principle of synthesis. In my talks with Lou things became clear to me that I might not have found by myself. . . . One felt the spark of genius in her.

Lou was fifty and Freud fifty-five when they met. She trained as a psychoanalyst with him but even while she was developing her own psychological insights, he perceived her as a muse. "Because you were not with me at the Saturday lecture, I was deprived of my fixation-point and spoke falteringly." He valued her understanding of him, which (he wrote) "while it goes beyond what was said is a correct inference." Freud saw her as an empty creative vessel for his unspoken thought.

In the last third of Lou's life she practiced psychoanalysis and maintained stimulating professional friendships with the leading thinkers of her time. One of them described Lou at seventy:

The extraordinary woman was still blond and she moved with the supple movements of a young tree. . . . She was endowed with a graceful, searching or groping empathy and she lacked the too strongly masculine predominance of the female intellectual. . . . It was a great relief to me to notice even in her book on Freud that because of her own originality she was entirely free of psychoanalytical dogmatism.

Lou's friendship with Freud (continuing to her death in 1937) did not limit her to his views; she valued some of Jung's concepts, despite the intense disagreement between Freud and Jung. Her own writings reveal original insights on man-woman relationships. In 1912 she suggested a complex fourfold interaction of man-woman/anima-animus going beyond concepts of both Freud and Jung at that time:

I think that just because male and female are basic constituents of *all* life, they both enter at some point into the formation of the man as well as the woman . . . In love and in submission we are given the gift of ourselves, we are made more actual, more encompassing, more wedded to ourselves, and this alone is the true efficacy of love, giving life and joy. . . . Only when there is a twofold alternation between masculinity and femininity can two persons be more than one, no longer regarding each other as a goal (like miserable halves which need to be stuck together to form a whole) but rather committed together to a goal outside themselves. Only then are love and creation, natural fulfillment and cultural activity no longer opposites, but one.

Although history may value Lou Andreas-Salomé only as an "empty-vessel" to Nietzsche, Rilke, and Freud, the translator of her *Freud Journal* asserts that her "spirit . . . insinuated itself into the writings of all of them." The books she wrote about them demonstrate her own brilliance and originality. She also wrote novels, plays, and poetry as well as reviews, articles, and writings on philosophy and analytical psychology. The daring conviction with which she lived and her independent creativity qualify her as a heroine.

The steps from muse to heroine are accomplished by very few. Many women trained as architects marry architects. No longer the woman behind the man, the woman architect in partnership with her husband may nevertheless be barely visible beside (or slightly behind) the hero.

The man's creative output and recognition are often inflated; credit for the partner-wife is frequently omitted. This situation is compounded by the woman's projection of her own potential for visible achievement onto the real-life man who acts and is perceived as the hero-animus. The two are further bound in work and love by the man's projection of his anima or generative source of creativity onto his real-life partner.

Aino Marsio (1894–1949). The Aaltos are one such example. Aino Marsio received her architectural degree in 1920, moving from her first job to the office of Alvar Aalto; they married in 1924. A Finnish monograph on her life concludes, "It is very often difficult to distinguish their respective contributions in the work of their office."[4] Goran Schildt describes their collaboration:

Aino Aalto was an extremely skilled, sure and patient draughtsman. . . . In addition she understood the facts and limitations of everyday life better than Aalto, who at times flew high above reality. . . . Alvar was able to let loose his architectural visions, for he knew that Aino would bring them back to earth.[5]

Although Alvar received greater recognition, in a sense this is a reversal of roles: Alvar as the muse and Aino as the one giving ideas tangible form.

Together the Aaltos founded the furniture and design firm Artek, with Aino as its managing director. In a workshop, with her own hands, she created much of the famous "Aalto furniture." But she remains in the shadow of her husband and is mistakenly considered only the designer of interiors of buildings credited to her husband alone.

Marion Mahony (1871–1961). Marion Mahony left a clearer creative identity, although she consciously took the role of "woman behind the man" in her partnership with her husband. The first woman to receive the B.S. in architecture at MIT, she was also the first woman to be licensed as an architect in Illinois.[6]

During her fourteen years in Frank Lloyd Wright's office (from 1895 to 1909) she designed several of her own commissions, clearly indicating her ability for overall conception, but historians have perceived her merely as a designer of details and furniture. In fact, Mahony's furniture was fully integrated with the architecture and determined the "flow" of interior spaces.

There is no doubt of her contribution to the Wasmuth publication of Wright's work in 1910; of twenty-seven attributable drawings, seventeen were by Mahony and ten were by Mahony and others.[7] A colleague in Wright's office wrote:

The style of these drawings of Miss Mahony's was determined only in a general way by Mr. Wright, he having in mind, of course, the artistic character evident in Japanese prints. The picture compositions were initiated by Miss Mahony, who had unusually fine compositional and linear ability, with a drawing "touch" that met with Mr. Wright's highly critical approval. She was the most talented member of Frank Lloyd Wright's staff.[8]

In 1916, Wright included two Decatur houses (designed and built while he was in Europe with Mrs. Cheney) in an exhibition of his work at the Chicago Art Institute. The two houses were "entirely Marion Mahony creations, but they are chiefly remarkable for the completeness with which they reproduce Wright's style."[9] Is it sacrilegious to suggest that Mahony may have had a part in creating "Wright's style"? She was twenty-four and he twenty-six when she began working for him. (I tend to accept Mahony's claims concerning designs in Wright's office that were "wholly" hers or Griffin's and not dismiss them as exaggerations resulting from Wright's later ill treatment of Mahony and her husband.[10])

In 1911, Mahony married Walter Burley Griffin, a colleague in Wright's office, and with him won the competition for the Australian capital of Canberra. She wrote: "I was proud to have the prize come our way. Proud for my husband's sake. I can never aspire to be as great an architect as he but I can best understand and help him and to a wife there is not greater recompense."[11]

Marion Mahony's capacity ranged from the design of rich detail, to the development of interior/exterior spatial concepts of buildings, to the planning of entire towns (the latter demonstrating her boldness in large-scale concepts as well as her sensitivity to environmental relationships). Yet in her professional partnership with her husband she was reluctant to assume a separate psychic identity and acknowledge her own creativity.

A number of women find a creative identity independent of husband-partners. But the creative image of these women, by their own choice or otherwise, is often considerably more modest than that of a comparably creative man.

Julia Morgan (1872–1957). Julia Morgan also shunned the limelight, but since she had an independent practice of heroic proportions, and never married, her creative identity is distinct. Even so, her work was not recognized by historians who publicized the work of contemporaries Maybeck and the Greene brothers and is only now fully documented in a book published last year.[12]

From 1904 when she became the first woman architect registered in California, until 1951 when she closed her office, Morgan carried on an independent practice of the highest professional standards. She showed her dedication and courage when, with her sense of balance damaged by ear surgery, she inspected structural work at exposed heights on her hands and knees. Perhaps that was to be expected from the woman who had squared off against the French government, and won, when she became in 1898 the first woman of any nationality to be accepted at the Ecole des Beaux-Arts to study architecture. She placed thirteenth from a field of three to four hundred.

The scope and value of Morgan's work is only beginning to be appreciated. In more than eight hundred buildings Morgan demonstrated a mastery of light, of space, and of scale. Her architecture proclaims her as original and innovative, and an unacknowledged pioneer of the California Shingle style. Yet her extreme modesty probably kept her from being perceived as the heroine she unquestionably was.

Ellamae Ellis League (b.1899) and Jean League Newton (b.1919). Ellamae League's forty-one-year practice in Macon, Georgia, from 1934 to 1975, joined full-time by her daughter Jean for its last thirty-one years, could hardly have been expected from a pretty "southern belle" once described as demure.

At twenty-two, divorced from the lieutenant she had married during World War I, Ellamae League was left with two children she was determined to educate. The fact that her uncle was the family's fourth generation of architects pointed the way toward architecture. With only a year of college, she apprenticed in a local firm for ten years to qualify for registration exams. (She also took the correspondence course of the Beaux-Arts Institute of New York and an academic year at Fontainebleau.) When her mentor William Franklin Oliphant died in 1934, she took over his office, becoming the first woman licensed to practice architecture in Georgia.

For many years the only woman in the Georgia chapter of the AIA, Ellamae League served as its first and second vice president. In 1963 she was first president of the statewide Georgia Council (now Georgia Association) of the AIA. When she became a Fellow in 1968, the entire Atlanta chapter, including colleague John Portman, chartered a bus to the party given her by the Macon chapter.

Jean League was one of the first Radcliffe students to get credit for studio work at the Cambridge School. She continued there until women were admitted to Harvard, receiving her M.Arch. degree from Harvard in 1944. Her Bauhaus training complemented her mother's Beaux-Arts training, and was a vital asset for the six-person firm. Neither of Jean's daughters is an architect but a nephew continues the family tradition in the seventh generation. Jean League Newton has held every office of the AIA chapter in Macon, where she has her practice. These two women have pioneered in forging a strong two-generation link between independently creative women architects.

A shift in the perception of women's creative image has occurred, as men no longer need to be macho extroverts and women can move confidently into leading roles.

Adèle Naudé Santos (b.1938). In 1982, Adèle Naudé Santos became the first woman chairman of the department of architecture at the University of Pennsylvania—the first at any Ivy League architecture school. She has the London Architectural Association diploma (1961), an M.Arch. in urban design from Harvard (1963), and both the M.Arch. and M.C.P. from the University of Pennsylvania (1968).

The chairman's job requires her to be highly visible and articulate, a role she plays with imagination and flair. She has organized summer studios in India, and in Colombia (where students designed housing for earthquake victims), bringing a fresh breath of humanism to the more formal aspects of architecture.

At the same time Adèle has made a breakthrough in her independent practice (begun in 1979 as Adèle Naudé Santos Architects) by winning the competition for a cultural center in Hawaii. Her six-year practice with husband-partner Antonio de Souza Santos, ending in 1974 with

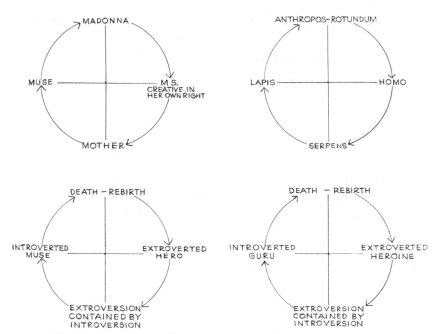

(TOP LEFT) *Four feminine roles: the mother gives biological birth to offspring who bear the father's name: the muse as "vessel" gives birth to man's creativity; the Madonna gives birth from "spiritual" impregnation (similar to Isis and other myths); and the Ms. or heroine gives birth to her own creativity in her own name. (TOP RIGHT) The process of psychic healing, described by Carl G. Jung as four symbolic stages in a continuous cycle beginning and ending with "death" and "rebirth" (anthropos-rotundum). The path toward wholeness passes through deeper and deeper levels of the unconscious mind and, in a sense, back in time to "lower" levels of evolution: through man (homo) to serpent (serpens) as healing natural instinct, through plant forms to the philosopher's stone (lapis) and through the four basic elements—fire, air, earth, and water—to dissolution and a new synthesis (anthropos-rotundum). (BOTTOM LEFT) The starting place of introverted muse and extroverted hero in Jung's cycle of individuation, showing the hero's direction toward introversion and the muse's toward extroversion through "death" and "rebirth." (BOTTOM RIGHT) The new position in Jung's cycle for the woman transformed to extroverted heroine and the man to introverted guru. Drawings by Anne Griswold Tyng*

their divorce, was followed by her five-year practice as Interstudio in Houston.

Adèle Naudé Santos is meeting the challenge of individual creative identity with a bold and humanistic spirit.

Joan Goody (b.1936). Joan Goody, as the principal architect in the fifty-member firm Goody, Clancy & Associates, is personally responsible (at this writing) for a twenty-story downtown office building; a massive restoration of a city housing project; and a sports complex, renovation, and additions on three major campuses. Multi-million dollar commissions—and awards for excellent design—are not new to her.

Joan entered Harvard Graduate School of Design in 1956, the year Marvin Goody (then teaching at MIT) started his practice. They did not meet and marry until 1960. When Joan joined his firm that year, Marvin was ten years ahead of her professionally.

Marvin died of a heart attack in 1980, and Joan has assumed his role as the most visible partner of the firm. The challenge of work helped her through the tragedy. "It made me open up more to the world. Mourning can drive you out and make you much more alert and aware."[13]

A difficult step in the psychic process is required to break out of the muse-hero bond. The four phases of the creative cycle I have proposed[14] correspond with the four stages in Carl Jung's cycle of individuation.[15] My research convinces me that these cycles move from simple containment of energy through expanding complexity following a natural flow of the law of entropy. (This law states the probable tendency toward loss of order and energy within a closed system.) In the process of individuation, consciousness and energy turn inward to deeper and deeper levels of the unconscious mind. The natural entropic flow toward "death" involves a gradual letting-go of the ego and opening up to previously unknown contents of the unconscious. "Rebirth" is experienced as a spontaneous breakthrough—a synthesis of accumulated unconscious contents in a new conscious balance of what is known and unknown.

Experiencing the death of the husband-partner (or divorce as another kind of death) is a pattern common to Naudé Santos, Goody, and a number of other women architects. The new men in their lives are involved in introverted work, freeing these women from the role of introverted muse for husband-partner-hero and allowing them to assume the extroverted heroic role themselves.

A woman must experience a crisis (usually some kind of loss or death) in order to break out of the muse-hero bond and move forward in the psychic cycle. If a man moves forward in psychic development from the extroverted stage of the cycle, however, he follows a natural flow toward entropy and introversion. This may be experienced by him as a regression: a loss of energy and a loss of control over his environment. It is not hard to see why men resist this psychic development, although many find rewards in the introverted role of teacher or guru as a rounding-out of an excessive emphasis on extroversion.

In contrast to a man's natural psychic flow toward entropy (moving from the conditioned male extroversion toward an introverted phase), the move from the conditioned female introversion toward the extroverted and heroic phase is counter-entropy; a woman must pass through a psychic death and rebirth to do so. It is easy to see why a woman can get stuck in the introverted role of muse.

Joanna Steichen, widow of photographer Edward Steichen, writes empathetically of "The Widow-of-the-Great-Man Syndrome" in response to the recent suicide of Jacqueline Picasso.[16] Faced with her sudden oblivion as a forgotten widow, a woman may find the lack of her own identity devastating. Yet I believe that the role of muse to a great man can be just as inflated as the role of hero. Like the whale that swallowed and spewed Jonah, the muse has contained the hero. She harbors the comforting thought that if she can produce greatness in the hero, she has the potential for greatness within herself, without of course having to test herself. Many of us remain whales in the watery domain of the feminine principle. And while, as a whale, one might have been a land mammal in some past millennia, one knows instinctively that a beached whale is in trouble.

When a woman reclaims her own animus or is aware that she has projected it onto someone outside herself, when a man assimilates his own anima or becomes similarly aware of his projection, both become more complete and more creative.

Women are no longer prisoners of conditioning as introverted shadow figures, and men are no longer prisoners of macho extroverted conditioning. Extroverted masculine and introverted feminine principles are different modes of creativity available to both men and women. Continuous movement through the psychic cycle offers a rounding-out of consciousness and a renewal of energy for more creative men and women architects to make better architecture.

In opening up for rebirth, we turn ourselves inside-out, like the glove of the subjective left hand turned inside-out to become a glove for the more dexterous extroverted right hand.

We give birth to ourselves.

Notes

1. Carl G. Jung, "Approaching the Unconscious," in *Man and His Symbols* (Garden City, N.Y.: Doubleday, 1968), 30–31.

2. For information on Alma Schindler Mahler, I have drawn largely on the excellent biography by Karen Monson, *Alma Mahler, Muse to Genius, From Fin-de-Siècle Vienna to Hollywood's Heyday* (Boston: Houghton Mifflin, 1983).

3. My resources on Lou Andreas-Salomé include the absorbing biography of H. F. Peters, *My Sister, My Spouse: A Biography of Lou Andreas-Salomé* (New York: W. W. Norton, 1962), and the revealing *The Freud Journal of Lou Andreas-Salomé* trans. Stanley A. Leavy (New York: Basic Books, 1964).

4. Riitta Nikula, "Aino Marsio-Aalto" in *Profiles: Pioneer Women Architects From Finland*, trans. Harald Arnkil (Helsinki: Museum of Finnish Architecture, 1983): 56.

5. Ibid. and quote from Goran Schildt, *The White Table* (1982), 133.

6. Susan Fondiler Berkon, "Marion Mahony Griffin" in *Women in American Architecture: A Historic and Contemporary Perspective*, ed. Susana Torre (New York: Whitney Library of Design, 1977), 75.

7. H. Allen Brooks, "Frank Lloyd Wright and the Wasmuth Drawings" in *Art Bulletin* 48 (June 1966): 202.

8. Ibid., 195, note 14.

9. David T. Van Zanten, "The Early Work of Marion Mahony Griffin" in *Prairie School Review* 3 (2d quarter 1966): 17.

10. Ibid., 10.

11. Marion Mahony, *The Magic of America* (1949, unpublished) 7: 339.

12. Sara Holmes Boutelle, *Julia Morgan, Architect* (New York: Abbeville Press, 1988).

13. Otile McManus, "A Reputation Built, Architect Joan Goody's Designs For Life," in *Boston Globe Magazine*, 5 October 1986.

14. I first proposed eleven cycles of collective creativity based on changing styles in the history of architecture, in "Geometric Extensions of Consciousness," in *Zodiac 19* (Milan, Italy: Edizioni di Communitá, 1969): 130–62; I have elaborated both individual and collective creative cycles in "Individuation, Entropy and Creativity: Cycles in the History of Architecture" in *C. G. Jung and the Humanities: Toward a Hermeneutics of Culture*, Karin Barnaby and Pellegrino

D'Acierno, eds. (Princeton: Princeton University Press, 1989).

15. C. G. Jung, *The Collected Works* (New York: Pantheon, 1959), vol. 9, II, *Aion, Researches into Phenomenology of the Self*, 248.

16. Joanna Steichen, "Jacqueline Picasso and Me: The Widow-of-the-Great-Man Syndrome," in *Ms.* 15 (March 1987): 76.

Ad-Architects

Women Professionals

in Magazine Ads

DIANE FAVRO

Vicariously balanced between actual and enhanced depictions of "real life," the people appearing in ads embody both perceived and desired social identities. As demographics have changed, so have advertisements. More and more ads today use images of professionals to promote products, and in recent years advertisers have increasingly selected the architect as a positive and desirable spokesperson. Architects appear in printed ads hawking cigarettes, hotels, liquor, newspapers, courier services, fashions, beer, computers—and more. The images range from the architect as road-racing adventurer to the architect as computer-bound technician. These images mirror popular conceptions and misconceptions about architecture professionals and conversely put forth idealized images about these individuals.

Advertisements celebrate women architects. In architecture today, 94 percent of the practitioners are male,[1] but in the world of printed advertisements a disproportionate number are women.[2] The increased number of ad-architects partially reflects a fad; the profession is suddenly "hot" in popular culture. (Several current movies and best-sellers portray architects, and the most popular of all media, television, has a situation comedy with a woman practitioner.)[3] Given this exposure, it is not surprising that representations of women architects also appear in print advertisements. How these images are used, what they depict, and where they appear all serve to clarify contemporary conceptions of the profession and the role of women in it.

I will begin with my own preconceptions. I expected to find ads celebrating the creativity of women architects and their association with the home, specifically through interior design. Similarly, I postulated that advertisers would exploit the artistic side of the profession, using female architects to model more trendy fashion than the staid business suits of their peers in law and business. Neither premise proved true. Ads emphasize the business acumen of female practitioners, not their creativity or social concerns. While male architects may appear in less conservative dress than other professionals, women are generally shown in suitlike attire, frequently with necktie. Even fashion ads emphasize the woman architect's practicality and propriety rather than her style or flair. The message is clear. A female ad-architect is above all a professional.

What kind of professional? What identifies an architect? What locales and activities are associated with this occupation? While ads stress professional identification, they make few references to famous architects (and none to well-known buildings), and consider only superficially the actual working methods of contemporary architects.

Ad-architects are identified by standard icons such as the triangle, drafting table, and template. Most popular is the ubiquitous T-square, easily recognized by the public as an attribute of the architect, but supplanted in actual practice by the parallel rule. Blueprints also commonly appear as props in ads, yet most architects have abandoned these fugitive reproductions for more durable blue-lines. Equally misconceived are calipers, yardsticks, and ball-point pens. Conversely, some items commonly used in the office today appear only infrequently in advertisements, notably electric erasers, tracing paper, study models, and calculators. And despite increasing use of computers in architecture, only the computer companies show architects at terminals.

Locales and activities also identify the architect. Advertisements are crowded, so full views of design offices are rare. Offices are extremely neat, with the requisite drafting table, flex lamp, and white decor. Male architects often lean over a drafting table with rolled-up sleeves, while

The female ad-architect is not usually shown in the act of designing; instead her work is implied. Advertisement reproduced courtesy of Evan-Picone

such a pose is infrequent for women practitioners; hawking fashions, women more commonly stand inactive, the entire body visible. Representations of women professionals consistently stress cerebral activity rather than the physical act of designing. At a drafting table, women appear as passive thinkers rather than active designers; work is implied. (An Evan-Picone ad, for example, runs a banner headline "Clothes that work" above a female architect standing at a drafting table. To provide a sense of action, she holds a telephone.)

Outside the studio-office, women are depicted as more active. Ads frequently show female ad-architects on the move, striding assuredly from one appointment to the next. A favored scenario has the woman architect, smiling and confident, making a presentation to male clients in an opulent business environment. But the architecture profession also allows novel settings: a few advertisements show women architects wearing hard hats and giving orders at construction sites.

These activities and locales are entirely appropriate for the architect in the 1980s. However, like icons, they are highly selective. Ad-architects operate exclusively in the corporate world and work on large, nonresidential projects. Nothing demonstrates concern with any social issues like low-cost housing. Ads portray the architect as an independent individual, working for personal goals, although in reality practitioners often work together on a project and collaborate closely with consultants, clients, and building users. Female ad-architects interact with others more frequently than their male counterparts, but like the men they are generally shown as authority figures, not collaborators.

Overall, ads exclude any negative image. They do not depict women architects *en charrette*, working frantically amid mountains of crumpled tracing paper. Similarly, they make no allusion to the long hours spent fighting for building permits, hustling for clients, and suing for payments. Only in rare instances are female ad-architects allowed to admit the demands of the profession.[4]

Since male architects are the expected norm, advertisers use these spokespersons to draw different associations. Advertisements show males doing physical work and referring to occupational discomforts. Where female ad-architects often interact with others, males generally stand alone in the tradition of the architect-individualist Howard Roark from

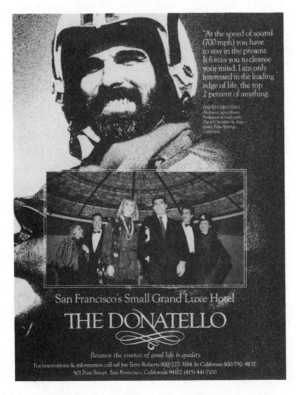

Male ad-architects are frequently rugged and self-assured individualists. Advertisement reproduced courtesy of Donatello Hotel

Ayn Rand's *The Fountainhead*. Male architects are depicted not so much as professionals, but as creative and self-assured individualists. They sell an attitude or lifestyle as much as a given product; the reader is meant to identify with the independent, affluent, confident male individual. While female ad-architects are always identified by specific professional tools and settings, independent males are shown in other contexts— relaxing at home or enjoying sports—their occupation identified by a few words. (One notable ad depicts a bearded man in a racing helmet, identified in small type as "architect, adventurer, professional road racer.")

Advertising copy further clarifies and shapes the popular image of the architect. In both male and female representations, advertisements associate the architect with success, upward mobility, and discerning taste. The professional's self-assured image is evident in such slogans as "You're on your way to the top" (Michelob); "Nobody does it better" (Winston); and "Taste of success" (Vantage). Other text emphasizes the architect's sophistication in such terms as "civilized" (Hennessy), and "elegant" and "discreet" (Chimère). In several cases, ads associate male practitioners with self-determination by telling mini-stories about setting goals and working hard. An ad for the Donatello Hotel has an architect saying, "I am only interested in the leading edge of life, the top 2 percent of anything."

With female architects, the ad copy generally continues to stress professionalism. Descriptions include "authoritative," "clout," "winning," "success," and "professional." A few ads use copy to explore other possible facets of the architect's character. One ad for the *Wall Street Journal* runs the headline, "Here's to the dreamers," identifying people motivated by a more personal and less status-conscious vision of success; as exemplars the ad shows a developer, a cowboy, a scientist, a bicycle-shop owner, a vintner, and a woman architect.

Ad-architects represent both the stereotypical female professional and the stereotypical male individualist. All are white, Caucasian, and youthful. Depictions of nonwhite architects occur primarily in magazines with a focused audience (such as *Ebony*[5]), or in ads for products with a specific ethnic association. (For example, a campaign for Puerto Rican rum shows three successful male architects: one white, one black, and one Hispanic.) Notable by omission from all advertisements are architects of Asian descent. Also ignored are older professionals. Today fewer than 10 percent of male and 30 percent of female architects are under thirty years of age, yet ad-architects are invariably twenty-five to

Chimère
Perfume.
To the world.
it's discreet.
elegant.

But up close,
it's something
else.

PRINCE MATCHABELLI

Ad-architects often hawk upscale products. Advertisement reproduced courtesy of Chesebrough-Pond's Inc., owner of the registered trademark CHIMÈRE

A female architect is among those motivated by a search for personal success. Advertisement reproduced courtesy of Fallon McElligott, for Dow Jones, Inc.

Here's to the dreamers.

There are certain people in American business whose motives for working are a bit out of the ordinary.

They don't work just to pass the time, or to keep food on the table, or to pay the mortgage.

They're motivated by something more powerful.

The American dream. The dream of turning their brains, their sweat and their talent into a very personal kind of success.

It is to these men and women that we dedicate The Wall Street Journal.

Every business day, The Journal brings you precisely what you need to nourish your own dream.

We bring you the most comprehensive report of business news in the world.

We bring you down-to-earth analysis of what the news means to you.

We bring you regular columns on subjects of wide-ranging interest.

And we bring you advance notice of trends that might catch the less observant quite unaware.

To start your subscription to The Wall Street Journal, call 800-872-5466.

We'll show you how to dream with your eyes wide open.

The Wall Street Journal.
The daily diary of the American dream.

thirty-five years of age.⁶ And though young, they are all prosperous, selling upscale goods and appearing in expensive clothes and successful environments. This affluent image reflects the popular misconception that architects earn as much as other professionals. In truth, the average salary of architects is far below that of doctors and lawyers.⁷

Product association further shapes the architects' image. Ad-architects are used to promote products and services of interest to any professional. A large number are luxury items such as expensive perfume, liquor, and hotels. When promoting more plebian goods (e.g., beer, pantyhose), advertisers use architects to make a clear association with upward mobility. (Ads for Michelob beer depict a whole range of young professionals, including a female architect, "on [their] way to the top.") Other promotions incorporate actual practitioners to demonstrate the benefits of life once the top is reached. *Working Woman* combines short articles on successful professionals with fashion layouts showing dress-for-success ensembles far beyond the means of the average practitioner.⁸

Architects are popular models for clothing because they are easily identified by a few unobtrusive props and are not hampered by a professional uniform (e.g., doctor's coat). Yet female ad-architects must follow conventional fashion. Their clothing is practical and appropriately conservative. An ad for Bullock's claims that knits are perfect for the woman architect "whose day may include hours at a drawing board and a meeting with clients." A businesswoman or lawyer may spend the same amount of time sitting and moving; once again, the specific requirements of an architect are minimized in favor of a broader appeal to professionals in general. No mention is made of the architect's need for clothing appropriate to the specific tasks of her job. Ad-architects often wear cumbersome jewelry and billowing sleeves at the drafting table and suits with skirts at the job site.

The public more readily accepts men in a broad range of professional activities. A male ad-architect can be shown in an elegant suit socializing over cocktails or in a hard hat talking about comfortable shoes. Furthermore, men are identified with many related occupations; they appear as contractors, developers, and engineers. Frequently the reader cannot definitively identify the role depicted. Several ads use the same icons for architect and engineer, while other ads consciously blur the distinction between architect, client, and developer. The ambiguity of roles allows viewers to make their own associations. Significantly, all interpretations are positive, all are desirable.

The man is clearly an architect, but the woman's role is ambiguous: is she coworker, client, secretary, or friend? Advertisement reproduced courtesy of Schieffelin & Co.

Female ad-architects are often shown on the move, competing in the business world, and in this case winning out over male peers. Advertisement reproduced courtesy of Ramada Inc.

A similar openness of interpretation is found in several ads show-ing women architects. One for Ramada Inns depicts a woman carrying rolled drawings. She is clearly a professional but she could be an archi-tect, businesswoman, engineer, interior designer, or any other person who travels and uses drawings. Women in ads cannot readily be identi-fied as engineers or contractors.[9] For the general public, these jobs still remain the domain of men. Much more acceptable is a woman as an interior designer; this occupation has traditionally been considered a sub-domain of architecture—an auxiliary (and hence a less prestigious) realm occupied primarily by women. For advertisers promoting their products to a female audience, the depiction of interior designers lacks both the positive recognition of a professional and the shock value of a woman operating in a male domain. Few examples occur. More posi-tive are the more exotic representations of women in architecture-related jobs, like the site-search expert examining property in Hawaii.[10]

Positioning and role playing also determine how ad-architects are interpreted. Again, multiple readings are possible. An ad for Hennessy shows a man after hours sitting at a drafting table while an attractive woman gives him a drink. His role as the professional is clear; hers is not. She could be a colleague, a secretary, or a friend. The same ques-tion arises in ads with a woman carrying rolled drawings: is she the archi-tect or is she a messenger? Copy often clarifies the situation. In the Ramada Inns ad, the accompanying story credits the woman with know-ing how to deal more successfully with travel arrangements than her male competitors—here is a successful professional. Some ads simulta-neously exploit professional and personal concerns; Tab runs an ad showing a suited woman in hard hat who carefully considers both the skill of her construction crew and the caloric content of her soft drink.[11]

Whom do advertisers hope to reach with representations of female architects? Ad distribution provides a clue. Many ads appear in general interest journals (such as the *New Yorker* and *Newsweek*), which are directed at educated readers of both sexes. In these publications, the advertisers target the broadest possible audience. Instead of concentrating exclu-sively on female ad-architects, these ads frequently include a woman architect among several male professionals. Larger spreads and a larger number of examples are found in women's magazines (such as *Glamour* and *Working Woman*), which are aimed at fashion-conscious, career-oriented women. Few ads appear in homemakers' periodicals. Clearly, advertisers exploit ad-architects to attract an educated, primarily female market. Marketing research has revealed three relevant facts: (1) women

to do what the big kids do.

Mattel Preschool Wonder Blocks are built for little kids.

Easy-to-work-with shapes.

Little kids just love to play with those finicky interlocking blocks. But their little hands have trouble putting them together and taking them apart. And that's no fun.

That's why Mattel Preschool makes Tuff Stuff™ Wonder Blocks. They're big chunky shapes. Perfect shapes for tiny fingers.

Tuff Stuff Wonder Blocks build confidence.

Interlocking Wonder Blocks are simple to put together and simple to take apart. So it's easy for little kids to make big statements. And that's constructive to their development and growth.

Ordinary blocks just go up and down. Wonder Blocks, on the other hand, can also go around. Yes, in circles. They have rounded edges that actually turn corners.

As a result, the architectural possibilities are almost endless. Kids can get really creative.

Small wonders.

Your little Frank Lloyd Wright can build in circles constructing imaginary coliseums, skyscrapers, or, of course, old-fashioned castles. Square or round, whatever your little one dreams up.

Tuff Stuff Wonder Blocks go in circles, too.

Architects build round buildings. Kids should be able to, also.

The ways your kids can play with Wonder Blocks are endless, too. They can link them together to create anything from a zigzag to a slinky make-believe train.

And to insure your little ones will enjoy Tuff Stuff Wonder Blocks for a long time, we make them out of the perfect building material. It's a practically indestructible plastic. Tough enough to stand up to all the ways today's kids play.

There are three different sets of Wonder Blocks to collect: starter, intermediate and master.

Want some constructive advice? The best building blocks for your preschoolers are Tuff Stuff Wonder Blocks. They're built for little kids.

Preschool

MATTEL

Toys for today's kids

© Mattel, Inc. 1986. All Rights Reserved.

Addressing yuppie parents, Mattel identifies the little girl as "your little Frank Lloyd Wright." Advertisement reproduced courtesy of Mattel Toys

wield almost 75 percent of all purchasing power; (2) women audiences respond favorably to representations of females in nontraditional, professional roles; and (3) affluent career women are the largest magazine-reading segment of the population. Print advertisers wisely select women architects as representative professionals to portray the psychographic traits most admired in a career woman: efficiency, intelligence, self-assurance, and creativity.[12]

What makes the female architect a more desirable spokesperson than other professionals? According to research by advertising agencies, the public thinks of architects quite favorably. Doctors and lawyers are well known to most individuals but are irrevocably associated with adversity. In contrast, most people have little direct contact with architects, and these professionals therefore have a more idealized and positive image.[13] The general public envisions the architect as creative, independent, youthful, professional, and financially well-off. Advertisements mirror this image, portraying the ad-architect as the ultimate Yuppie. Such a portrayal appeals specifically to the market segment with great-

est purchasing power—the affluent "Baby Boomers" who readily identify with ambitious young urban professionals.[14] For this group of over-
achievers, architecture seems a desirable occupation. Several ads
specifically address Baby Boomer parents. Promoting building blocks,
for instance, Mattel identifies a young girl as "your little Frank Lloyd
Wright."

Architecture professionals offer advertisers another significant
advantage: shock value. Representations of women in business, medicine, and law have become advertising clichés, but the depiction of
women architects in the 1980s is still novel. Readers experience cognitive dissonance when they see a woman presenting an architecture
project to a client or giving orders at a job site, yet such representations
are not beyond the realm of acceptability. Advertisers apparently select
female architects first to grab attention and then to encourage the reader
to view the female ad-architect as a generic "professional," not as a member of a particular occupation with a long history and unique characteristics.

Few ads specifically address the relatively small audience of actual
practitioners. Specialized jargon is avoided. When using quotations by
famous architects, copy editors select well-known examples that may be
familiar to the general public, but can in any case stand on their own
merit. Thus a fashion spread on a woman architect in *Working Woman*
includes the statement, "Less is more when it comes to what you carry
in your [hand] bag," repeating the famous epigram of Mies van der Rohe.
Similarly, an ad for Epson Computers incorporates Louis Sullivan's
famous line in the ad-architect's statement, "I admire a design that sat-
isfies function without ignoring form." Several ad campaigns co-opt the
term "architect" to evoke appealing associations. Architects build,
design, create; they shape our environment. Similarly, women consumers are urged to be in charge of their own appearance; Ralph Lauren
ads challenge women to design "the architecture of a beautiful face,"
and *Working Woman* urges readers to "architect an image."

Advertisers address architects directly in professional journals such
as *Progressive Architecture* and *Domus*. Not surprisingly, professional ads
are filled with representations of practitioners. Also, not surprisingly,
almost all are white males; neither female ad-architects nor real female
practitioners are common in professional journals. Ads here depict
women in three main roles. First, they appear as sex objects or adorn-
ments; significantly, examples of this *retardataire* role are most commonly
found in European publications even though Europe has traditionally

offered female practitioners more opportunities than has the United States.[15] Second, women are shown as interior designers carrying fabric swatches and furniture catalogs. Third, women occur in ambiguous roles and can be variously identified as secretaries, friends, or architects.

The deliberate omission of women in professional ads reflects the realities of the profession in the 1980s. Women make up only a small percentage of practitioners. Furthermore, they are generally not in high-level positions and are thus less likely to have the authority to purchase the products advertised. Ads in architecture journals confirm and per-petuate the image and reality of architecture as an old-boys' club.

Advertisers dealing with the general public, then, find representa-tions of architects extremely versatile. Architects can be identified eas-ily by a few unobtrusive icons; they can be depicted in a variety of indoor and outdoor settings; they can promote either tools of the trade or upscale goods; they can project a macho, hard-hat image or champagne sensibilities; they can wear trendy designer fashions or conservative suits. Most importantly, they can be female. Advertisers use women ad-architects as attention-grabbers and as representative professionals.

Print advertisements depict a distinct personality profile for the architect in the 1980s. To the lay person, architects of both genders are young white professionals, upwardly mobile and affluent. They are styl-ish individualists, discriminating in taste, adventuresome in action; they work independently, collaborating only from positions of authority.

Architecture practitioners should take advantage of advertising images. By understanding these images, architects can improve interac-tion both between themselves and the lay public and between profes-sionals of different gender. For example when Morris*Aubry Architects realized that the image of heroic misfit promoted by advertisements was a liability with clients, the firm published its own advertisements stress-ing a commitment to such unheroic issues as budget restrictions, user satisfaction, and regulatory approval.

The positive image of women professionals in advertisements should also be exploited. In ads, female practitioners run their own offices, command work crews, and openly display their well-deserved success. They are consummate professionals. Such a contrived portrait is naturally misleading. It does not deal with actual working practices, with negative aspects of the profession, or with any of the social issues inherent in architectural problems. Yet, this idealized, popular image does more for women in architecture than many affirmative action plans. Bombarded with images of female architects in advertisements, the public gradually is becoming more comfortable with women architects. The same is not true within the field of architecture itself; inclusion of more and positive depictions in the ads in architecture journals would likewise enhance the status of women among their professional peers.

Internally, the profession remains inhospitable to women. A recent article read by career-oriented women[16] listed architecture as one of the ten worst careers for women, noting that one out of four female practitioners would choose a different profession if she could start over. Yet externally, in the world of printed advertisements, women architects are repeatedly seen as successful and valuable contributors to the profession. Each positively depicted female ad-architect not only promotes a particular product, she also promotes women's place in architecture.

Notes

1. The AIA's 1985 update of the comprehensive survey on women in the profession states that women make up only 5.9 percent of contemporary practitioners. Using diverse criteria, other surveys give similarly low percentages ranging from 6.7 percent (U.S. Department of Labor, 1981) to 11 percent (*Working Woman* 11, July 1986: 73).

2. The same advertisements are repeated in several journals. Including repetitions, 40 percent of the ad-architects in general interest magazines (*Newsweek* and the *New Yorker*) are women. In specialized women's magazines (*Working Woman* and *Glamour*), the percentage is in the 90s. These figures are based on a survey of journals published from 1980 to 1986. Depictions of architects also occur in other types of periodicals, e.g., business and homemakers' magazines.

3. In the 1980s male architects appear in the movies "Tempest," "Hannah and Her Sisters," "That's Life," "Bedroom Window," "Electric Dreams," "Hanky Panky," and several others. They are also primary characters in the recent books *The House* by Tracy Kidder and *Paradise* by Donald Barthelme. Women architects are portrayed in the television movies "Anatomy of a Seduction" and "Sins," in the situation comedy "Family Ties," and in several commercials.

4. Depictions of actual practitioners strengthen the advertisers' message. Real professionals hawk *TV Guide*, Rums of Puerto Rico, Clarks Shoes, and the Donatello Hotel. Safeway Stores photographed architect Toby Levy, AIA, of San Francisco for its campaign "I work an honest day. I want an honest deal." In some instances, advertisers provide an illusion of actual endorsement by using quotations without identifying the architect.

5. Advertisers frequently use different models in the same layout to reach different audiences. Thus Michelob runs an ad with a white woman architect in general magazines like *Newsweek* and a black woman architect in the same stage set for *Ebony*.

6. Figures are based on the AIA's 1983 membership survey: the mean age of male architects was forty-two years; of women, thirty-five years. While rare in advertisements, older architects are not unusual in films as evidenced by "The Tempest" and "That's Life."

7. In 1986, the average starting salary for a beginning architect was $16,200; for a lawyer, $31,000. In 1987, the beginning salary for doctors was $44,400. *Occupational Outlook Handbook 1988–1989* Bulletin 2300 (Washington, D.C.: U.S. Department of Labor, Bureau of Labor Statistics, April 1988), 60, 87, 131. Women in these professions generally earn below the average.

8. One such article stressed the need for appropriate professional clothes to justify the purchase of a $2,500 bleached-rhinoceros-skin suit for an important presentation; *Working Woman* 10 (September 1985): 149.

9. An ad for "Comfort Stride" pantyhose depicts a woman in a hard hat carrying rolled drawings as she climbs the stairs of a storage tank; she could be an engineer or a secretary. Borg-Warner uses a woman construction worker to demonstrate the light weight of its pipes.

10. *Working Woman* 10 (March 1985): 98–105.

11. On positioning and sex roles in advertising see Erving Goffman, *Gender Advertisements* (Cambridge: Harvard University Press, 1979).

12. On psychographics in advertising see William Meyers, *The Image Makers: Power and Persuasion on Madison Avenue* (New York: Times Books, 1984), 136; Rena Bartos, *The Moving Target: What Every Marketer Should Know About Women* (New York: The Free Press, 1982), 73–74, 111, 135, 254–58.

13. Leber Katz Partners Advertising surveyed the reaction to images of different professionals in 1982 and was surprised to find that lawyers ranked low in respect and confidence, while architects ranked high. This research was conducted for a Vantage cigarettes campaign. With surprise, Vice President Robert Hirsch noted, "The architect has become a sort of hero"; *Metropolitan Home* 15 (May 1983): 14; Letter to author, 26 March 1985.

14. Advertisers use psychographic research systems to target different markets. According to the VALS (Values and Life-Styles) system, representations of architects would appeal specifically to emulator-achievers, prosperous middle-class materialists who wield close to 50 percent of the nation's purchasing power (Meyers, 18–19, 219).

15. Andrea O. Dean. "Women in Architecture: Individual Profiles and a Discussion of Issues," *AIA Journal* 17 (January 1982): 47.

16. "Architecture" by Iris Cohen Selinger, in "The 10 Worst Careers for Women," *Working Woman* 11 (July 1986): 73.

17

A Feminist

Approach to

Architecture

Acknowledging Women's

Ways of Knowing

KAREN A. FRANCK

The qualities that seem to character-
ize women's ways of knowing and analyzing appear variously in
social–architectural research conducted by women, in alternative communities proposed by women, and in projects designed by women.[1] Evidence that such qualities exist or that they distinguish women from men
is suggestive at best. The test for this essay, however, is not in the scientific persuasiveness of the evidence but in the degree to which the
descriptions resonate with women's own experiences, in architecture
and in everyday life. One goal is to help women in architecture to identify qualities and concerns in themselves that are often unrecognized
or suppressed in architectural education, research, and practice. A second goal is to celebrate these qualities and concerns; a third is to work
toward a profession that is more hospitable to feminist practitioners
and that produces an environment more attuned to people's needs.[2]

"Knowing" is discussed here as an act of creating. We construct
what we know, and these constructions are deeply influenced by our
early experiences and by the nature of our underlying relationship to

the world. As the early experiences of women and men and their relationship to the world differ in significant ways, so too will their charac-
teristic ways of knowing and analyzing. Many writers in the past decade
have pointed out that women's underlying relationship to the world is
one of connection while men's is one of separation.[3] This fundamental
tenet of much feminist thought is based on object relations theory (as
expounded by Nancy Chodorow in *The Reproduction of Mothering*).
Chodorow holds that since the daughter is of the same gender as the
mother, development of the daughter's self-identity centers on attachment to the main parenting figure and thereby to the generalized "other"
and the world. In contrast, development of the son's self-identity requires
differentiation and separation from the mother, leading to separation
from the "other" and the world.

That masculinity is defined in terms of the denial of connection,
and that femininity is defined as self-in-relationship, has important implications for cognitive activities and hence for western science, philosophy, and architecture. Evelyn Fox Keller suggests in *Reflections on Gender
and Science* that the nature of science mirrors the nature of masculinity;
the scientific method requires the scientist's separation from, and dom-
ination of, the objects of research. Emotion and subjectivity, as qualities of connectedness, are demarcated from reason and objectivity, with
the former given little credence in scientific endeavors. As an alternative to this "static objectivity," Keller describes "dynamic objectivity."
This approach acknowledges and relies on the connectedness between
researcher and observed world, and is demonstrated in the work of the
geneticist Barbara McClintlock; her premise for research was to "listen
to what the material has to tell you" rather than to impose an answer on
it.[4]

In provocative works, Carol Gilligan has used the definition of the
feminine identity as self-in-relationship to interpret observed differences
between women and men in resolving moral dilemmas.[5] She finds that
women and girls draw upon a "reflective understanding of care" requiring that no one be hurt and that one respond to the needs of others,
whereas men and boys are concerned that everyone be treated fairly.
Gilligan calls the first, women's "ethic of care" and the second, men's
"ethic of justice."

Nancy Hartsock, in her article "The Feminist Standpoint," relates
the development of male self-identity to the masculinist tendency to
degrade everyday life and to value abstraction. The masculinity that boys
must achieve is an ideal not directly experienced in the home and fam-

ily but reached only by escaping into the masculine world of public life, which remains distant from the child's experience. Boys thus see two worlds: one "valuable, if abstract and deeply unattainable, the other useful and demeaning, if concrete and necessary."[6] In contrast, the female sense of self is achieved within the context of home and family, and hence embraces and values everyday life and experience.

Connectedness applies to analyzing as well as to knowing. Since analyzing is the activity of distinguishing between elements, it can easily lead to seeing distinctions as being divisions—to seeing elements that are different as being separate, distant, and disconnected. In the masculinist world view, based on separations, this is particularly true.[7]

The tendency to see only division and separation takes its most extreme form in dualistic thinking, where only two categories are posited in opposition to each other, and where one category is often valued more highly than the other. Nancy Hartsock suggests that the masculinist dualism between the abstract and the concrete is replicated in many other combative and hierarchical dualisms: ideal/real, stasis/change, culture/nature, man/woman. In her feminist materialism she sees variety, connectedness, continuity, and unity between manual and mental work as marking a new social synthesis. Sandra Harding similarly questions the dichotomous structures of culture/nature, mental/manual, and abstract/concrete. She sees an opportunity in feminist thinking to integrate what are traditionally seen as separate categories. She posits a feminist way of living and understanding that will unify the labor of hand, head, and heart. In addition, Harding advocates the valuation of change in her proposal for a feminist materialism, and she praises the instability of categories in feminist theory.[8]

These writings from recent feminist literature in psychoanalysis, psychology, philosophy, and philosophy of science suggest seven qualities that characterize feminine or feminist ways of knowing and analyzing: (1) an underlying connectedness to others, to objects of knowledge, and to the world, and a sensitivity to the connectedness of categories; (2) a desire for inclusiveness, and a desire to overcome opposing dualities; (3) a responsibility to respond to the needs of others, represented by an "ethic of care"; (4) an acknowledgment of the value of everyday life and experience; (5) an acceptance of subjectivity as a strategy for knowing, and of feelings as part of knowing; (6) an acceptance and desire for complexity; and (7) an acceptance of change and a desire for flexibility. These same characteristics appear in social/architectural research conducted by women, in utopian and alternative communities proposed by women, and in architectural projects designed by women.

Connectedness and Inclusiveness. —Synthesism, or the integration of categories, is one alternative to dualistic thinking.[9] Another, perhaps a prerequisite for greater connectedness, is to recognize the dualisms and other forms of categorization that exist and to study their origins, their status, and the consequences they have for everyday life, for research, and for design. Researchers in the field of environment and behavior are beginning to do this and to indicate how an unreflective categorization precludes the recognition of variety, complexity, and change.[10] One eventual consequence of such research should be the spurning of oppositional and hierarchical dualisms and the development of more inclusive, more complex, and more changeable categories.

Analysis of the categories used in urban theory, planning, and design is the hallmark of recent feminist analyses of the contemporary, designed environment in Great Britain and the United States. The writings of Susan Saegert, Ann Markusen, Linda McDowell, Suzanne MacKenzie, and Damaris Rose reveal the pervasive influence of the dualisms of public/private, city/suburb, work/home, and production/reproduction, which are habitually and unthinkingly aligned with each other and with men/women in urban theory and design.[11]

These dichotomies are applied in theory and in practice as if they were separate and unrelated; in fact, in each case, they are interdependent and overlapping. Industrial capitalism depends on the home/work, reproduction/production, and women/men divisions for the large-scale consumption of goods generated by the needs of separate households in suburban locations[12] and for the biological and psychological renewal of the wage labor force in the home setting.[13] Industrial capitalism helped to create and continues to enforce the spatial separations that accompany these categories in contemporary communities in the United States.

By examining the daily lives of women, it is possible to see that the simple dichotomies are not an accurate reflection of women's experience. The home has always been a place of work for women; women habitually frequent public settings; and the quality of idyllic retreat romantically associated with the suburban home is more myth than reality.[14] The ideology of separation between the spheres of public/private, men/women, and work/home makes everyday activities more difficult to pursue precisely because of the spatial distances that the ideology has generated.[15] In addition to revealing the existence and consequences of these dualisms, commentators have called for a greater degree of analytic synthesis between the categories and for a greater degree of overlap between the spatial domains that this dualistic thinking has generated in the built environment.

The desire for greater connectedness between different types of activities and the spaces to support them appears in many feminist visions of utopian or alternative communities. In Marge Piercy's utopian novel *Woman on the Edge of Time*, work takes place within walking distance of people's cottages and of all other centers of activity. Dolores

Dolores Hayden's proposal for reorganization of a typical suburban block through rezoning, rebuilding, and relandscaping, from Redesigning the American Dream, 1984. *At the top (in A) are ten single-family houses (1) on their private lots (2). Next (in B) are the same houses (1) but now with smaller private lots (2) after a backyard rehabilitation program has created a village green (3) at the heart of the block. Finally (in C) are the same houses (1), but with the village green (3) surrounded by a new zone (4) for childcare, elderly care, laundry, and food service, as well as new accessory apartments. A new sidewalk or arcade (5) rings the entire green, and new street trees (6) border the whole block. The village green can contain a play area, flower and vegetable gardens, and outdoor seating. The narrow ends of the block can be emphasized as collective entrances (with gates and keys for residents). In extremely dense situations, the central area (3) can be designed as an alley and parking area, if existing street parking and public transit are not adequate. Drawing by Dolores Hayden reproduced from Dolores Hayden,* Redesigning the American Dream: The Future of Housing, Work, and Family Life *(New York: W. W. Norton, 1984), courtesy of D. Hayden and W. W. Norton*

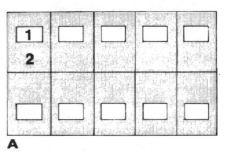

A

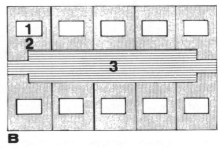

B

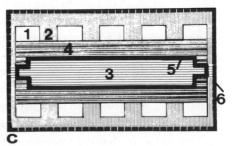

C

205

Hayden, in her proposal for the redesign of forty suburban houses into a community, connects social activities, wage work, and home life through the provision of on-site jobs, good public transportation, and shared services and facilities. Suzanne MacKenzie imagines a future where women themselves have integrated home and work by redesigning their homes into a combination of dwelling and workshop and by substituting the exchange of services for money.[16]

A closer spatial connection between activities currently separated is one way of reducing the extreme dichotomy between private and public domains. This dichotomy enforces the traditional sexual division of labor. Thus at the heart of any feminist alternative must be the goal of lessening the separation between public and private, and between wage work and home life. Piercy lessens the private/public split by envisioning small and highly localized communities where all residents know each other; there is no anonymous public realm. MacKenzie's vision also does away with the anonymous realm: home and local community become the domain for all daily activities. In Hayden's proposal, private yards are redesigned to be shared, and many services and some sources of employment are placed within the residential setting. The integration of services with housing, as a way of reducing the current distance between activities and between the private and public domains, is also advocated by Gerda Wekerle, Susan Saegert, and Jacqueline Leavitt.[17]

In designing, connectedness takes several forms. One form is a close relationship between designer and client or designer and user.[18] Designing from a feminist perspective is likely to blur role distinctions between designer and client and designer and user. This is the approach taken by Matrix, a group of feminist architects in England.[19]

A second form of connectedness is the desire for closer spatial or visual connections between spaces. The Matrix group has identified among its women clients an interest in connecting spaces and activities in buildings and in connecting the people who use the building. Thus, a waiting room in a community health center becomes a café so that women can meet and share experiences; in a community center, large windows in an interior wall allow people to see activities inside a workshop. The clients for Susana Torre's House of Meanings were also women. Each version of the house she designed for them creates a spatial continuity between spaces conventionally kept separate and distinct. Moreover, the house allows opposites (including private/public, individual/shared, outside/inside) to interact rather than to remain in opposition.[20] Thus, a third form of connectedness in designing is the integration of opposite types of spaces. A fourth type of connectedness is the integration of what are usually seen as opposing design approaches. Julia Robinson proposes a design process, called "design as exploration," that will create "a dialogue between the subjective and the objective, the intuitive and the rational."[21]

Ethic of Care and Value of Everyday Life. —These are prominent characteristics of the alternative communities proposed by women, and they appear in social and architectural research by women as early as the housing reforms of Catherine Bauer and Edith Elmer Wood. The attention given to issues of family life in early public housing is attributed to these reformers.[22] Similarly, Elisabeth Coit was paramountly concerned with the daily lives of families in her surveys and observations of conditions in New York public housing between 1938 and 1940.[23]

Subsequently, Jane Jacobs showed how people's everyday activities and needs were being ignored or frustrated by the large-scale, single-use, superblock developments so popular in urban renewal. Her concern was daily experience and the ways in which the designed environment could support and enhance that experience—a far cry from the abstract concepts and geometric site planning of urban renewal plans. More recently, researchers such as Clare Cooper have taken a similar approach: focusing on the everyday lives and perceptions of residents and comparing these with the intentions and expectations of architects.[24] Hayden's *Redesigning the American Dream* demonstrates a similar sensitivity, to daily life, particularly that of women and children and the elderly whose needs have long been ignored or misunderstood by planners and architects.

Attention to everyday activities and the ethic of care appear in women's design work as well. The winning entry in the recent New American House Competition, designed by Troy West and Jacqueline Leavitt, demonstrates a strong concern for the special needs of different kinds of parents and children, as well as a desire to bring neighbors together. Architects in the Matrix group draw upon their own experience and that of their clients so that daily experiences rather than abstract concepts become the source material for design. Eileen Gray and Lilly Reich designed furniture and spaces that were especially sensitive to mundane needs. Gray's acknowledgment of unmade beds, and eating or reading in bed, led her to design the first colored sheets! And her awareness of

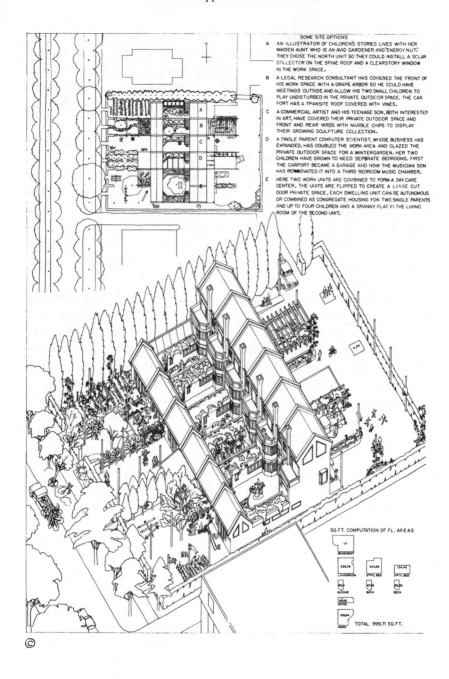

SOME SITE OPTIONS

A AN ILLUSTRATOR OF CHILDREN'S STORIES LIVES WITH HER MAIDEN AUNT WHO IS AN AVID GARDENER AND ENERGY NUT. THEY CHOSE THE NORTH UNIT SO THEY COULD INSTALL A SOLAR COLLECTOR ON THE SPINE ROOF AND A CLEARSTORY WINDOW IN THE WORK SPACE.

B A LEGAL RESEARCH CONSULTANT HAS COVERED THE FRONT OF HIS WORK SPACE WITH A GRAPE ARBOR SO HE COULD HAVE MEETINGS OUTSIDE AND ALLOW HIS TWO SMALL CHILDREN TO PLAY UNDISTURBED IN THE PRIVATE OUTDOOR SPACE. THE CAR PORT HAS A TRANSITE ROOF COVERED WITH VINES.

C A COMMERCIAL ARTIST AND HIS TEENAGE SON, BOTH INTERESTED IN ART, HAVE COVERED THEIR PRIVATE OUTDOOR SPACE AND FRONT AND REAR YARDS WITH MARBLE CHIPS TO DISPLAY THEIR GROWING SCULPTURE COLLECTION.

D A SINGLE PARENT COMPUTER SCIENTIST, WHOSE BUSINESS HAS EXPANDED, HAS DOUBLED THE WORK AREA AND GLAZED THE PRIVATE OUTDOOR SPACE FOR A WINTERGARDEN. HER TWO CHILDREN HAVE GROWN TO NEED SEPARATE BEDROOMS. FIRST THE CARPORT BECAME A GARAGE AND NOW THE MUSICIAN SON HAS RENOVATED IT INTO A THIRD BEDROOM MUSIC CHAMBER.

E HERE TWO WORK UNITS ARE COMBINED TO FORM A DAY CARE CENTER. THE UNITS ARE FLIPPED TO CREATE A LARGE OUT DOOR PRIVATE SPACE. EACH DWELLING UNIT CAN BE AUTONOMOUS OR COMBINED AS CONGREGATE HOUSING FOR TWO SINGLE PARENTS AND UP TO FOUR CHILDREN AND A GRANNY FLAT IN THE LIVING ROOM OF THE SECOND UNIT.

SQ. FT. COMPUTATION OF FL. AREAS

BASEMENT

236.78 LIVINGROOM   224.26 2ND FL BED   134.40 3RD FL BED

ALCOVE   BATH   DECK

SPINE

WORK   TOTAL 999.71 SQ.FT.

Guest alcove off the living room in House E-1027, Rocquebrune, France, 1926–1929, designed by Eileen Gray and Jean Badovici. Note adjustable bed table and storage for pillows and other items. Photograph courtesy of Eileen Gray Archives

(ON LEFT) First place, "A New American House" competition, 1984, Troy West and Jacqueline Leavitt. The task was to create six small units of urban housing (1000 square feet in each) that would be workplace, too, for at least one occupant of each unit. The workplaces, here, are approached from the street; the living units, from the alley. Connecting the workplace and the living area are linear kitchens that look out onto protected outdoor areas. Many of the 346 submissions to this competition were designed by women, and women comprised 36 percent of all who won awards. Drawing by Troy West

the ever-present need for storage generated ingenious designs, including drawers that pivot.[25]

The furniture of Lilly Reich, who collaborated with Mies van der Rohe, showed a similar attentiveness to human comfort; Reich's chairs featured backs contoured to the body while Mies's took idealized lines.[26] Margrit Kennedy lists as a female principle in architecture a greater emphasis on functional issues and a lesser emphasis on formal ones, and Jane Thompson makes the concern for human comfort and growth a goal of feminist architecture.

Value of Subjectivity and Feelings. —The acceptance of subjectivity as a strategy for knowing allows personal experience and knowledge to be sources of information and design. Many of Jane Jacobs's insights were drawn from her own experience of living on Hudson Street in Greenwich Village. In other instances, environmental autobiographies are used as a way for individuals, including architects, to become aware of their own preferences as these derive from life experiences. Cooper Marcus explores the deep-seated meanings of house and home by using Gestalt techniques whereby respondents role-play their own homes, speaking as their homes might speak.[27] In a recent course on architecture for utopia, I asked students to list their own complaints about current social and physical arrangements, to imagine more desirable arrangements, and to develop them in an illustrated narrative.[28] Robinson, in her proposed design process, presents a more systematic way of using personal experience in design—through making one's preconceptions conscious and using these preconceptions, and revisions to them, as sources for design ideas.

The importance of feelings (and, relatedly, of intimate relationships) is recognized in women's proposals for alternative communities. The attitudes commonly associated with mothering—expressiveness, caring, affection, attachment—are part of all relationships in Piercy's utopian community. Happiness, love, anger, conflict, and depression are all dealt with as openly and as considerately as possible. Many writers acknowledge the importance of informal, intimate, and caring relationships between people and favor designed settings and programs that reinforce such relationships.[29]

And it is the lack of emotion and lack of intimacy that Eileen Gray decried in modernism in 1929: "Modern designers have exaggerated the technological side. . . . Intimacy is gone, atmosphere is gone. . . . Formulas are nothing; life is everything. And life is mind and heart at the same time."³⁰

Value of Complexity and Flexibility. —Eileen Gray attributed this lack of intimacy to the substitution of simplification for simplicity. Women architects since then have voiced their desire for greater complexity. Margrit Kennedy lists complexity among her female principles in architecture; Sheila de Bretteville sees complexity and ambiguity as desirable design qualities because they undermine control and invite user participation.³¹ And Jane Thompson calls for an architecture that embraces both the aesthetic of the industrial age (valuing simplification) and the earlier aesthetic embodied in religion and magic (valuing complexity).

The desire for complexity is allied with an attention to multiple use, and more generally with awareness of change and the need for flexibility and transformation. Eileen Gray's understanding of the use of an object over time allowed her to design a table that could be used as coffee table, side table, or bed table. Flexibility or the anticipation of change also guided Lilly Reich's design of an open-plan apartment where she divided the apartment across the narrow dimension to give areas for rest, study, and meals; the furniture could be rearranged to change divisions or to unite the entire room. In contrast, Mies's open plan generated a hierarchical set of spaces, main and subsidiary spaces, for fixed functions: the living space could not serve as a minor space because of its central placement in the formal composition.³² Multiple use of space and transformation of space were guiding principles in Torre's House of Meanings and in West and Leavitt's New American House.

These qualities of connectedness, multiple use, flexibility, and complexity find expression in designing space as a matrix. The idea of the matrix fulfilling women's design proclivities is implied by several authors. De Bretteville identifies quilts and blankets as examples of women's work that grow over time, are organized with many centers, and do not have beginnings or ends. They are examples of designing a matrix.³³ Designing her House of Meanings as "matrix space" allowed Torre to achieve her objectives of overcoming opposing dualisms, of creating multifunctional spaces, and of combining completeness with the opportunity for transformation. Given the potential usefulness of the idea of matrix for women's concerns in architecture, it is fitting that the original meaning was uterus or womb, coming from the Latin word "mater" or mother. (Later it came to mean a place or medium in which something is produced or bred; most recently, the rectangular arrange-ment of quantities.)

Although this essay follows earlier feminist thinking in architec-ture and other fields, it is still only part of a fledgling effort to outline a feminist approach to architecture. Some of the qualities that a feminist approach to architecture might well encourage have been discussed in this essay. Other qualities that could be explored are cooperation and collaboration, organic systems of spatial organization and form-making, and metaphors based on hearing and touching (this last, to balance the exclusive reliance on the metaphor of vision in western philosophy and architecture).[34] Similarly, the activities of analyzing, proposing alterna-tive communities, and designing are only some of the activities of archi-tecture; others would include teaching and professional practice, and advocacy. At first glance, the qualities discussed here seem to apply to these other activities as well. I have noticed that my teaching has come to possess some of them and I see some of them reflected in the work of early women architects such as Eleanor Raymond and Mary Jane Col-ter, as well as in the concerns of more recent ones including Dolores Hayden and Joan Forrester Sprague.[35]

Finally, this essay has drawn entirely upon literature from and about western industrialized capitalist society. The qualities and concerns described may only be true of women in this society and of a limited segment of those women (those with economic and educational resources). One way for women to express their desire for greater and different forms of connectedness is to explore the qualities and con-cerns of women in other societies and in other circumstances.[36] If it is true that women in architecture in this society are less likely than men to be distanced from other people by perceived differences, and if it is true that we wish to overcome opposing dualities, then there is less to stop us from discovering both our similarities and our differences with women elsewhere in the world.[37]

Notes

1. Research for this essay was supported in part by a grant from the New Jersey Department of Higher Education, award number 87-990780-2494. I would like to thank my research assistant Nancy Bartlett for her help and Cathie Comerford for her encouragement. This essay is dedicated to these two young women in architecture and to others like them.

2. The spirit of this essay follows earlier proposals of female principles in architecture. See: Jane Thompson, "The World of Double Win," *Feminist Art Journal* (Fall 1976): 16–20 and Margrit Kennedy, "Toward a Rediscovery of Feminine Principles in Architecture and Planning," *Women's Studies International Quarterly* 4(1981): 75–81. Other feminist approaches to architecture focus on the importance of understanding how the designed environment oppresses women and the need for environments that respond to women's needs. See: Leslie Kanes Weisman, "Women's Environmental Rights," *Heresies* 3 (1981): 6–8; Nunzia Rondanini, "Architecture and Social Change," *Heresies* 3 (1981): 3–5; and Jos Boys, "Is There a Feminist Analysis of Architecture?" *Built Environment* 10 (1984): 25–34. The framework described in the present essay complements and can encompass these other approaches. Discussions of feminine or feminist aesthetics in other fields may have implications for architecture. See, for example: Gisela Ecker, ed., *Feminist Aesthetics*, trans., Harriet Anderson (Boston: Beacon Press, 1985) and Naomi Schor, *Reading in Detail* (New York: Methuen, 1987).

3. Dorothy Dinnerstein, *The Mermaid and the Minotaur* (New York: Harper and Row, 1976); Nancy Chodorow, *The Reproduction of Mothering* (Berkeley: University of California Press: 1978); Carol Gilligan, "Women's Place in Man's Life Cycle," *Harvard Educational Review* 49 (November 1979): 431–46; Evelyn Fox Keller, *Reflections on Gender and Science* (New Haven: Yale University Press, 1985); Nancy Hartsock, "The Feminist Standpoint" in *Discovering Reality*, eds., Sandra Harding and Merrill B. Hintikka (Dordrecht, Holland: D. Reidel, 1983).

4. Keller, *Gender and Science*, 138. Others have proposed that connectedness with the object to be known is the most developed form of "women's knowing." See Mary F. Belenky, Blythe Clincy, Nancy Goldberger, and Jill Tarule, *Women's Ways of Knowing* (New York: Basic Books, 1986).

5. Gilligan, "Women's Place." See also Carol Gilligan, *In a Different Voice* (Cambridge: Harvard University Press, 1982).

6. Hartsock, 297.

7. Keller contrasts this propensity with the approach of Barbara McClintlock, who was willing to accept complexity and connectedness and who saw anomalous evidence as indicative not of disorder but of a larger and more complex pattern.

8. Sandra Harding, "The Instability of the Analytical Categories of Feminist Theory," *Signs* 11 (1986): 645–64. See also: Hilary Rose, "Hand, Brain and Heart: A Feminist Epistemology for the Natural Sciences," *Signs* 9 (1983): 73–90.

9. Lynda Glennon, "Synthesism: A Case of Feminist Methodology," in *Beyond Method*, ed., Gareth Morgan (Beverly Hills: Sage Publications, 1983).

10. Karen A. Franck, "A Call for Examining Categories in Environmental Design Research," in *The Costs of Not Knowing*, eds., Jean Wineman, Richard Barnes, and Craig Zimring (Washington, D.C.: Environmental Design Research Association, 1986); Karen A. Franck, "When Type is Stereotype (and What to Do About It)" (Paper presented at University of Minnesota conference "Type

and the Possibilities of Convention," May 1987 in Minneapolis); Eileen Bradley and Maxine Wolfe, "Where do the 65-year-old Latina Jewish Lesbians Live?" in *Public Environments*, eds., Joan Harvey and Don Henning (Washington, D.C.: Environmental Design Research Association, 1987).

11. Susan Saegert, "Masculine Cities and Feminine Suburbs," in *Women and the American City*, eds., C. R. Stimpson, E. Dixler, M. J. Nelson, and K. B. Yatrakis (Chicago: University of Chicago Press, 1981); Ann Markusen, "City Spacial Structure, Women's Household Work and National Policy," in *Women and the American City*, eds., C. R. Stimpson et al (Chicago: University of Chicago Press, 1981); L. McDowell, "Towards an Understanding of the Gender Division of Urban Space," *Environment and Planning D* 1 (1983): 59–72; Suzanne MacKenzie and Damaris Rose, "Industrial Change, the Domestic Economy and Home Life," in *Redundant Spaces in Cities and Regions*, eds., J. Anderson, S. Duncan, and R. Hudson (London: Academic Press, 1983).

12. R. Miller, "The Hoover in the Garden" *Environment and Planning D*, 1 (1983): 73–87.

13. McDowell, "Towards an Understanding"; MacKenzie and Rose, "Industrial Change."

14. Leonore Davidoff, Jean L'Esperance and Howard Newby, "Landscape with Figures," in *The Rights and Wrongs of Women*, eds., Juliet Mitchell and Ann Oakley (New York Penguin, 1976); Saegert, "Masculine Cities and Feminine Suburbs."

15. Dolores Hayden, "What Would a Non-sexist City be Like?" in *Women and the American City*; Dolores Hayden, *Redesigning the American Dream* (New York: Norton, 1984); Karen A. Franck, "Social Construction of the Physical Environment: The Case of Gender," *Sociological Focus* 18 (1985): 143–70.

16. Marge Piercy, *Woman on the Edge of Time* (New York: Fawcett, 1976); Hayden, "What Would a Non-sexist City be Like?"; Suzanne MacKenzie, "No One Seems to Go to Work Anymore," *Canadian Women's Studies* 5 (1985): 5–8.

17. Jacqueline Leavitt, "The Shelter Service Crisis and Single Parents," in *The Unsheltered Woman*, ed., E. L. Birch (New Brunswick, N.J.: Center for Urban Policy Research, 1985); Gerda Wekerle "Neighborhoods that Support Women," *Sociological Focus* 18 (1985): 79–95; Susan Saegert "The Androgenous City," *Sociological Focus* 18 (1985): 79–95.

18. Jane Thompson ("The World of Double Win") refers to women designers' empathy with the user; Margrit Kennedy ("Toward a Rediscovery of Feminine Principles") suggests that one female principle in architecture is to be more user-oriented than designer-oriented.

19. Frances Bradshaw, "Working with Women," in *Making Space*, ed., Matrix (London: Pluto Press, 1984).

20. Susana Torre, "Space as Matrix," *Heresies* 3 (1981): 51–52. Elsewhere, Torre contrasts this view of opposites-as-complementary with the more prevailing belief in their irreconcilability. See: Susana Torre, "The Pyramid and the Labyrinth,"

in *Women in American Architecture: A Historic and Contemporary Perspective*, ed., Susana Torre (New York: Whitney Library of Design, 1977).

21. Julia Robinson, "Design as Exploration," *Design Studies* 7 (April 1986): 67–78. See also Julia Robinson and Stephen Weeks, *Programming as Design* (Minneapolis: School of Architecture and Landscape Architecture, University of Minnesota, 1983).

22. Eugenie Birch, "Women-made America," in *The American Planner*, ed., D. Krueckberg (New York: Methuen, 1983).

23. Mary Otis Stevens, "Struggle for Place," in *Women in American Architecture*.

24. Jane Jacobs, *The Death and Life of Great American Cities* (New York: Random House, 1961); Clare Cooper, *Easter Hill Village* (New York: Free Press, 1975). While Cooper's approach is now fairly common in environment-behavior research, her book was an early and influential example.

25. Jacqueline Leavitt, "A New American House," *Women and Environments* 7 (1985): 14–16; Deborah Nevins, "Eileen Gray," *Heresies* 3 (1981): 67–71; J. Stewart Johnson, *Eileen Gray* (London: Debrett's Peerage Ltd. and The Museum of Modern Art, 1979). Johnson points out the close resemblance between Joe Colombo's 1968 design of pivoting drawers and Gray's small chest, published in 1939. See also: Peter Adams, *Eileen Gray: Architect/Designer* (New York: Harry N. Abrams, 1987).

26. Deborah Dietsch, "Lilly Reich," *Heresies* 3 (1981): 73–76.

27. Clare Cooper Marcus, "Home-as-Haven, Home-as-Trap," in *The Spirit of Home*, ed., Patrick Quinn and Robert Benson (Washington, D.C.: Association of Collegiate Schools of Architecture, 1986). Cooper Marcus is currently writing a book based on this research.

28. Elsewhere in the field of architecture, the personal narrative is being used as a way to generate design. See, for example: John Hejduk, *Mask of Medusa* (New York: Rizzoli, 1985). Misuse of this approach can become purely narcissistic, especially when it is not coupled with an ethic of care (and the empathy that this entails).

29. Hayden, "What Would a Non-sexist City be Like?"; Wekerle, "Neighborhoods that Support Women"; MacKenzie, "No One Seems to Go to Work Anymore"; Saegert, "The Androgenous City"; Leavitt, "A New American House."

30. Deborah Nevins, trans., "From Eclecticism to Doubt," *Heresies* 3 (1981): 72.

31. Sheila de Bretteville, "A Reexamination of the Design Arts from the Perspective of a Woman Designer," *Women and the Arts* 11 (1974): 115–23.

32. Dietsch, "Lilly Reich."

33. See also: Lucy Lippard, "Centers and Fragments," in *Women in American Architecture*.

34. Evelyn Fox Keller and Christine Grontkowski, "The Mind's Eye" in *Discovering Reality*.

35. Doris Cole, *Eleanor Raymond* (Cranbury, N.J.: Associated University Presses, 1981); Virginia L. Grattan, *Mary Colter: Builder Upon the Red Earth* (Flagstaff, Ariz.: Northland Press, 1980); Dolores Hayden, Gail Dubrow, and Carolyn Flynn, *The Power of Place: Los Angeles* (Los Angeles: The Power of Place, 1985), available from Graduate School of Architecture and Urban Planning, University of California; Joan Forrester Sprague, *A Manual on Transitional Housing* (Boston: Women's Institute for Housing and Economic Development, 1986).

36. The idea that women have a desire for greater connectedness to ideas, people, and nature is developed by Catherine Keller, *From a Broken Web* (Boston: Beacon Press, 1986). A more global view of feminism is emerging, as evidenced by recent comparisons between different cultures. See Susan Bassnett, *Feminist Experiences* (Winchester, Mass.: Allen and Unwin, 1986) and Kumari Jayawardena, *Feminism and Nationalism in the Third World* (London: Zed Books/Kali for Women, 1986).

37. I appreciate comments from Setha Low and Jody Gibbs that inspired this conclusion.

PART IV.

ENVISIONING

FUTURE

ROLES

Introduction

Long before most of us heard
about Julia Morgan in the past, we knew about Chloethiel Woodard
Smith in the present; whenever the dearth of women architects was discussed, her name came up. To understand this stalwart professional's
stand against gender labeling, we must consider the possibility that having been for years automatically classified as a "woman architect" she
may have been denied full appreciation simply as an excellent architect: dedicated, innovative, and durable.

Rochelle Martin, calling architecture "the difficult path" for women,
believes that women are marginal in architecture, both quantitatively
and substantively, and will not be legitimate members of the profession
as long as this marginality remains. But she suggests that marginal people of both sexes can more readily question the assumptions, standards,
and practices of the profession. She envisions a new kind of professional—male and female alike—emerging from the questioning brought
by women.

Denise Scott Brown describes her own difficult path when, in mid-career, she married a colleague and saw him become a star, to some extent through their joint work and the work of their firm. Her experiences have led her to formulate an interpretation of sexism and the star system in architecture. She acknowledges that her interpretation is speculative, but few are likely to dispute it. We can wonder, with her, how her theory might be updated in another dozen years. Will the same star system still prevail? Will the same patterns of sexism at the upper levels of the profession still exist?

Matilda McQuaid, first archivist for the new AIA collection on women in architecture, demonstrates that looking to the past is one way of building a better future. Although the history of women in the field is relatively young, the growing treasury of books, photographs, portfolios, letters, and articles is in rich measure responsible for a climate of opinion increasingly aware of the significance of women's contributions. The record shows ever more persuasively that architecture is indeed a place for women.

Anne Vytlačil points out that the most unabashed instances of discrimination toward women in the schools of architecture are a thing of the past, but she sees more subtle forms of sexism operating today. If women in school now have more subtle problems, they also have more promising prospects. Vytlačil suggests that "women's tendency to approach design issues with greater flexibility and greater aesthetic tolerance for social implications" may be peculiarly suited to contemporary practice. Women may find that their "particular ability to adapt and accommodate," says Vytlačil, gives them a "competitive edge" in this constantly changing field.

18

Architects

without Labels

The Case against All

Special Categories

CHLOETHIEL WOODARD SMITH

When I was invited to submit an essay for this book, I initially said no. "I am afraid I must express my dissent," I replied. "Fragmentation of the profession into categories based on sex (or race, color, creed, or previous condition of servitude) seems wrong to me. I do not believe it will serve the profession as a whole or the best interests of the individual members."

But then I agreed to write my dissenting opinion. Surely I should be able to explain why I did not think that the word "architect" should be modified by "woman," or by any of the currently recognized minorities—Afro-American, Hispanic, American Indian, Asian, Pacific Islander, or Aleut. (Increasing pressures for homosexual "rights" may someday add new categories.) Such fragmentation is undesirable for the profession, I believe, in that members of the separate groups may tend to think of themselves primarily as belonging to the subgroup and only secondarily as belonging to the profession as a whole. Such fragmentation is also undesirable for the individual, in that those who declare themselves "special" seem to be calling attention to themselves simply for becoming architects, regardless of the quality of work they may then do as architects.

I am a woman and I have practiced architecture for many years. I am called a "woman architect" and I have disliked that title—I have resented it—for its implication that women have some physical or mental impediment they have remarkably overcome in managing to practice architecture. I do not object to the label "woman" in other respects. I have always enjoyed my role as a woman—as a wife, mother, and grandmother—but I do not see any reason why this role should be confused with my professional role.

The more militant feminist movements came along after I started to practice architecture. I have not participated in group activities to seek special consideration in the profession just because I am a woman. I have refused the many requests to write or speak about how I was discriminated against. (I do not think I was.) I have avoided joining women's architectural associations or committees. I have tried to be as good an architect as I was capable of being. I have tried to serve the profession. I do not find justification for more than one professional organization.

There were women students in the two undergraduate and graduate architecture schools I attended. But we never considered ourselves a group apart. Men and women alike were dedicated to an exciting profession and we weren't very interested in politics. In the summer I worked in the offices of architects who took me to lunch with other architects and took me to their jobs under construction; sometimes I was left for the day to watch working drawings get translated into three dimensions—sometimes details I had done. When I went to another city for graduate work, friends wrote to architects there and they took me to see their offices and jobs. These experiences and many since that time did not prepare me to fight for "rights" or seek special consideration because I was a woman. I did not feel I needed special consideration.

It will come as no surprise, therefore, that I take the negative side in the following debate: "Resolved: women have been neglected in the architectural profession and they must fight to establish their qualifications as architects and to increase their numbers greatly."

Let me begin with the AIA's Women in Architecture Committee and its extensive report issued in 1983. This report puts primary emphasis on problems that seem to be the fault of men (who do not allow full representation of women in the profession, do not pay them as much as men, do not advance them to high positions as rapidly as men, and also behave in ways that alienate women from the AIA). But blaming men does not seem to be a step in the right direction. It is perhaps not coincidental that this 1983 *Report on the Status of Women in the Profession* is mostly concerned with women employees and has little discussion of women as principals.

Why not do as the AIA's Minority Resources Committee did in its 1984 Public Policy Statement, saying merely that the "architectural profession and the AIA are entirely and equally open to all persons regardless of sex, age, race, color, religion or national origin"? Legislation would seem to have taken care of these matters and further affirming would seem to be unnecessary. (I was surprised recently to receive a letter from a federal department with "an equal opportunity employer" printed on the envelope. If they were not that, I would think, they would be in real trouble.)

Among the programs put forward by the Women in Architecture Committee are architectural licensing seminars "to help young women practitioners achieve this important step in career advancement." (I question the use of the word "practitioner" since one must be licensed in order to "practice" architecture.) For many years, however, there have been programs to prepare applicants for registration exams. Both women and men have participated. There are no limitations on the sex of applicants eligible to take these exams. The statement that women are "dramatically underrepresented in the ranks of registered architects" implies that women have somehow been prevented from becoming registered. Yet it is noted in the report that registered architects are much more likely to rank in the higher income brackets. Why, then, do women not rush to take the exams and become registered architects as soon as possible? Do *they*, perhaps, believe they are handicapped in some way and would find it especially difficult to pass the exams? To accept the label "woman architect" is to accept the idea of a handicap. From this follows the need to blame someone else for one's status, real or imagined, and the need to depend on someone else for deliverance.

There is wide variation in the capabilities of those who pass the registration exams, whether women or men. The determination of what skills, what knowledge, what capabilities are essential for the practice of architecture is a difficult task, but if we are to define an architect we must somehow find a way to determine whether an applicant can qualify. Since it is assumed that women can qualify equally with men, is there any justification whatsoever for a special designation as a "registered woman architect"? Do women want special exams for the disadvantaged, of the kind suggested by some colleges?

While it is possible (and necessary) to test a person for professional qualification as an architect, I think it is impossible (and unnecessary) to differentiate between the qualities possessed by female and male architects. We can scarcely describe great architecture. How, then, can we expect to set forth the characteristics that define a great architect—let alone the characteristics that might be attributed to sexual differences?

Some say that women architects are different from men—that they are more sensitive, have a deeper understanding of life, are more human, have a more profound knowledge of space, and possess many other special qualities. Some say that they design better residences. Some even say that they design better kitchens because they understand cooking. But if participation in cooking were a prerequisite for designing the place in which to cook, then a man who cooks should be able to design a better kitchen than a woman who does not cook. Is it significant that the Women in Architecture Committee does not address these complex issues? I suggest that we do not know enough as yet to create such check lists for each sex. I suggest further that we would do a great disservice to the men who are our colleagues by not allowing them the possibility of being as "human" and "sensitive" and "understanding" as our species is capable of being.

Parenthetically, the public perception of "an architect" is interesting in that the word is frequently used to describe someone who is not a designer of buildings and in charge of their construction, but is the designer of policies and in charge of their implementation—the architect of our foreign policy, the architect of our fiscal policy, the architect of our criminal justice system, etc. Have we ever seen the words "woman architect" in connection with a policy, even though women are increasingly sitting in the seats of power in many areas of public and private activity?

If women architects' differences from men could be clearly defined, and were deemed to be good differences capable of leading to the advancement of the art and science of architecture, perhaps a high-powered public relations firm could launch a major campaign to persuade prospective clients or employers that their successes in architecture would be greatly increased if they hired women. Clients and employers would then rush to hire women; and more modest programs to promote increases in the numbers of women, in their salaries, and in their participation in the AIA would not be needed. Or are we to wait for clients and architectural firms to respond to feelings of guilt that they have not given women their "just due"? That could take a very long time. It could take a very long time even to define "just due." As a third alternative, are we to hold out for the goal of having women be 50 percent of all architects because women are 50 percent of the population? Attempts to relate employment goals to percentages of minorities in the population have been made, but not without problems.

At one point I thought it might be amusing to include a little game with my essay. I would collect a series of small photos of buildings— each numbered, but none identified with the name of the architect. The rules of the game would be simple. The winner would be the one who correctly identified all the women-designed buildings. If there were one or more winners, the losers would buy the winners drinks. If all players scored 100 percent, there would be no free drinks, but since this result would prove the existence of recognizable characteristics in the buildings done by women architects, someone would surely bring forth a bottle to celebrate.

Ah, but who would select the buildings for my little game? If I did, someone would be certain to say that I favored the women in some way because I am a woman. If I did not do the selecting, the scales would be considered unbalanced in some other way. If a committee selected the buildings, each submission of photos by committee members would undoubtedly require a test vote and—depending on the results—produce a demand for more representative committee members on the other (male or female) side.

In 1986, I received a letter from a university describing a proposed archive devoted to the work of women architects and including the following:

We will collect photographs and drawings of architectural and art work, as well as personal information, letters, documents, written works and audiovisual formats. The collection will contain executed or project works of independent practitioners, of employees in architectural firms, of teams with women participants and any related archival material. The scope of the archives will be international and will include work from the beginning of women's involvement in architecture in any capacity up to the present time.[1]

The selection of works by employees of firms and by members of teams would seem to be particularly difficult tasks. Also, if the archives are to include work from the beginning of women's involvement in architecture, are we to go back to caves and lake dwellings? The time and effort required for all of this does not appear to be justified. Carefully selected material on *architecture* as we know it today (and including our best buildings, not just those by women) would seem to be preferable. The three most recent polls on outstanding architecture of the past seem to show that the most significant works of architecture in our history are overwhelmingly those done by men.[2] Would it serve the profession of architecture as a whole to collect and publicize only buildings done by women?

The recently opened National Building Museum in the nation's capital is "devoted solely to the building arts whose programs would contribute to improving the built environment of America." It is an exciting new institution that should be welcomed by all architects as well as by all others involved in improving the quality of life in the United States. Would the overall goals of this institution be served by dividing its programs into those for women and/or minorities? Conversely, would a proliferation of museums devoted to the work of special groups serve the national interest of improving the built environment throughout the country?

The new building for the Canadian Center for Architecture, now under construction in Montreal and scheduled to open in 1988, has been designed "to make a case for architecture, to make people aware of what they have as their heritage . . . ," as the *New York Times* describes the purposes of the Center. Would this Center "make a case for architecture" if it limited itself to architecture by any one sex or minority?

As I write this essay, the current issue of the AIA's *Memo* has two important articles by AIA presidents—a 1986 year-end report by the retiring president, John A. Busby, Jr., and a statement looking forward to 1987 by the incoming president, Donald J. Hackl. I am delighted that neither article mentions women (or minority) architects, or architecture by women (or minorities). Perhaps both omissions were oversights, but I hope not. I hope that the profession will heed the words of the Institute's recent statement calling for a fundamental shift in the AIA's direction "from a primary concern for architects to a primary concern for architecture—from a service-oriented association to a knowledge-based national institute concerned with the advancement of the art and science of architecture and the advocacy of design excellence."[3]

As we look ahead to the twenty-first century it would be stimulating to review all of the twentieth century—evaluating the progress that the full profession has made in achieving the *well*-built environment and in learning more about the impact that the settings for life have on life itself. I would like to propose, for the year 2000, a great exhibit of

Architecture by Architects, to be held in the National Building Museum and to be accompanied by a major book on One Hundred Years of United States Architecture. Women would be represented in that exhibition and book, but they would be "architects" and not "women architects."

I would like to propose, too, that the final ten years of the twentieth century be designated the Decade of the Architect and a series of special programs be scheduled to challenge all of those responsible for creating the setting for life. Women would be involved in these programs, but they would not be the only "human" and "sensitive" and "understanding" members of the profession to be engaged in the search for a finer quality of life.

With the greatly expanded role of women in the workplace in all fields, now and in the future, it will be less and less justifiable to single out women for special attention. The current celebration of women in architecture will, I hope, be viewed as the ill-advised and obsolete celebration I believe it to be—a curiosity left over from the days when women thought they needed special recognition.

I cannot know whether I have won this debate that is the subject of my essay. Perhaps that depends on the sexes of the judges. Let it be recorded, however, that an "architect" and not a "woman architect" has proposed to do away henceforth with all modifiers, and has proposed an alternative celebration for all architects.

Notes

1. Virginia Polytechnic Institute and State University (International Archive of Women in Architecture organized by Milka Bliznakov, professor of architecture and urban design).

2. None of the following lists of significant works of architecture included any buildings designed by women. In 1976, the *AIA Journal* reported on an informal poll of a group of practitioners, historians, and critics, who nominated a total of thirty proud achievements of American architecture over the previous 200 years. In 1982, celebrating the first 125 years of the AIA, the Institute honored six outstanding buildings built during that time. In 1985, honoring 100 years of the AIA College of Fellows, the Fellows selected the ten best buildings of that century.

3. "Shift in AIA Priorities," *AIA Journal* 71 (April 1982): 16.

19

Out of

Marginality

Toward a New Kind

of Professional

ROCHELLE MARTIN

An average of one hundred persons a year over the past decade, roughly one-quarter of them women, earned the doctorate in architecture and environmental design. I am one of this group; my dissertation, completed in 1986, is titled "The Difficult Path: Women in Architecture." Although it is impossible to compress five years of research and 162 pages of dissertation into this brief essay, I can describe some of my findings and suggest where women now find themselves on this still-difficult path.

First, a word about my own history and my decision to pursue this subject. When I began to study architecture, I fantasized that this career would be socially significant and at the same time would involve personal growth and creative expression. My previous experience gave me every confidence that I could accomplish my goals. My "consciousness" was so low that I did not perceive either the overt or subtle discrimination occurring in school.

My first foray into the professional world was a part-time job during my senior year with a small firm run by a former professor. The office consisted of the principal, another architect, and two women students. The four of us would often lunch together comfortably. I was convinced that this was the real world of the profession, contradicting the observations of one of my professors that as a woman I would have difficulty finding a job and that if employed I would feel isolated from all others in the office.

When the dean asked me to teach an architectural history class, I accepted with pleasure; I would be able to integrate my education in cultural and social history with my training in architecture. But now my sanguine perceptions began to change. I was told by male colleagues not to "waste" a good grade on women students because they were "just cute little things who would only end up as wives." I was also told by male colleagues that unless an individual made a "total commitment," the person would not make a "good" architect. Unless this standard was maintained, professional excellence would suffer. During these years from 1975 to 1978, I saw women students ignored, patronized, and discouraged from pursuing the profession.

These experiences led me to a conscious search for the roots of women's professional identity. What does it mean to be a woman in architecture? Are women architects part of the community of architects? What kind of human being does the profession nourish?

Concentrated work on my dissertation began in 1982 when I interviewed forty women architects between the ages of twenty-six and sixty. From this group, I selected six for additional interviews.[1] Covering education, professional experiences, and the relationship of work to personal life, these interviews provide a detailed picture of the problems and satisfactions of women in the profession. Several interwoven themes appear frequently in these discussions: belonging, image, and ambivalence.

Women continually express a lack of confirmation as architects; they lack the sense of belonging that accompanies an accepted and welcome member of the professional community. From their first jobs, when it was truly "an oddity" to be a woman *and* a draftsman or architect, they always felt "different." They did not relate to the women; they did not relate to the men. This sense of being an outsider has colored the professional life of women architects and profoundly affected identity, performance, and achievement.

In architecture a collegial atmosphere is essential. Work is often organized in teams, and cooperation and communication among team members is crucial. The team is like a family; when team members have difficulties establishing rapport, it affects both individual and team performance. Women tend to feel that men are afraid to get really close to them, and that this inevitably affects their work, denying them the working relationship needed to do their best.[2]

Acceptance and support of supervisors and employers are essential for professional advancement. But women find it difficult to obtain the attention and help needed to advance in the firm. They are not part of the old boys' network and do not have the same opportunity as men to have older members of the firm take them under their wing.[3]

Employers frequently assign to women small jobs that do not challenge ability or increase experience. A woman may not realize until long afterward (or may deny it even then) that having been offered the projects that were "the most fun" or gave her the most independence actually limited her potential and restricted her ability to attract large projects when on her own.

Professional identity, the internalization of a professional image that becomes a significant aspect of one's self-concept, is derived from standards established by the professional elite and from the organizations and institutions associated with it.[4] For the architect, official standards consist of the degree and the professional registration. Membership in professional organizations also links the individual to the professional establishment, enabling the individual to learn the appropriate roles and required behavior of the professional as well as the shared values, attitudes, and assumptions of the profession. But are these roles appropriate to women, and are these values shared by women?

Architects, like other professionals, subscribe to the "mystique of the expert": individual practitioners are considered strong, independent, and all-knowing, having specialized knowledge unknowable to the lay person. For women architects, establishing credibility as experts is one of the most problematic areas of professional identity. Women must accommodate themselves to the male-determined standards or be found lacking in the qualities attributed to a professional.[5] In situations with colleagues, clients, and construction workers, women architects continually encounter stereotypes of women as less competent than men. For many women, each time they go out on a job, they sense that the men are testing them. Women architects have a difficult task because they must overcome stereotypes of both women and architects. Male colleagues are largely unaware of the ways in which they increase the identity problems of women architects; many assumptions held by male architects have been held too long without being reexamined.

Intersecting with problems of belonging and image are feelings of ambivalence. Women who choose both career and family invariably experience a conflict between the traditional expectations and image of a professional and those of a wife and mother. The resulting ambivalence is reinforced by the narrow definition of the professional, which gives great importance to the satisfactions derived from professional life and denigrates those derived from personal life.[6]

Women who have devoted themselves solely to their careers, attaining positions of prestige in their firms, feel that they can afford total commitment only if they are not married. This echoes a belief in the traditional career path that is structured to fit the male pattern—a young man works long hours at the beginning of his career to establish his reputation and gain necessary skills and knowledge. His entire focus is on his career, often to the exclusion of family and personal life. The degree to which an individual accepts the validity of this career pattern is the degree to which it describes reality. A woman with a family is usually not free to follow this pattern and she suffers by seeing herself, as well as by being seen, as not quite a "real" architect.

For many women architects, personal relationships and families are very important. Women architects have often found alternatives to the traditional male career path, choosing practice in joint partnership with their husbands, or part-time work from their homes, or employment situations with fewer demands on their time. Through their continued commitment to a career, these architects have demonstrated that the traditional idea of total commitment is not the only career course for a professional.

Women are marginal in a quantitative sense, as evidenced by their low numbers and consequently their absence (with few exceptions) from professional boards, from tenure positions at professional schools, and from partnerships with large firms or as principals of their own firms. Women are also marginal in a substantive sense, in not being considered part of the group and upholding its standards. As long as both forms of marginality remain, women will not be legitimate members of the profession.

The prevailing norms that define the professional serve both to produce and sustain this marginality. Women become—and remain—marginal when the architect is seen as an "expert" possessing esoteric and specialized knowledge in which male competence is held as the norm. Women become—and remain—marginal when the hierarchical and elitist nature of the profession (relying on conformity and "old boy" connections) serves to exclude women from opportunities for advancement and achievement. Finally, women become—and remain—marginal when the emphasis on "commitment" places professional life ahead of personal life, creating conflict for women who desire both career and family.[7]

Although I have focused on the more problematic areas for women in the profession, some positive aspects have recently emerged. Efforts of women architects in academia have increased student awareness of women as creators and as consumers of the built environment. Efforts by the architectural press have brought accomplishments of women architects to the notice of the professional community. Nevertheless, recent discussions with former students currently employed in practice suggest that the problems faced by women architects are essentially unchanged, at least in the Midwest.

The current panacea for changing the status and role of women in the profession—as proposed by the AIA—is networking. But this solution is inadequate and inappropriate. Networking does not alter the basic institution and in fact perpetuates some of its detrimental features; the cronyism of the "old boys' club" is merely replaced by that of the "old girls' club."

The best route for women in architecture, according to a spokeswoman for the AIA, is "mainstreaming," or working for change within the established organizations and institutions. But this view, too, seems inappropriate, assuming as it does that women have similar goals, values, and aspirations to male practitioners.

If real change is to occur, it will have to come from outside—from the marginal people, men and women, who question the standards and assumptions and practices of the profession. A new kind of professional must be envisioned, one who can balance a desire for professional excellence with an ability to pursue personal interests and commitments. Restructuring of professional career paths is not a concession to women. Men also need second careers, retraining periods, and the redefinition of goals making possible a more balanced and rewarding life.

Changes in professional practice that promote new modes of office practice (cooperatives, and ad hoc groups formed exclusively for a particular project) would be more responsive to the needs of women and men alike. In addition, changes that provide work-based child care and more flexible working arrangements (in terms both of hours and leaves of absence) would ease the burden of family members, male or female, who are responsible for child care.

The concepts and standards of the profession are currently defined by men. If the values of the profession are to include the concerns of women, then women must have a clear vision of their goals and must be able to communicate them. Women must go beyond the issues of salaries and hiring policies to define the relationship of the professional to the profession—and indeed to the larger society. Clearly, a developed awareness of these matters need not be restricted to women. Nor can it be achieved solely by women. The task presumes the collaboration of men, in education and practice, who also wish to see a redefinition of the practice and profession of architecture. Women will not be the only beneficiaries.

Notes

1. The six include: An East Coast principal of her own firm, forty-three, unmarried, trained in Europe; a Midwest project architect at a medium-sized firm, forty-five, married, three children, educated at a state university in the Midwest; a freelance designer-draftsperson, working from her home, sixty, married, three children, educated at a university in the Midwest; an in-house corporation project manager, thirty-seven, married, two children, educated at an East Coast technical college; an East Coast principal in partnership with her husband, forty-eight, married, two children, educated at an East Coast technical college; an East Coast principal of a 400-person firm, forty-two, unmarried, educated at an East Coast design school.

2. To be the only woman on a team has special difficulties. Carol Wolman and Harold Frank, studying the dynamics of the solo woman in a professional peer group, found in 1975 that one professional woman in an otherwise male group tends to be classified as an isolate, or a low-status member, or a deviate. She can become paired as the satellite of a flirtatious or patronizing male group leader, or become isolated as a "weak" group member (perhaps with a supportive male sharing her isolation). But for a woman to become "one of the boys" is difficult; becoming group leader is next to impossible. Carol Wolman and Harold Frank, "The Solo Woman in a Professional Peer Group," *American Journal of Orthopsychiatry* 45, 1 (January 1975): 164–70.

3. According to Sara Ruddick and Pamela Daniels, discussing the findings of Daniel Levinson in his book *The Seasons of a Man's Life* (New York: Alfred A. Knopf, 1977), "the ideal mentor is not an awesomely senior patron, 'guru,' or parent figure, but rather an experienced, somewhat older co-worker who, not only by example—a mentor is more than a role model—but through regular professional contact and direct encouragement, criticism, and support of work-in-progress, introduces a younger person to a specific work world and 'shows

the way'. The currency of a developmentally significant mentor relationship is not deference and distance but a sort of 'dailiness' and the ever more equal give-and-take that generates colleagueship—such that the younger person learns what he or she needs to learn to work alone, choose new colleagues, and eventually become a mentor to others. Given the sociology of the professions, most women do not benefit from this kind of tutelage and support in their work. By and large, women still must make it on their own, and part of the price of success is a well-defended isolation." Sara Ruddick and Pamela Daniels, eds. *Working It Out* (New York: Pantheon Books, 1977), 59.

4. Erik Erikson postulates that identity is located "in the core of the individual and yet also in the core of his communal culture." Erik Erikson, *Identity: Youth and Crisis* (New York: W. W. Norton and Company, 1968), 22.

5. Shulamith Firestone writes, "A woman who participates in (male) culture must achieve and be rated by standards of a tradition she had no part in making—and certainly there is no room in that tradition for a female view, even if she could discover what it was." Shulamith Firestone, *The Dialectic of Sex* (New York: William Morrow and Company, 1970), 159.

6. A 1969 book includes one woman among the several "typical" architects in various types of practice. Discussing the difficulties facing this woman in a predominantly male field, the authors describe the series of jobs she held before she got married and temporarily left the field. She continued to do renderings at home after starting a family, and when her children were older she returned to work; her income from this job, however, was much less than the income received by someone practicing without interruption. Although feminist thinking and writing were present in the society at the time this book was published, they do not appear in this book (the result of the publisher's timidity, according to the authors). The book reinforces traditional thinking about women, stressing the home and family as the wife's responsibility. No alternative scenario is offered for the female who wants a career in architecture. Carl Meinhardt, Carolynn Meinhardt, and Alan E. Nourse, *So You Want to Be an Architect* (New York: Harper & Row, 1969), 59–69.

7. The need to be "perfect," to prove oneself constantly, stems from a sense of insecurity created by the marginal position of women in the profession, says Virginia Valian, a psychologist: "My preoccupation with my ability seemed to imply a need to be perfect, which is both a sign of arrogance and of weakness. It says, in effect, 'I am so smart I can demand perfection of myself, something impossible for lesser mortals'. But it also says, 'I have so little confidence in my personal worth that professional imperfection is symbolic of personal unworthiness'." As quoted in Ruddick and Daniels, *Working It Out*, 172.

20

Room at

the Top?

Sexism and the Star

System in Architecture

DENISE SCOTT BROWN

Most professional women can recount "horror stories" about discrimination they have suffered during their careers. My stories include social trivia as well as grand trauma. But some less common forms of discrimination came my way when, in mid-career, I married a colleague and we joined our professional lives just as fame (though not fortune) hit him. I watched as he was manufactured into an architectural guru before my eyes and, to some extent, on the basis of our joint work and the work of our firm.

When Bob and I married, in 1967, I was an associate professor. I had taught at the Universities of Pennsylvania and Berkeley, and had initiated the first program in the new school of architecture at UCLA. I had tenure. My publication record was respectable; my students, enthusiastic. My colleagues, mostly older than I, accorded me the same respect they showed each other, and I had walked the same corridors of power they had (or thought I had).

The first indication of my new status came when an architect whose work I had reviewed said, "We at the office think it was Bob writing, using your name." By the time we wrote *Learning from Las Vegas*, our grow-ing experience with incorrect attributions prompted Bob to include a note at the beginning of the book asking that the work and ideas not be attributed to him alone and describing the nature of our collaboration and the roles played by individuals in our firm. His request was almost totally ignored. A body of theory and design in architecture apparently must be associated by architecture critics with an individual; the more emotional their criticism, the stronger is its focus on one person.

To avoid misattributions, our office provides an information sheet describing our preferred forms of attribution—the work to our firm, the writing to the person who signed the article or book. The result is that some critics now make a pro forma attribution in an inconspicu-ous place; then, in the body of the text, the *design* of the work and the *ideas* in the writing are attributed to Robert Venturi.

In the Japanese journal *Architecture and Urbanism*, for example, Hideki Shimizu wrote:

A review of his plan for the Crosstown Community suggests that Venturi is not so much affording his theory new development as giving the source of his architectural approach clear form in a fundamental attitude toward city plan-ning. . . . Venturi's position in relation to city planning is the thing that enables him to develop his basic posture in relation to architecture. The Crosstown Community reveals a profound mood of affectionate emotion.[1]

This would be fine except that the Crosstown Community was my work and was attributed as such in our book; I doubt whether, over a period of three years, Bob spent two afternoons on it.

When Praeger published a series of interviews with architects,[2] my name was omitted from the dust jacket. We complained and Praeger added my name, although objecting that this would spoil the cover design. On the inside flap, however, "eight architects" and "the men behind" modern architecture were mentioned. As nine were listed on the front, I gather I am still left out.[3]

There have been exceptions. Ada Louise Huxtable has never put a foot wrong with me. She works hard at reporting our ideas correctly too. A few critics have changed their methods of attribution in response to our requests, but at least one, in 1971, was on the warpath in the oppo-site direction, out to prove that Great Art can only be made by one Man, and that Robert Venturi (read Howard Roark) is led astray when "he joins his wife Denise Scott Brown in praising certain suburban practices." And the consort and collaborator of a famous architect wrote to me that, although she sees herself in his work, the work owes its quality to his individual talents and not to her collaboration. When real artists collaborate, she claimed, their separate identities remain; she gave as an example the *lieder* of Schubert and Goethe. We countered with the Beatles.

The social trivia (what Africans call *petty apartheid*) continue too: "wives' dinners" ("We'll just let the architects meet together, my dear"); job interviews where the presence of "the architect's wife" distressed the board; dinners I must not attend because an influential member of the client group wants "the architect" as her date; Italian journalists who ignore Bob's request that they address me because I understand more Italian than he does; the tunnel vision of students toward Bob; the "so you're the architect!" to Bob, and the well-meant "so you're an architect too?" to me.[4]

These experiences have caused me to fight, suffer doubt and confusion, and expend too much energy. "I would be *pleased* if my work were attributed to my husband," says the designer wife of an architect. And a colleague asks, "Why do you worry about these things? We know you're good. You know your real role in the office and in teaching. Isn't that enough?" I doubt whether it would be enough for my male colleagues. What would Peter Eisenman do if his latest article were attributed to his co-editor, Kenneth Frampton? Or Vincent Scully, if the book on Newport houses were attributed to his co-author, Antoinette Downing—with perhaps a parenthesis to the effect that this was not intended to slight the contribution of others?

So I complain to the editor who refers to "Venturi's ducks," informing him that I invented the "duck." (He prints my letter under the title "Less is a Bore," a quotation from my husband.) But my complaints make critics angry, and some have formed lasting hostilities against both of us on this score. Architects cannot afford hostile critics. And anyway I begin to dislike my own hostile persona.

That is when self-doubt and confusion arise. "My husband is a better designer than I am. And I'm a pretty dull thinker." The first is true, the second probably not. I try to counter with further questions: "How come, then, we work so well together, capping each other's ideas? If my ideas are no good, why are they quoted by the critics (even though attributed to Bob)?"

We ourselves cannot tease our contributions apart. Since 1960 we have collaborated in the development of ideas and since 1967 we have collaborated in architectural practice. As chief designer, Bob takes final design responsibility. On some projects, I am closely involved and see many of my ideas in the final design; on others, hardly at all. In a few, the basic idea (what Lou Kahn called the What) was mine. All of our firm's urban planning work, and the urban design related to it, is my responsibility; Bob is virtually not involved with it, although other architects in the firm are.[5]

As in all firms, our ideas are translated and added to by our coworkers, particularly our associates of long standing. Principals and assistants may alternate in the roles of creator and critic. The star system, which sees the firm as a pyramid with a Designer on top, has little to do with today's complex relations in architecture and construction. But, as sexism defines me as a scribe, typist, and photographer to my husband, so the star system defines our associates as "second bananas" and our staff as pencils.

Short of sitting under the drawing board while we are around it, there is no way for the critics to separate us out. Those who do, hurt me in particular but others in the firm, too, and by ignoring as unimportant those aspects of our work where Bob has interfaced with others, they narrow his span to meet the limits of their perception.

Although I had been concerned with my role as a woman years before the rebirth of the movement, I was not pushed to action until my experience as an architect's wife. In 1973 I gave a talk on sexism and the star system to the Alliance of Women in Architecture, in New York City. I requested that the meeting be open to women only, probably incorrectly, but for the same emotional reasons (including hurt pride) that make national movements initially stress separatism. Nevertheless, about six men came. They hid in the back and sides of the audience. The hundred or so women identified strongly with my experience; "Me too!" "My God, you too?" echoed everywhere. We were soon high on our shared woe and on the support we felt for and from each other. Later, it struck me that the males had grown glummer as we grew more enthusiastic. They seemed unable to understand what was exercising us.

Since then I have spoken at several conferences on women in architecture. I now receive inquiries of interest for deanships and departmental chairs several times a year. I find myself on committees where I am the only woman and there is one black man. We two tokens greet each other wryly. I am frequently invited to lecture at architecture schools, "to be a role model for our girls." I am happy to do this for their young

women but I would rather be asked purely because my work is interesting.

Finally, I essayed my own interpretation of sexism and the star system in architecture. Budd Schulberg defines "Star Quality" as a "mysterious amalgam of self-love, vivacity, style and sexual promise."[6] Though
his definition catches the spirit of architectural stardom, it omits the
fact that stardom is something done to a star by others. Stars cannot
create themselves. Why do architects need to create stars? Because, I
think, architecture deals with unmeasurables. Although architecture is
both science and art, architects stand or fall in their own estimation
and in that of their peers by whether they are "good designers," and
the criteria for this are ill-defined and undefinable.

Faced with unmeasurables, people steer their way by magic. Before
the invention of navigational instruments, a lady was carved on the prow
of the boat to help sailors cross the ocean; and architects, grappling
with the intangibles of design, select a guru whose work gives them personal help in areas where there are few rules to follow. The guru, as
architectural father figure, is subject to intense hate and love; either way,
the relationship is personal, it can only be a one-to-one affair. This
accounts for the intensely *ad hominem* stance of some of "Venturi's" critics. If the attribution were correct the tone would be more even, as one
cannot easily wax emotional over several people. I suspect, too, that for
male architects the guru must be male. There can be no Mom and Pop
gurus in architecture. The architectural prima donnas are all male.

Next, a colleague having her own difficulties in an American Studies department brought the work of Lionel Tiger to my attention. In
Men in Groups, he writes that men run in male packs and ambitious
women must understand this.[7] I recalled, as well, the exclamation of the
French architect Ionel Schein, writing in *Le Carré Bleu* in the 1950s: "The
so-called studio spirit is merely the spirit of a caste." This brings to mind
the upper-class origins of the American architecture profession, the differences between upper-class and middle-class attitudes to women, and
the strong similarities that still exist today between the architecture profession and a men's club.

American architectural education was modeled on the turn-of-the-
century, French Ecole des Beaux-Arts. It was a rip-roaring place and
loads of fun, but its organization was strongly authoritarian, especially
in its system for judging student work. The authoritarian personalities
and the we-happy-few culture engendered by the Beaux-Arts stayed on

in Modern architecture long after the Beaux-Arts architectural philosophy had been abandoned; the architecture club still excludes women.

The heroically original, Modern architectural revolutionary with his avant-garde technology, out to save the masses through mass production, is a macho image if ever there was one. It sits strangely on the middle-aged reactionaries who bear its mantle today. A more conserving and nurturing (female?) outlook is being recommended to the profession by urban planners and ecologists, in the name of social justice and to save the planet. Women may yet ride in on this trend.

The critic in architecture is often the scribe, historian, and kingmaker for a particular group. These activities entitle him to join the "few," even though he pokes them a little. His other satisfaction comes from making history in his and their image. The kingmaker-critic is, of course, male; though he may write of the group as a group, he would be a poor fool in his eyes and theirs if he tried to crown the whole group king. There is even less psychic reward in crowning a female king.

In these deductions, my thinking parallels that of Cynthia F. Epstein, who writes that elevation within the professions is denied women for reasons that include "the colleague system," which she describes as a men's club, and "the sponsor-protégé relationship, which determines access to the highest levels of most professions." Epstein suggests that the high-level sponsor would, like the kingmaker-critic, look foolish if he sponsored a female and, in any case, his wife would object.[8]

You would think that the last element of Schulberg's definition of a star, "sexual promise," would have nothing to do with architecture. But I wondered why there was a familiar ring to the tone—hostile, lugubriously self-righteous, yet somehow envious—of letters to the editor that follow anything our firm publishes, until I recognized it as the tone middle America employs in letters to the editor on pornography. Architects who write angry letters about our work apparently feel we are architectural panderers, or at least we permit ourselves liberties they would not take, but possibly envy. Here is one, by an English architecture instructor: "Venturi has a niche, all right, but it's down there with the flagellant, the rubber-fetishist and the Blagdon Nude Amateur Rapist." These are written by men, and they are written to or of Bob alone.

I have suggested that the star system, which is unfair to many architects, is doubly hard on women in a sexist environment, and that, at the upper levels of the profession, the female architect who works with her husband will be submerged in his reputation. My interpretations are speculative. We have no sociology of architecture. Architects are unaccustomed to social analysis and mistrust it; sociologists have fatter fish to fry. But I do get support for my thesis from some social scientists, from ironists in architecture, from many women architects, from some members of my firm, and from my husband.

Should there be a star system? It is unavoidable, I think, owing to the prestige we give design in architecture. But the schools can and should reduce the importance of the star system by broadening the student's view of the profession to show value in its other aspects. Heaven knows, skills other than design are important to the survival of architecture firms. The schools should also combat the student's sense of inadequacy about design, rather than, as now, augmenting it through wrongly authoritarian and judgmental educational techniques. With these changes, architects would feel less need for gurus, and those they would need would be different—more responsible and humane than gurus are asked to be today.

To the extent that gurus are unavoidable and sexism is rampant in the architecture profession, my personal problem of submersion through the star system is insoluble. I could improve my chances for recognition as an individual if I returned to teaching or if I abandoned collaboration with my husband. The latter has happened to some extent as our office has grown and our individual responsibilities within it take more of our time. We certainly spend less time at the drawing board together and, in general, less time writing. But this is a pity, as our joint work feeds us both.

On the larger scene, all is not lost. Not all architects belong to the men's club; more architects than before are women; some critics are learning; the AIA actively wants to help; and most architects, in theory at least, would rather not practice discrimination if someone will prove to them that they have been and will show them how to stop.

The foregoing is an abridgment of an article I wrote in 1975. I decided not to publish it at the time, because I judged that strong sentiments on feminism in the world of architecture would ensure my ideas a hostile reception, which could hurt my career and the prospects of my firm. However, I did share the manuscript with friends and, in *samizdat*, it achieved a following of sorts. Over the years I have received letters asking for copies.

In 1975, I recounted my first experience of the new surge of women in architecture. The ratio of men to women is now 1:1 in many schools. The talent and enthusiasm of these young women has burst creatively

into the profession. At conferences today I find many women participants; some have ten years or more in the field.

Architecture, too, has changed since I wrote. My hope that architects would heed the social planners' dicta did not pan out, and women
did not ride in on that trend. Postmodernism did change the views of
architects but not in the way I had hoped. Architects lost their social
concern; the architect as macho revolutionary was succeeded by the
architect as *dernier cri* of the art world; the cult of personality increased.
This made things worse for women because, in architecture, the *dernier
cri* is as male as the prima donna.

The rise in female admissions and the move to the right in architecture appear to be trends in opposite directions, but they are, in fact,
unrelated because they occur at either end of the seniority spectrum.
The women entrants are young; the cult of personality occurs at the
top. The two trends have yet to meet. When they do, it will be fascinating to see what happens. Meanwhile, affirmative action programs have
helped small female-owned firms get started but may have hindered the
absorption of women into the mainstream of the profession, because
women who integrate large existing practices gain no affirmative action
standing unless they own 51 percent of the firm.

During the eighties there has been a gradual increase of women
architects in academe. (I suspect that the growth has been slower than
in other professions.)

I now receive fewer offers of deanships, probably because there are
more female candidates than before and because word is out that I am
too busy to accept. I have little time to lecture. As our office has grown,
Bob and I have found more, rather than less, opportunity to work
together, since some of our responsibilities have been delegated to the
senior associates and project directors who form the core of our firm.

During this period, we have ceased to be regarded as young turks
and have seen a greater acceptance of our ideas than we would have
dreamed possible. Ironically, a citation honoring Bob for his "discov-
ery of the everyday American environment" was written in 1979 by the
same critic who, in 1971, judged Bob lacking for sharing my interest in
everyday landscape.

For me, things are much the same at the top as they were. The discrimination continues at the rate of about one incident a day. Journalists who approach our firm seem to feel that they will not be worth their
salt if they do not "deliver Venturi." The battle for turf and the race for
status among critics still require the beating-off of women. In the last

twenty years, I cannot recall one major article by a high-priest critic about a woman architect. Young women critics, as they enter the fray, become as macho as the men and for the same reasons—to survive and win in the competitive world of critics.

For a few years, writers on architecture were interested in sexism and the feminist movement and wanted to discuss them with me. In a joint interview, they would ask Bob about work and question me about my "woman's problem." "Write about my work!" I would plead, but they seldom did.

Some young women in architecture question the need for the feminist movement, claiming to have experienced no discrimination. My concern is that, although school is not a nondiscriminatory environment, it is probably the least discriminatory one they will encounter in their careers. By the same token, the early years in practice bring little differentiation between men and women. It is as they advance that difficulties arise, when firms and clients shy away from entrusting high-level responsibility to women. On seeing their male colleagues draw out in front of them, women who lack a feminist awareness are likely to feel that their failure to achieve is their own fault.

Over the years, it has slowly dawned on me that the people who cause my painful experiences are ignorant and crude. They are the critics who have not read enough and the clients who do not know why they have come to us. I have been helped to realize this by noticing that the scholars whose work we most respect, the clients whose projects intrigue us, and the patrons whose friendship inspires us, have no problem understanding my role. They are the sophisticates. Partly through them I gain heart and realize that, over the last twenty years, I have managed to do my work and, despite some sliding, to achieve my own self-respect.

Notes

1. Hideki Shimizu, "Criticism," *A + U (Architecture and Urbanism)* 47 (November 1974): 3.
2. John W. Cook and Heinrich Klotz, *Conversations with Architects* (New York: Praeger Publishers, Inc., 1973).
3. The architects originally listed were Philip Johnson, Kevin Roche, Paul Rudolph, Bertrand Goldberg, Morris Lapidus, Louis Kahn, Charles Moore, and Robert Venturi. Also omitted from the dust jacket was the architect Alan Lapidus,

interviewcd with his father, Morris. Alan did not complain; at least he's up there with those men behind the architecture.

4. The head of a New York architecture school reached me on the phone because Bob was unavailable: "Denise, I'm embarrassed to be speaking to you because we're giving a party for QP [a well-known local architect] and we're asking Bob but not you. You see, you *are* a friend of QP and you *are* an architect, but you're also a wife, and we're not asking wives."

5. Bob's intellectual focus comes mainly from the arts and from the history of architecture. He is more of a specialist than I am. My artistic and intellectual concerns were formed before I met Bob (and indeed before I came to America), but they were the base of our friendship as academic colleagues. As a planner, my professional span includes the social sciences and other planning-related disciplines that I have tried to meld into our critique and theory of architecture. As an architect, my interests range widely but I am probably most useful at the initial stages of a design as we work to develop the *parti*.

6. Budd Schulberg, "What Price Glory?," *New Republic* 168 (6 and 13 January 1973): 27–31.

7. Lionel Tiger, *Men in Groups* (New York: Random House, 1969).

8. Cynthia F. Epstein, "Encountering the Male Establishment: Sex-Status Limits on Women's Careers in the Profession," *American Journal of Sociology* 75 (May 1970): 965–82.

21

Educating for

the Future

A Growing Archive on

Women in Architecture

MATILDA MCQUAID

An archive is made up of discoveries of the past, but it speaks to the future by forever developing our awareness of what has already been learned. The AIA Archive on Women in Architecture offers countless opportunities to find an explanation, to locate the missing link in a chain of events, to substantiate a fact.[1] These are the experiences that an archivist treasures.

My initial responsibility as AIA's keeper of records on women in architecture was to discover whether Louise Blanchard Bethune was, in fact, the first woman to join the American Institute of Architects. This mission to validate her centennial proved not only successful but also gratifying, when I went on to add more names to Bethune's. As the archive grew, I began to set long-term goals.

One of the most important was to dispel the belief that there have not been many women architects. Invariably, when I described the archive to friends or visitors, they would express amazement that there have been enough women in the profession to warrant a special place in an archive.[2] In the same breath they would ask me to recall the name

The Junior League Building (now Kossuth House), 1931–1933, Washington, D.C., Gertrude Sawyer, architect. This little gem, one of Miss Sawyer's first buildings on her own, is the only Art Deco building on Dupont Circle. Photograph by Glen Leiner

of the woman in California who was responsible for designing San Simeon or the name of Philip Johnson's relative who built two schools in Connecticut. Julia Morgan and Theodate Pope were the only women architects they came close to recognizing. My response, like a response in the *Architect and Engineer* in 1914, is that "women architects are no longer a novelty."[3]

The surprise and unfamiliarity about the history of women in architecture indicated to me that people equate the contributions women have made to the profession with the small number of women in the profession. I began to suspect that women would not make any impression on public awareness until they achieve greater numbers, especially in the only professional organization of architects in the country. Statistics show that the cumulative total membership of women in the AIA did not top one hundred until 1949 and did not reach one thousand until the early 1980s.[4] Only forty-five women have been elected to the AIA's College of Fellows since Louise Bethune became the first Fellow in 1889.[5]

Looking at the women themselves and not their numbers, however, I could see that their lives are truly outstanding and their dedication to architecture is, despite their relatively solitary existence in the profession until the 1970s, truly impressive.

Gertrude Sawyer is one woman committed to architecture. And perhaps because of her devotion she discounts any prejudices toward her sex.[6] In a telephone conversation I had with her in 1986, she told me that several women's organizations had contacted her, knowing her to be one of the pioneer women architects. But when she told them, "I was always treated fairly, and throughout my career had a very good time building and designing," they never called back. She did not work harder because she was a woman, but because she was a good architect. It was this ability that got her such long-standing clients and admirers as the Jefferson Patterson family. She was their "family" architect—working

First farm manager's complex, 1932–1933, Point Farm (now the Jefferson Patterson Park and Museum), St. Leonard, Md., Gertrude Sawyer, architect. Miss Sawyer worked until 1955 on the twenty-six new buildings for Point Farm, doing extensive research on functional requirements as well as on the architecture of Tidewater Maryland and Virginia. The entire property is on the National Register of Historic Places. Photo shows manager's residence at bottom; darker barn at rear is not by Gertrude Sawyer but was moved to the site and expanded by her. Photograph by Fairchild Aerial Surveys, Inc., courtesy of Jefferson Patterson Park and Museum

Old Harbor Village, 1935–1940, South Boston, Massachusetts, Howe, Manning & Almy, architects. The first public housing project in Boston, it is currently considered the best one by the Boston Housing Authority; many aspects of the design contribute to the well-being of tenants and buildings alike. Photograph by Doris Cole

Providence Academy, 1856–1873, Vancouver, Washington, Mother Joseph (Esther Pariseau). Built for the sisters' various medical, spiritual, and educational ministries, this was once the largest brick building in the Washington territory. Photograph courtesy of Sisters of Providence Archives, Seattle, Washington

St. Peter Hospital, 1887–1889, Olympia, Washington, Mother Joseph (Esther Pariseau). When Mother Joseph entered the convent in Montreal at the age of twenty, her carriage-maker father said she could "do carpentering" and handle a hammer and saw as well as he could. She led an arduous trek to the West, and from the 1850s through the 1890s she designed and built many buildings for the sick and needy throughout the Northwest. To raise funds for construction she went into mining camps on what she called her "begging tours." Photograph courtesy of Sisters of Providence Archives, Seattle, Washington

for three generations of Pattersons on a range of challenging projects. It was also her ability as an architect that got her the important job of building 4,000 temporary facilities for naval families in Washington, D.C.

In order to make people aware of women's history in architecture, and of the productive lives of women like Gertrude Sawyer, it is necessary to provide something to read, to see, and to remember—books, photographs, portfolios, letters, and articles by and/or about women. The Archive on Women in Architecture is constantly acquiring more of this material.

The archive is concerned with collecting documentation on women in and out of the AIA. But without a full-time archivist and considerably more money and space, acquisitions must be selective. The AIA archivist will advise on the proper location of materials that cannot be taken into the collection, and will record their whereabouts. The col-

The Lookout, ca. 1914, Grand Canyon National Park, Mary Elizabeth Jane Colter, architect. Visitors view the canyon and purchase photos and postcards from the Lookout, which was designed to resemble ancient Indian dwellings of the region. Photograph courtesy of University of Arizona Library, Special Collections Department

lection is thus becoming a clearinghouse for researchers on the subject of all women in architecture, serving as a directory for researchers interested in locating information on a specific topic or individual.

For example, the AIA Archive has an index to the office records (permanently housed at the MIT Museum) of the first women's architecture firm in Boston: Howe, Manning & Almy. Lois Lilley Howe began her individual practice in 1893, joining forces with Eleanor Manning in 1913 and with Mary Almy in 1926. Noted for its efficient and well-designed houses, Howe, Manning & Almy built hundreds of projects in the New England area.

A very interesting woman only modestly represented in the archive—but with full information about her own archive in Seattle—is Mother Joseph (1823–1902), one of the Sisters of Providence and a pioneer builder in the Northwest.[7] She served as architect, construction supervisor, and fundraiser for numerous hospitals, schools, and orphanages in the Northwest;[8] one of her first buildings, Providence Academy, is on the National Register of Historic Places. In 1953 the American Institute of Architects declared Mother Joseph "the first architect in the

Fireplace at Hermit's Rest, 1914, Grand Canyon National Park, Mary Elizabeth Jane Colter, architect. Using indigenous timber and boulders, Colter built a resting spot for sightseers. The stones within the fireplace were covered with soot to make the building look centuries old. Photograph courtesy of University of Arizona Library, Special Collections Department

Architecture students at Massachusetts Institute of Technology, 1898. Woman on the left is Henrietta C. Dozier, '99, who was lionized during her school years for being one of the few women. She went on to have a lively practice and to become the first southern woman in the AIA. Photograph courtesy of MIT Museum

Pacific Northwest."9 In 1980 she became the fifth woman inducted into Statuary Hall of the Capitol in Washington, D.C.

In many cases, little information has been uncovered about the women in the AIA archive. All would make excellent subjects for monographs, articles, theses, or dissertations. From the archive, here are a selection of the women who will someday be well known:

Katharine C. Budd (1860–1951), architect and writer. Miss Budd designed houses for such prestigious clients as John D. Rockefeller, Jr. and wrote many articles concerning architecture. Her most important project came during World War I when she was "responsible for the designing and development of that new type of architecture, the YWCA Hostess Houses."10 (Sites for the Hostess Houses were chosen by a woman contractor, a Miss Maye—first name unknown.)

Frances Benjamin Johnston (1864–1952), architectural photographer. She is known for her photographs of historic buildings in the South under the Carnegie Survey (1933–40). More than seven thousand negatives resulted from this survey, and they are significant both for their artistic beauty and their historic value; her photographs are the only documentation that exists for many of these buildings.

Mary Elizabeth Jane Colter (1869–1958), architect. Miss Colter worked from 1902 to 1942 as an architect, designer, and decorator for the Fred Harvey Company, which was responsible for building many of the hotels and restaurants along the Santa Fe Railroad. Colter's most outstanding work was at the Grand Canyon where she designed lodges, dormitories, watchtowers, and other park concessions for the company. These buildings reflect her great sensitivity to native materials and her freedom from the more popular historical styles. Her design philosophy was that a building should grow out of its setting, embodying the history and flavor of the location.11 Indeed, her architecture is in harmony with the boulders that dominate the landscape of the Grand Canyon, and her buildings honor the early inhabitants of the region.

Henrietta Cuttino Dozier (1872–1947), architect. Miss Dozier, also known as "Cousin Harry," "Harry," or "H. C. Dozier," was the third woman to join the AIA, in 1905, and the first from the South. She graduated from MIT in 1899 and soon began her own practice in Atlanta. Her most notable work in Atlanta was a chapel for All Saints Episcopal Church in 1903. She was one of the charter members of the Atlanta chapter of the AIA and was chosen as its delegate to the Eighth International

Congress of Architects in Vienna (1908). "There were about 500 delegates, several hundred of them women," she recalled in an interview.[12] "I don't mind adding that the men had altogether the best of it when it came to getting particular good from the Congress . . . the women were packed off on some excursion about town. None of that for me. I did my own sightseeing." She moved to Jacksonville, Fla. in 1916 where she obtained some of her best commissions—a Federal Reserve Bank (as associate architect), and numerous residences and apartment buildings. She bolstered her practice in the 1930s with work as a delineator for the Historic American Buildings Survey and documented many of the historic buildings in St. Augustine. She applied for a patent on a safety device for planes in the 1940s.

Fay Kellogg (1871–1918), architect. Miss Kellogg was one of the few women who fought for admission, for herself and other women, into the Ecole des Beaux-Arts. Although she ended up studying architecture in private ateliers, she "could not forget the injustice of those doors barred to my sex."[13] In her work she was especially concerned with improving the working environment of women, both in the home and in the factory. Her largest project was designing the Hostess Houses for all the southeastern camps.

Georgina Pope Yeatman (1902–1982), architect. Miss Yeatman opened her own office in 1929 and undertook a variety of commissions, from residences and schools to alterations for the Philadelphia Country Aviation Club. Not interested in publicity and too busy to prepare for publication of her work, she nevertheless became in 1936 the most publicized woman architect when she was appointed Philadelphia's city architect. The job entailed advisory and supervisory work along with the design of a number of WPA projects.[14]

Fascinating topics beckon from the archive. Very little research has been done on women's buildings and the women's clubs and organizations that sponsored them. The most famous example is Sophia Hayden and the Woman's Building at the World's Columbian Exposition in Chicago (1893). But there are other women's buildings. In 1914 the Women's Council of St. Louis made plans to build "a manless office building." To be designed by a woman, the building would have prohibited men as tenants or employees. "Women will run the elevators and officiate as window cleaners and janitors. . . . They will also look after the boilers and the machinery in the cellar. . . . [The] intention seems to construct, so far as possible, a monument to the new feminism."[15]

On the other side of Missouri at the same time, the Women's Commercial Club of Kansas City and a "woman capitalist" were planning to finance a ten-story office building. Only women would be employed; "male stenographers need not apply."[16]

What triggered this desire to build an environment for women only? Was it a wish to retaliate against a society that disapproved of women working outside the home? Was it an opportunity finally to coalesce and support one another at work? Whatever the cause, the reaction gives us a flavor of the time, and something of what it was like to be a woman in the early twentieth century. The present becomes more meaningful, and the future richer, with this knowledge.

Attitudes are a potent part of archival materials. I came across an article in the AIA archive on the considerable accomplishments of Elisabeth Coit (1892–1987), an architect and important housing reformer during the 1930s. An AIA scholarship in 1937 allowed her to study the ways in which recent construction and equipment in architecture could meet the needs of low-cost housing.[17] One has only to read the title to understand the attitudes of her day—"Houses Are Her Children: Men May Build Skyscrapers, Elisabeth Coit Designs Houses for Living."[18] Procreation was a woman's duty, whether the offspring was a child or a home. It would be difficult to imagine an item written in 1938 with a similar analogy to fatherhood.

People continue to live on, in an archive. Think, with me, of the Boston architect Ida Annah Ryan. In 1906 she wrote a letter to Glenn Brown, Secretary of the AIA at the time, requesting a membership application and some professional advice—how could she obtain admission to the national AIA organization if her local chapter in Boston would not accept women? (Membership in a local chapter was a criterion for membership in the national organization.)[19] She asked whether a separate chapter for women would be possible. The reaction to Miss Ryan's application stirs us still. Seth Temple protested not because "I know the person, but because I am repelled by the name, against the presentation of a woman's name for membership in the Institute."[20] Mr. C. H. Blackall protested against admitting Miss Ryan and other women to the Institute "unless they have achieved some substantial success, not in their studies but in actual practice." (His excuse for Lois Lilley Howe's admission to the AIA in 1901 was that most of the members voted for her because they thought Lois was a man's name.)[21] Others protested because she was not a member of the Boston chapter. Ryan's application was accepted in 1921. A persistent woman.

The stories have not ended. Collecting materials on women in architecture is an ongoing process, and as the archive grows, the collection reveals the unusual and wide-ranging accomplishments of these women. Their achievements go beyond architecture. Helen Allen (1878–?), for example, a graduate of the Cambridge School who began her own practice in 1927, served as a plane spotter during both World Wars. Elizabeth Nedved became a naval architect for a California shipbuilder during World War II. Viola S. R. Prassas received a certificate of service for her efforts as a special investigator on the War Production Board and Civilian Production Administration.

When Henrietta Dozier became a fellow of the American Institute of Genealogy in 1939, she set an example for her colleagues. Tracing and preserving history, whether it pertains to family or architecture, is important for future generations. We need to know who preceded us.²²

Notes

On behalf of the AIA Archive on Women in Architecture, I would especially like to thank Mrs. Jefferson Patterson, who made it possible for me to continue my research at the archive when other sources of funding had ceased. And I am forever grateful for discovering Ellen Perry Berkeley, who always amazed me with her patience, diplomacy, and thoroughness in editing this book. She has been a true mentor. All materials used for this essay, unless otherwise indicated, are in the AIA Archive on Women in Architecture.

1. The AIA Archive on Women in Architecture is part of the larger archives of the AIA in Washington, D.C. The AIA Archives is the official repository of all records produced by the AIA in its day-to-day operation and consists of several thousand linear feet of material. The Archive on Women in Architecture (referred to, in this essay, as "the archive") has acquired approximately fifty linear feet of material since 1984. It is open to the public by appointment only. Those interested may contact Tony P. Wrenn, archivist at the AIA, for further information.

2. I knew very little about the history of women in architecture until I took a graduate seminar at the University of Virginia, "Nineteenth and Twentieth Century Patronage and Taste in Architecture." After this seminar I pursued an internship at the AIA to study women in architecture and, at the same time, to gather information for an archive and an exhibition on the subject. It was at the AIA Archives that I met my best instructor and guide to the subject, Tony

Wrenn. With an enthusiasm unequalled by anyone, he helped to create a sense of the singular importance of this project.

3. "More Women Architects," *Architect and Engineer* 36 (April 1914): 116.

4. These statistics were obtained in January 1986 by going through AIA membership directories since 1887. The statistics are accurate only to the extent that women's names can be discerned from the membership directories. The task was easy, for the most part, during the early twentieth century, when etiquette demanded a title of "Miss," "Mrs." or "Mr." During the mid-1960s, however, titles were forgotten, anonymity was more acceptable, and initials occasionally replaced first names.

5. The following women architects have been elected to the AIA's College of Fellows: Louise Bethune (1889), Lois Lilley Howe (1931), Elisabeth Coit (1955), Marion Manley (1956), Chloethiel Woodard Smith (1960), Lutah Maria Riggs (1960), Eleanor Raymond (1961), Victorine duPont Homsey (1967), Ellamae Ellis League (1968), Elizabeth K. Thompson (1968), Elizabeth S. Close (1969), Gertrude Lempp Kerbis (1970), Jean Roth Driskel (1971), Betty Lou Custer (1972), Natalie Griffin DeBlois (1974), Lillian Scott Leenhouts (1975), Maria F. Bentel (1976), Shirley Jane Vernon (1976), Anna M. Halpin (1976), Anne Griswold Tyng (1976), Mildred F. Schmertz (1977), Lavone Dickensheets Andrews (1977), Christine Fahringer Salmon (1978), Marjorie McLean Wintermute (1979), Sarah P. Harkness (1979), L. Jane Hastings (1980), Diane Serber (1980), Norma Merrick Sklarek (1980), Beverly A. Willis (1980), Taina Waisman (1981), Judith Edelman (1981), Laurie M. Maurer (1983), Zelma G. Wilson (1983), Judith D. Chafee (1983), Iris S. Alex (1984), Yvonne Warner Asken (1984), Audrey Emmons (1984), Mary Caroline Cole (1985), Barbara Neski (1985), Cathy Simon (1986), Frances Halsband (1986), Elizabeth Bobbitt Lee (1986), Nancy A. Miao (1987), Jane L. Landry (1988), Carole J. Olshavski (1988), and Carolina Ying Shi Woo (1988).

6. Gertrude Sawyer (1895-), now in her nineties and living in California, graduated from the Cambridge School and practiced architecture in Washington, D.C. until her retirement in 1969. She designed the Junior League Building (now Kossuth House, owned by the Hungarian Reformed Federation), which is the only Art Deco Building on Dupont Circle. (She never thought of it as "Deco Art," she says.) She intimated to me that she occasionally had to win the respect of her employees, especially when building Point Farm.

7. Information and publications are available from the Sisters of Providence Archive [4800 37th Avenue, SW, Seattle, Wash., 98126], which is supervised by Sister Rita Bergamini.

8. St. Joseph Hospital (Vancouver, Wash.), first hospital in the Northwest, was built by Mother Joseph and was followed by many others in Washington, Montana, and Oregon. In her forty-six years of service to church and architecture, she constructed twenty-nine major buildings. Her last work, Providence St. Genevieve (New Westminister, Canada), was completed in 1900.

9. James Stevens, *The Seattle Times*, 14 June 1953 (from the Sisters of Providence Archives). The American Institute of Architects held its 1953 national convention in Seattle on the theme of wood processing and the uses of wood in architecture. When a question arose as to who could be considered the first architect of the Northwest region, the majority of architects supported Mother Joseph. (The West Coast Lumberman's Association have honored her as "the first white artisan to work with wood in the Pacific Northwest.")

10. From an unidentified and undated (ca. 1920) newspaper clipping, given to the AIA Archive on Women in Architecture by Vicky Opperman. Miss Budd was not the only woman commissioned to design YWCA Hostess Houses; Fay Kellogg and Julia Morgan also designed this type of building widely used during the war.

11. Virginia L. Grattan, *Mary Colter: Builder Upon the Red Earth* (Flagstaff, Ariz.: Northland Press, 1980), 59. This book includes a complete list of her buildings.

12. Mabel Drake, "Miss Henrietta C. Dozier, Architect, Talks to Congress in Vienna," an unidentified and undated (ca. 1908) newspaper article given to me by Mrs. Thomas Palmer, a relative of Miss Dozier. (Miss Dozier wanted to will her library to the AIA; unfortunately, the AIA had neither an archive nor a library at the time.)

13. Fay Kellogg, "Women as Builders of Homes," *Southern Architect and Building News* 29 (June 1912): 18–20. Miss Kellogg was not aware that Julia Morgan had already been admitted to the Ecole des Beaux-Arts in 1898.

14. Elisabeth Coit, "Georgina Pope Yeatman," *The Technology Review* 39 (1937): 255.

15. "A Manless Office Building," *Architect and Engineer* 41 (June 1915): 108.

16. "Skyscraper for Women by Women," *Southern Architect and Building News* 33 (October 1914): 28.

17. She was awarded an extension of her Langley Scholarship in 1938. This study resulted in an important and unpublished 136-page document with exquisite drawings by Miss Coit, *Notes on Design and Construction of the Dwelling Unit for the Lower-Income Family*," AIA Archives RG 801 SR 7 Box 7 Folder 6.

18. From an unidentified newspaper clipping, 6 August 1923. AIA Archives, RG 801 SR 7 Box 4 Folder 17.

19. Letter from Ida Annah Ryan to Mr. Glenn Brown, Secretary of the AIA, 4 November 1906, AIA Archives RG 803 Box 10 Folder 14.

20. Letter from Seth J. Temple of Temple, Burrows and McLane Architects (Davenport, Iowa) to Glenn Brown, Secretary of the AIA, 6 September 1907, AIA Archives RG 803 Box 10 Folder 15.

21. Letter from C. H. Blackall, Architect (Boston, Mass.) to Glenn Brown, 7 September 1907, AIA Archives RG 803 Box 10 Folder 2.

22. Many repositories have fine collections and are in extremely capable hands. I am especially grateful to the MIT Museum and Heidi Saraceno, who was always so helpful in providing me with information about MIT graduates,

and to Katherine Warwick, director of the Hill-Stead Museum (Farmington, Conn.), who gave me a greater insight into the life of Theodate Pope. And we can watch with interest the development of the International Archive of Women in Architecture, founded by Milka Bliznakov at Virginia Polytechnic Institute and State University, Blacksburg, Va. For further information, contact Laura H. Katz, archivist.

22

The Studio

Experience

Differences for Women

Students

ANNE VYTLACIL

The number of women in architecture schools, both students and faculty, has increased substantially in recent years.[1] At the same time, because of persistent efforts of women and enlightened academic administrations, the visible presence of women specifically in design education has increased greatly. Although the attitudes influencing studio performance are an extension of cultural perceptions not unique to women (or to the profession of architecture), this essay will focus on the special problems and opportunities encountered by women in the design studio. It is the studio that has always been, and continues to be, at the center of all architectural education.

Assuming that overt discrimination toward women students and faculty has been generally overcome, the question arises as to whether psychological mechanisms, conscious or unconscious, may remain to affect the woman student's learning experience and successful performance in the studio.[2] Conversely, what new possibilities and potential benefits may result from the participation of more women students and faculty in design education? Can women's special qualities and concerns be integrated into the architectural learning experience in such a way as to improve that experience for all students? To answer these questions and to assess the general experience of women in the design studio, I have consulted a group of women instructors from various schools and a group of my own former students from California Polytechnic State University, San Luis Obispo. My appreciation is extended to all who assisted me in exploring these sensitive and difficult issues.[3]

Architectural education has one special aspect not found in most academic areas: the creative nature of design precludes definitive or correct solutions to assigned problems. Because of the preeminence of design in the architecture curriculum, success in the design studio is mandatory for success as a student, yet design excellence can neither be accurately quantified nor objectively judged or explained. The standard academic approach is for the student to engage exclusively in the study of aesthetics or "pure design," and for competence in design to develop through an understanding of theoretical abstractions as an expression of personal artistic creativity. The necessary working knowledge of the mundane realities of practice and construction is expected to be acquired later in the professional office. Under this system, the program head or instructor is a prominent architect (or "star") with an established reputation as a designer. If this is the traditional model for design education, it is also a traditionally masculine preparation for entry into a male-dominated profession.[4] Women until recently have played little or no part in the development of curriculum or teaching methods.

The strength of self-image is of course critically important to successful performance in this atmosphere. Confidence in personal judgment is essential in order to evaluate the merits of possible approaches and solutions to theoretical design problems. As an experienced woman instructor wrote:

Development of design competence is at the same time a very personal and very social development—personal because solutions to given problems are based on individual values, and social because one must depend on constant communication with others in design development and communication. Emotional composure is required, for stress can severely limit a student's ability to achieve that almost complete focus on the whole mind that design demands.[5]

For all design students, competition with peers for individual achievement is a significant motivating force. Students and former students
responding to my questions agree on the importance of this factor to
their own studio performance. They suggest that all students fear negative criticism and that everyone receives too little positive reinforcement in design education; fear of failure limits every student's willingness to experiment creatively. But women are likely to feel this fear more
deeply, sensing that the consequences of failure are greater because of
the greater pressure to prove their ability and serious purpose.

It is indicative of improvement in women's status in the studio that
most current and recent women students do not see themselves as exceptions, but tend to regard discrimination as a battle fought and won by
previous generations. Women instructors today see male students accepting women as part of the normal studio experience. A few women students, on the other hand, still note instances of negative or condescending attitudes from male peers; in fact, women students report more
negative treatment from male students than from male instructors. This
is in marked contrast to earlier women (former students and instructors) who recall incidents from their own experience in which it was
evident that as women they were not expected actually to *practice* architecture or to design real buildings (houses, of course, did not qualify as
"real" buildings). The common perception was that architectural training was useless for women and that their presence in the studio was a
waste of everyone's time. Competing demands of marriage and childrearing would probably render practice impossible; if not, patterns of
discrimination in the profession would severely limit career opportunities. If women were to persist in pursuing a career in this field, it should
be in the peripheral role of writer, teacher, or historian.

Although full acceptance of women in the studio is certainly important, the higher goal must be the recognition and integration of women's
special abilities in the design process. Two diverging theoretical views
of architecture will probably remain difficult to reconcile: Is design primarily a creative art or is it first a social responsibility? These two perspectives are not gender-specific, but the weight of psychological
research seems to separate them neatly into male and female principles. Recent educational theory has explored ways in which the self-
orientation and psychological perspective of women seem to be basically
different from those of men: " . . . male and female voices typically speak
of the importance of different truths, the former of the role of separa-

tion as it defines and empowers the self, the latter of the ongoing process of attachment that creates and sustains the human community."[6]

In architectural education, then, the intuitive and self-developmental process of learning design would appear to create a fundamental conflict for women between a motivation for individual achievement and a concern for cooperative relationships and responsibilities. Further application of psychological theory to analysis of male and female approaches in visual design suggests a related set of differences:

Traditionally inside represents female, outside male. Attention has already been drawn to the male concern with facade and monument, the female concern with function and environment; the male concern with permanence and structural imposition, the female concern with adaptability and psychological needs . . . [7]

Standard architectural education would seem to fit this pattern quite well—focusing on the masculine side of the equation. The particular qualities defined as feminine, in fact, may appear as liabilities in the traditional studio environment. Women's psychological sensitivity and responsiveness, while valued by society, may be interpreted in the studio as oversensitivity to criticism or "taking things personally." A flexible or accommodating approach to design—a willingness to compromise in order to reconcile differing viewpoints—loses its rationale in the absence of a real client or user group; this attribute may be seen as a lack of aesthetic conviction and creative strength. It seems possible, then, that the woman student's development may be constrained through psychological factors inherent in the learning objectives themselves, objectives that favor male expression at the expense of female self-image. It is worth noting that behavioral mechanisms based on "invisible discrimination," with the true cause hidden, can be at least as damaging as open expression. Possibly more so, since there remains latitude for self-doubt as to whether the discouragement from instructors or fellow students may be justified.

These observations explain much without addressing the fundamental question of whether women's nature may be innately different from men's or whether behavioral variations may be learned characteristics acquired as adaptation to the demands of an assigned social position. Choice of the assumption that male and female natures are basically the same—that characteristics typically identified as feminine actually develop from efforts to resolve conflicting and diverse social roles[8]—seems to have special implications for design education. Women are not *naturally* uncomfortable in the studio learning process but are confronted with a dual problem described by more than one instructor as a dichotomy between the professional and the feminine self-image. Social standards of feminine behavior must be reconciled with the expression of ego necessary for development of personal creativity. In this context, to succeed as a talented designer is plainly desirable but to succeed too well may be unfeminine and stimulate negative reactions. The student's self-confidence and thus optimum performance are necessarily dependent on the integration of the two self-images.

There has been one experiment—in an architecture program designed by women exclusively for women—that explored how women might approach design education if not bound by a conventional curriculum and traditional teaching method. In the summers of 1975–79 the Women's School of Planning and Architecture (WSPA) offered an alternative learning process which sought, among other things, to approach design in an experiential and personal way based on attention to the needs of users. (Through a nonhierarchical structure, and through the form and content of all courses and other activities, participants were also able to approach a more satisfying integration of their feminine and professional identities.) Looking back on this aspect of the WSPA experience, it is possible to conclude that design solutions developed in response to individual needs and applied to social aspects of architecture may indeed prove to be most comfortable with women's values.

In a field dominated by masculine prototypes, women's experience has not often included the supportive relationships of WSPA. A scarcity of female role models is consistently identified as a major obstacle to a constructive learning environment for women in standard design education. Cultural perceptions that have traditionally defined women as appropriate nurturers and teachers of the young are in conspicuous contrast to women's absence as role models in professional education. Thus a demonstration that women can achieve full standing in the profession becomes an important teaching objective in itself. On having encountered only male faculty in her education, one recent graduate comments: "I think this could be construed as reasonable preparation for a professional career in which there are practically no women role models and very few women peers!"

Many women speak of positive mentor relationships with a man. But when this relationship occurs with a woman it seems to have a special significance for personal development. One student feels that when working for a man she is working for his approval; with a woman, she is working to better herself. After graduation, attention seems to focus more closely (and sometimes more critically) on professional performance, as now the role model may set an example for actual behavior. A more personal relationship may develop with a female mentor, as she is now seen to be setting an example for balancing career and personal aspirations. Women who as students felt accepted by male peers also speak repeatedly of the value of supportive relationships with women colleagues in softening the shock of negative male attitudes encountered on entering the professional office.

Somewhat unexpectedly, the increasing presence of women in the studio is seen by women instructors as having both positive and negative aspects. Perhaps it is the nature of the student/faculty relationship that all instructors appear to be successful and accomplished in their careers. Counter to the positive contribution of a female role model is the observation that some women students tend to view a woman instructor with fear and awe—awe that the instructor has achieved a professional status the student feels she may never attain, and fear that the instructor will therefore be more demanding than a male instructor. Several experienced women instructors confirm that at times they ask more from women students, perhaps because they also ask more from themselves or perhaps because they feel more is required of a woman for success in a masculine profession. It is hoped that as greater numbers of women enter the architecture schools the suspicion will diminish that those few who succeed represent an example almost impossible to equal.

Women instructors seem to feel a special concern for their women students in several ways. In one context, they report that students seem unaware of potential cultural/social problems and anticipate no difficulty in combining a professional career with women's traditional family roles. Older women know that with or without patterns of discrimination this is difficult to do. In another context, women instructors suggest that women students are not represented in graduate schools in the numbers proportionate to those graduating with pre-professional degrees in architecture; women tend to drop out before completing professional training. Conflict seems still to occur between an awareness of new possibilities for career achievement for women and a traditional sense of appropriate role patterns for women.

How, then, does the studio experience differ for women students if the instructor is a woman? Current and recent students say they have rarely encountered a woman instructor. However, as is the case with mentors, the experience (when it occurs) often has special positive significance.9 Women instructors are seen by most women students as more sensitive and encouraging, as taking more interest in the student as an individual. One student reports, "They are just better instructors overall." Perhaps these observations reflect the frequent perception by women students that they are not taken seriously by male instructors, that the expectations for women students are lower. A woman instructor may be seen as more attentive to psychological needs—or simply as more impartial.

In general, the trend in the current studio experience is seen as positive for all participants, male and female. Women's increasing role in design education, both as students and as faculty members, is expected to have a beneficial influence on the learning experience and on the profession itself. Women can contribute cultural and social attributes which, when recognized and integrated into the design process, offer new and promising possibilities. As women students are accepted as equals in the studio, their male peers also have the opportunity to become better acquainted with—and more sensitive to— women's special qualities and concerns. The resulting understanding can be expected to affect not only the studio response of women students but also their performance later in the profession.

Reservations about priorities in the architecture curriculum are not expressed exclusively by women. Practitioners have a standard complaint that architectural education is inadequate for employment in the professional office; that most newly graduated students expect to acquire the necessary understanding of regulatory constraints, materials, and methods of construction during the apprenticeship period. In the reality of contemporary practice where legal, economic, and functional requirements are predominant, an employee with an incomplete education is not very useful. Furthermore, a set of construction documents is not prepared by any one person; effective collaboration with colleagues and consultants is essential to the success of the overall effort. A typical project may be reviewed by an assortment of government agencies, citizens' groups, and client committees, all of whom generate comments that must be resolved and incorporated if the project is to receive the approvals necessary to proceed. If design education can be better coordinated with these realities, both students and practitioners will be better served.

Compared with the individualistic and competitive academic view of architecture, women's tendency to approach design issues with greater flexibility and greater aesthetic tolerance for social implications seems clearly more appropriate to contemporary practice. The responsiveness and design accommodation that may be perceived as liabilities in the traditional studio may become advantages when applied to the practical realities of the profession. Sensitivity to existing context, combined with an understanding of user needs and a willingness to accept and incorporate varying opinions, can contribute substantially to the successful execution of a contemporary architecture project. As one woman expresses it: "Architecture today is a service industry." Paradoxically, the use of their particular ability to adapt and accommodate may offer women precisely the competitive edge needed for success in a field constantly subject to change.

Notes

1. For precise figures see AIA Women in Architecture Task Force, "Survey of Women in Architectural Schools," 1980. This was an informal survey of eighty-three schools, with forty-four responding (but not all had complete statistical data). As quoted in the 1980 survey, a 1977–78 annual survey by the National Architectural Accrediting Board indicated 16.4 percent of students were women (a 20.6 percent increase over 1975–76), and a 1978 Association of Collegiate Schools of Architecture survey of faculty indicated 9 percent were women (a 66.6 percent increase over 1973). By 1985–86, NAAB counted women students as 34 percent of total enrollment (31 percent of B.Arch. and 40 percent of M.Arch. degree candidates). The same survey indicates women as 20 percent of full-time faculty.

Schools vary, however, and women's representation on faculties can be considerably below these averages. For instance, the *Official Register 1987–1988* of the Harvard Graduate School of Design shows Academic and Adjunct Faculty to be made up of 40 men and 3 women (the latter: 2 full-time assistant professors of architecture and 1 adjunct professor of landscape architecture). Student composition, however, from the HGSD *Annual Report 1985–1986*, indicates that 35 of the year's 98 architecture degrees (or 36 percent) were awarded to women.

2. An *AIA Journal* survey of 1981 replicating the AIA Women in Architecture Task Force survey of 1974 concluded: "Women also report subtle discrimination in architectural schools, such as lower expectations from professors and

lack of support through scholarship and fellowships. Forty-six percent of the recent respondents cite discrimination from schools and 47.6 from teachers." Nora Richter Greer. "Women in Architecture: A Progress (?) Report and a Statistical Profile," *AIA Journal* 71 (January 1982): 40– 41. In the 1974 survey only 24 percent of respondents reported discrimination relating to school. The increase probably reflects an increased awareness of existing problems rather than an actual increase.

3. The following women were kind enough to contribute their thinking to this essay: Noel Phyllis Birkby, New York Institute of Technology, one of the founders of WSPA; Betsy Cann, Miami University, Ohio; Catherine Cresswell, Miami University, Ohio; Donna Duerk, California Polytechnic University (Cal Poly), San Luis Obispo; Joan Goody, formerly at Harvard University; Rosaria Hodgdon, University of Oregon; Sandra Lakeman, Cal Poly, San Luis Obispo; Peggy Woodring, University of California, Berkeley (all either current or former design-studio instructors); also, Laurie Barlow, Karen Black, Sharon Bonesteel, Kathleen O'Shaughnessy, Gail Pipal, Charlotte Sahara, Cynthia Snell (all recent graduates of Cal Poly, San Luis Obispo); and a group of women students at Miami University, Ohio, sophomore to graduate levels.

4. In considering my own education in the late 1950s and early 1960s, it is clear that the image of the architect was male. Women entering this environment (in very small numbers) saw themselves as having to perform in accordance with masculine standards—and perform better than men at the same tasks—in order to gain acceptance.

5. Rosaria Hodgdon. "Influences, Positive and Negative, On Women Entering the Profession," *AIA Journal* 66 (August 1977): 44.

6. Carol Gilligan. *In a Different Voice* (Cambridge: Harvard University Press, 1982), 156.

7. Lucy R. Lippard. "Centers and Fragments: Women's Spaces," in Susana Torre, ed., *Women in American Architecture: A Historic and Contemporary Perspective* (New York: Whitney Library of Design, 1977).

8. Elizabeth Janeway. *Man's World Woman's Place, A Study in Social Mythology* (New York: William Morrow and Company, 1971), 86–87.

9. Most of my own students stress the fact that I was the first woman architect they had ever met—living and encouraging proof that it could be done.

Index

An asterisk (*) indicates
women whose architectural
or planning work
(or professional activity
attendant to that work) is
mentioned in the text.

A

*Aalto, Aino Marsio, 177
Aalto, Alvar, 177
affirmative action: consequences of, xviii,
    244; program by AIA (1975) on, 118, 120–21,
    122, 123 n.1
*Allen, Helen, 257
Alliance of Women in Architecture (AWA),
    the, 117, 118, 240
*Almy, Mary, 81, 252
alternatives: to traditional career path, 232,
    233; to traditional education, 87–98,
    125–33; to traditional practice, xx, xxi-
    xxii, 233
American Academy in Rome, 52 n.30
American Institute of Architects (AIA), the:
    Archive on Women in Architecture,
    established (1984) by, 247–60; and
    Bethune, Louise Blanchard, 21, 28; defini-
    tion of architect (1906) by, 30–31; early
    campaign against builders by, 29–35;
    endorsement of academic education

(1901) by, 28–29; exclusion of women
(1906) by Boston chapter of, 256–57;
mainstreaming of women in, 233; mean
age of practitioners (1983) in, 200 n.6;
membership requirements (1901) of,
28–29; New York chapter, first woman
member of, 48; New York chapter, first
woman on executive committee of, 118;
resolution on status of women (1973)
passed by, 118; the South, first woman
member (1905) from, 254; Task Force on
Women in Architecture (1974)
established by, 119–23; "That Exceptional
One" (1988) exhibition by, xvii; women
as percentage of practitioners (1985)
in, 199 n.1; women elected to College
of Fellows (1889–1988) of, 248, 258 n.5;
Women in Architecture Committee
(1983), report of, 222–23, 224; women
members of, current figures, xvi, xvii,
xxiv n.5; woman members of, early
cumulative totals, 248

271

importance of 114–15; information lacking on, 107–11, 114; Julia Morgan Association, 111; repository of material on, 116 n.11

Mt. Vernon Ladies' Association of the Union, the, 160

N

National Park Service, the, 160, 164, 165, 168 n.18, 169 n.24
*Naudé Santos, Adèle, 180–82
*Nedved, Elizabeth, 257
*Newton, Jean League, 179, 180
*Nichols, Minerva Parker: defense of women architects by, 32–33, 47; successful career of, 33–34; support of, by builders, 34–35; views of, on practical experience, 33
number of women architects: (1900), 47; in the AIA (1987), xvi, xxiv n.5

O

old boys' club, the, 198, 231, 232, 233
Olmsted, Frederick Law, 49
*Open Design Office, the, xxi
Organization of Women Architects (OWA), the, 117

P

Peirce, Melusina, 160
percentage of women architects: (1985), xv; in the AIA (1987), xvii
Picasso, Jacqueline, 183
Piercy, Marge, 205, 206, 210
*Piomelli, Rosaria, xx
*Pope, Theodate, 248, 260 n.22
*Prassas, Viola S. R., 257
profession, the: assumptions and standards of, as defined by men, 231–33, 234; changes in, affecting women, 243–44; marginality of women in, 232–33, 235 n.7; similarities between a men's club and, 241, 242. *See also* American Institute of Architects; discrimination against women in architecture
professional, the: redefinition of, 233
professional identity, problems of, for

women: ambivalence between personal and professional lives, 232; mystique of the expert, 231; sense of belonging, 230–31
professionalization: campaign to make architecture distinct from the building trades, 27, 29, 34, 35; need for mediators between professional establishment and clients, 44; respect for professionalism by Tuthill, 10, 12; support of Architects' Licensing Bill by Bethune, 21

R

*Raymond, Eleanor, 94, 96 n.4, 212
*Reich, Lilly, 207–10, 211
Richardson, Henry Hobson, 43, 45, 59, 60 n.4
Roark, Howard, xxii, 190, 238
*Robinson, Julia, 207, 210
*Rogers, Eliza Jacobus Newkirk, 81
Rose, Damaris, 204
Ruffner-Russell, Linda, 164
*Ryan, Ida Annah, 256

S

Saegert, Susan, 204, 206
Saks Fifth Avenue, xxii
salary, average starting, of architects (1986), 200 n.7
*Sawyer, Gertrude, 96 n.4, 98 n.4, 249–51, 258 n.6
*Schiffelbein, Patricia, 120
Schulberg, Budd, 241
Sigourney, Lydia, 6, 13 n.22
*Simmons, Lynda, xx-xxi
Skidmore, Owings & Merrill, first woman partner of, xviii
"solo woman," the, 234 n.2
So You Want to Be an Architect (Meinhardt et al), 235 n.6
*Sprague, Joan Forrester, xxi-xxii, 120, 121, 212
star system, the: and the critics, 238, 240, 242, 244–45; definition of, 240, 241; possible changes in, 243; sexism and, 240, 241–42, 243, 244–45
Steichen, Joanna, 183
Sullivan, Louis H., 21, 58
Swallow, Ellen H., 79

About the editors

Ellen Perry Berkeley is an accomplished and widely published writer on architecture. She earned her undergraduate degree at Smith College and did graduate work at the Harvard Graduate School of Design and the Architectural Association's school in London. She has been a senior editor at *Architecture Plus* and *The Architectural Forum*. Matilda McQuaid is a curatorial assistant in the department of architecture and design at the Museum of Modern Art, New York. She received her B.A. from Bowdoin College and is working on a master's degree in architectural history at the University of Virginia.